"Those Who Call Themselves Jews"

Princeton Theological Monograph Series

Series Editor, K. C. Hanson

Recent volumes in the series

David A. Ackerman
Lo, I Tell You a Mystery

John A. Vissers
The Neo-Orthodox Theology of W. W. Bryden

Sam Hamstra, editor
The Reformed Pastor by John Williamson Nevin

Byron C. Bangert
Consenting to God and Nature

Stephen Finlan and Vladimir Kharlamov, editors
Theosis: Deification in Christian Theology

Richard Valantasis et al., editors
The Subjective Eye: Essays in Honor of Margaret Miles

Caryn Riswold
Coram Deo: Human Life in the Vision of God

Paul O. Ingram, editor
Constructing a Relational Cosmology

Mark A. Ellis, editor and translator
The Arminian Confession of 1621

"Those Who Call Themselves Jews"
The Church and Judaism in the Apocalypse of John

Philip L. Mayo

Pickwick *Publications*
An imprint of *Wipf and Stock Publishers*
199 West 8th Avenue • Eugene OR 97401

"THOSE WHO CALL THEMSELVES JEWS"
The Church and Judaism in the Apocalypse of John
Princeton Theological Monograph Series 60

Copyright © 2006 Philip L. Mayo. All rights reserved. Except for brief quotations in critical publications or reviews, no part of this book may be reproduced in any manner without prior written permission from the publisher. Write: Permissions, Wipf & Stock, 199 W. 8th Ave., Eugene, OR 97401.

ISBN: 1-59752-558-8

Cataloging-in-Publication data:

Mayo, Philip L.

"Those who call themselves Jews" : the church and Judaism in the Apocalypse of John / Philip L. Mayo.

Princeton Theological Monograph Series 60

x + 212 p. ; 23 cm.

Includes bibliography

ISBN: 1-59752-558-8

1. Bible. N.T. Revelation—Criticism, Interpretation, etc. 2. Christianity and other religions—Judaism—History. 3. Judaism—Relations—Christianity—History. 4. Judaism (Christian theology)—History of Doctrines—Early church, ca. 30-600. I. Title. II. Series.

BS2825.6 M37 2006

Manufactured in the U.S.A.

To Jolene
ἡ ἀγάπη . . . πάντα ὑπομένει

Contents

Acknowledgments / ix
Abbreviations / x

Introduction / 1

1. An Overview of Jewish-Christian Relations (70–150 CE):
   Factors in the Developing Schism / 27

2. "Those Who Call Themselves Jews":
   Conflict in Smyrna and Philadelphia / 51

3. The 144,000:
   Israel or Spiritual Israel? / 77

4. The Temple, the Two Witnesses, and the Heavenly Woman:
   The Church as Spiritual Israel / 107

5. The New Jerusalem as the Eschatological People of God / 164

6. Conclusion / 199

Bibliography / 205

Acknowledgments

It is only fitting that the completion of this project on the Apocalypse of John brings to an end a seven-year journey that began only as a vision and a call from God. In these seven years I have seen the hand of God in many ways—mostly through the people he has placed in my life. It is these individuals that deserve my thanks for the success of this journey and the completion of this project.

My tenure as a PhD student has been a time of growth and maturity as a person and as a scholar for which I am indebted to my PhD mentor, David Scholer. It is said that a person of integrity is one who has the same character in public as in private. David is this kind of person. I have come to know David both as a colleague and as a friend and have learned from him the meaning of being a teacher and a scholar. I have benefited from his deep respect for both students and colleagues and his commitment to exceptional scholarship, for which I thank him. His unwavering confidence, encouragement, and candid critique have made this project the success that it is.

I also would like to extend my thanks to the rest of the Fuller Seminary faculty. Special thanks go to James Bradley under whose guidance I first drafted the proposal for this project, and Donald Hagner for his suggestions offered as this project took shape and for his reading of the final product.

Of course, no acknowledgment would be complete without extending thanks to my friends and family who laughed with me, cried with me, prayed with me, and believed in me throughout the ups and downs of the past seven years. A special thanks goes to my wife, Jolene, and to my son, Josiah, who hopefully now knows the answer to that all-searching question, "Daddy, why are you always working at the computer?" It is to Jolene that I dedicate this project. It is her unflagging support and sacrificial devotion to me and our family that has truly guaranteed the success of not only this project but of the past seven years. She exemplifies more than anyone I know the character of Christ.

Abbreviations

Unless otherwise noted below, all abbreviations are taken from Patrick H. Alexander, et al., *The SBL Handbook of Style: For Ancient Near Eastern, Biblical and Early Christian Studies* (Peabody, Mass.: Hendrickson, 1999).

BECNT	Baker Exegetical Commentary on the New Testament
BRS	The Biblical Resource Series
IVPNTC	InterVarsity Press New Testament Commentary
LLJC	The Littman Library of Jewish Civilization
NT	New Testament
NTIC	The New Testament in Context
OT	Old Testament
PC	Proclamation Commentaries
SBLit	Studies in Biblical Literature
SCJ	Studies in Christianity and Judaism

Unless otherwise noted, all biblical quotations are taken from *The Holy Bible: New Revised Standard Version* (Nashville: Thomas Nelson, 1996, 1989). All Greek text quotations are taken from Eberhard Nestle and Kurt Aland, editors, *Novum Testamentum Graece,* 27th ed. (Stuttgart: Deutsch Bibelstiftung, 1993).

Introduction

THE nature of Jewish-Christian relations at the end of the first century has been a subject of serious study and considerable debate. It is of interest not only because of its historical significance in understanding the separation of the nascent Christian[1] church from its mother religion Judaism, but it also has in recent decades become of major interest in understanding the roots of anti-Semitism in the church. The time between approximately 70 and 150 CE is held to be a volatile time in that Jewish-Christian relations were quickly, although not uniformly, deteriorating. This is a time referred to as the "partings of the ways,"[2] when the church was emerging as a religion apart from Judaism.

The evidence for this period of Jewish-Christian relations is sparse, sometimes difficult to interpret and considerably one-sided since most of the evidence comes from Christian sources. This is likely a result of the church's preoccupation with its own self-definition in relation to Judaism. The increasingly Gentile church, in an attempt to stake out its own position on the vast religious field of Greco-Roman culture, began to vilify Judaism by laying claim to its scriptures and its place as the chosen people of God. This repudiation of Judaism, however, did not occur all at once

---

[1] There has been considerable angst in recent historical study of Jewish-Christian relations over using terms such as "Christian" and "Christianity" in opposition to "Jew" and "Judaism" for fear of being historically anachronistic. While one must be careful not to project twenty-first-century nomenclature or concepts on earlier centuries, one must adopt some kind of language for the discussion of this topic. The author recognizes that little evidence exists before the second century (e.g., the epistles of Ignatius) for the general use of "Christian" or "Christianity"; however, there is evidence that the former designation existed at least by the last quarter of the first century (Acts 11.26) and that even though the line between Judaism and Christianity was not yet clearly drawn at the end of the first century, some separation had already taken place in certain circles. Therefore, to ease the discussion, the terms "Christian," "Christianity," "church," and "Judaism" will be used throughout.

[2] This is a phrase used, for example, by James D. G. Dunn, *The Partings of the Ways: Between Christianity and Judaism and Their Significance for the Character of Christianity* (London: SCM, 1991).

but was an attitude that developed over several decades due to a variety of factors.

What are difficult to establish precisely are the factors that led to this eventual split between Judaism and Christianity and what particular factor or event, if any, precipitated the schism. By the end of the first and the beginning of the second centuries, the writings of the Apostolic Fathers already portray a dismissive attitude toward Judaism (e.g., *Barnabas*, the epistles of *Ignatius*) and by mid-second century the church proclaimed itself God's new Israel (Justin, *Dial.* 11.5).[3] In addition, there are several post-70 CE NT books such as the Gospel of John, Acts of the Apostles, and the Apocalypse of John[4] that arguably begin to sound an anti-Jewish tone. The Gospel of John implies a synagogue ban (9.22; 12.42; 16.2); Acts records violent Jewish opposition to the Christian mission (e.g., the martyrdom of Stephen, 7.54-8.1; the death of James, 12.1-3; 13.44-47; 14.1-7), and the writer of the Apocalypse calls the Jewish synagogue a "synagogue of Satan" (2.9; 3.9). These Christian texts do not, however, portray the Jews in a consistently negative light.

Of particular interest to the present study is the Apocalypse of John, since it was written in this dark and turbulent time in Jewish-Christian relations. This document will prove helpful because by its very nature it is a transitional document; that is, it is a decidedly Christian text written by a Jewish Christian author to likely predominantly Gentile churches. John,[5]

---

[3] For the first time in Christian literature the church is directly called God's "true spiritual Israel." Earlier Christian literature, however, had already made such inferences (e.g., *Barnabas*).

[4] Most scholars date these works after the fall of Jerusalem in 70 CE. J. A. T. Robinson, *Redating the New Testament* (Philadelphia: Westminster, 1976) attempts to put forth a serious challenge to this notion but his position has not been widely accepted. The dating of the Apocalypse will be discussed in more detail below since it has some bearing on the present discussion. For a discussion of the dating of the Fourth Gospel see Raymond E. Brown, *The Gospel According to John (I–XII): Introduction, Translation, and Notes,* AB 29 (Garden City, N.Y.: Doubleday, 1966) LXXX–LXXXVI; C. K. Barrett, *The Gospel According to St. John: An Introduction with Commentary and Notes on the Greek Text,* 2d ed. (Philadelphia: Westminster, 1978) 100–144. For a discussion of the dating of Acts see Joseph A. Fitzmyer, *The Acts of the Apostles: A New Translation with Introduction and Commentary,* AB 31 (New York: Doubleday, 1998) 51–55.

[5] The present author takes no position here with regard to the identity of the author of the Apocalypse. Whether the author is John the apostle, John the elder or some other John is notoriously difficult if not impossible to determine and has no direct impact on the present discussion. Since the author identifies himself within the Apocalypse as "John," he will be referred to in this manner throughout the present work. For a discussion of authorship see Isbon T. Beckwith, *The Apocalypse of John: Studies in Introduction with a Critical and Exegetical Commentary* (1919; reprinted, Grand Rapids: Baker, 1979) 343–53; G. R. Beas-

who is an ethnic Jew, seems to deny the very name "Jew" to his ethnic kin while accusing them of belonging to Satan (2.9; 3.9). Nevertheless, he does not abandon his own Jewish background and theology. He makes broad use of the Jewish scriptures and Jewish cultic imagery while maintaining a Christian understanding that Jesus is the fulfillment of God's salvific plan. What is of particular interest is how he adopts and adapts this imagery and language and applies it to the church. It is John's mix of Jewish imagery with a Christian message that may provide some insight into his perspective on the relationship between these two increasingly polarized sects. What exactly this perspective is, as John Court writes, "remains one of the most tantalizing of historical problems."[6]

John appears to see an unbroken line of fulfillment extending from the covenant promises of Israel through the Lamb (i.e., Jesus the Messiah) to his followers (i.e., the church). Several questions naturally arise. How much does John reflect the developing attitude of some segments of the church that the Jews have been replaced as God's people and that the Christian interpretation of their scriptures is the correct one? Does John hold out any hope for the salvation of ethnic Israel? These are questions not easily answered, but a close examination of John's apocalypse will allow one to offer some cautionary responses. Such an examination will make it possible to plot John's position on the grid of Jewish-Christian relations between 70 and 150 CE.

In order to respond to these critical questions and assess the value of John's apocalypse to the discussion of first-century Jewish-Christian relations, the present study will attempt in chapter 1 to establish a rudimentary framework which will outline the overall status of Jewish-Christian relations and the major factors that contributed to the developing schism between 70 and 150 CE. The development of this framework will involve examining both Christian and Jewish literature as well as any archaeological evidence relevant to establishing the developing nature of Jewish-Christian relations during this period, particularly in Roman Asia. This study, which could be a project within itself, will be only a brief overview but will provide the necessary background against which to measure John's apocalypse.

The subsequent chapters (2 through 5) will be comprised of an exegetical study of relevant passages (Rev 2.9; 3.9, the synagogue of Satan accusations; 7.1-17 and 14.1-5, the 144,000 and the innumerable multitude;

---

ley-Murray, *The Book of Revelation*, rev. ed., NCB (Grand Rapids: Eerdmans, 1981) 32–37; David E. Aune, *Revelation 1–5*, WBC 52A (Dallas: Word, 1997) xlviii–lvi.

[6] John M. Court, *Revelation*, NTG (Sheffield: JSOT Press, 1994) 109.

11.1-13, the measuring of the temple and the two witnesses; 12.1-17, the heavenly woman; 21.1-22.5, the new Jerusalem) in order to discern how John has adopted and adapted Jewish cultic imagery and texts and applied them to the church. Historical and literary critical approaches are used to understand how these apocalyptic texts and images function within the literary whole and how they portray John's particular perspective on Israel's and the church's place in God's economy. Once these passages have been examined, then some conclusions can be outlined with regard to what they reveal about John's theological perspective on Israel and the church. Upon completion of this task, his perspective can be integrated into the larger historical framework of the period and his contribution to the study of Jewish-Christian relations can be rightly evaluated.

The Dating of the Apocalypse

The attempt to place the Apocalypse within the ebb and flow of Jewish-Christian relations between 70 and 150 CE obviously assumes a date for its composition sometime within this time frame. A majority of modern scholars date the Apocalypse late in the first century around 95–96 CE, and this is the date assumed in the present work.[7] However, a number of scholars argue for an early date just prior to the fall of Jerusalem around 68–69 CE. Both sides garner important external and internal evidence to establish their position, and while neither date can be fixed with absolute certainty, the evidence for the later date is the most persuasive. Since the date of composition has some bearing on the present study, a consideration of the evidence is in order.

Irenaeus' Testimony

Much of the discussion over the external evidence for the date of the Apocalypse centers on Irenaeus' testimony that the Apocalypse was seen sometime near the end of Domitian's reign (*Haer.* 5.30.3). Since Domitian died in 96 CE, Irenaeus' testimony taken at face value lends credence to the

---

[7] The assumption is made here that the Apocalypse was written in its entirety at this time by one author. As Adela Yarbro Collins writes, "The unity of style and the complex but careful and deliberate design of the book as a whole make hypotheses about the compilation of extensive written sources or a series of editions superfluous" (*Crisis and Catharsis: the Power of the Apocalypse* [Philadelphia: Westminster, 1984] 54). See Richard Bauckham, *The Climax of Prophecy: Studies in the Book of Revelation* (Edinburgh: T. & T. Clark, 1993) 1–37, who has adequately proven the literary unity of the Apocalypse. Contra Aune, who argues for a three-stage, two-edition composition by one author or redactor (*Revelation 1–5*, cxviii–xxxiv).

argument that the Apocalypse was written late in the first century around 95–96 CE. Victorinus of Pettau, who wrote the oldest extant commentary on the Apocalypse, as well as Eusebius both follow Irenaeus' lead in dating the Apocalypse to the reign of Domitian. Although there are some later traditions indicating a date under Claudius, Nero or Trajan,[8] Irenaeus' testimony is the most significant external evidence but, of course, the reliability of his testimony is often questioned.

Irenaeus' testimony appears weighty when one considers the solid line of tradition from which it proceeds. He is a native of Asia Minor and purports to have known Polycarp who knew the apostle John (*Haer.* 3.3.4).[9] What is so damaging to Irenaeus' testimony, however, is his inaccuracy with regard to other matters related to the first century. For example, he remarks twice that John lived until the reign of Trajan (*Haer.* 2.22.5; 3.3.4), and he attributes the authorship of both the Fourth Gospel and the Apocalypse to the apostle John. J. A. T. Robinson makes much of this latter point observing that few scholars would accept that the author of both the Fourth Gospel and the Apocalypse are one and the same person and few would equally accept that that person is John the apostle. He further argues that even if one were to accept these two assertions, few could equally accept a late date for the Apocalypse since the apostle John would have been too old by the time of the writing.[10] Robinson believes that Irenaeus' inaccuracy in these matters impugns his testimony on the date of the Apocalypse.

Other critics have suggested that Irenaeus' testimony has been unduly influenced by Melito, bishop of Sardis (ca.160–170 CE).[11] Melito wrote a Christian apology, *To Antoninus*, which is quoted by Eusebius (*Hist. eccl.* 4.26) in which Melito portrays Domitian as a second Nero. It has been observed that Melito's judgment of Roman emperors is generally unreliable. He portrays Roman emperors who already had a bad reputation among Romans as anti-Christian simply because they were already considered evil.[12] Since Roman historians had already dubbed Domitian a second Nero, it was easy for Melito to follow their lead (Juvenal, *Sat.*

---

[8] See the discussion in R. H. Charles, *The Revelation of St. John,* 2 vols., ICC (New York: Scribner, 1920) 1:xcii-xciii; Robinson, *Redating,* 222–24.

[9] So Robinson, *Redating,* 221.

[10] Ibid., 222; cf. J. Christian Wilson, "The Problem of the Domitianic Date of Revelation," *NTS* 39 (1993) 597–98; John W. Marshall, *Parables of War: Reading John's Jewish Apocalypse,* SCJ 10 (Waterloo, Ont.: Wilfrid Laurier University Press, 2001) 94–95.

[11] E.g., Marshall, *Parables of War,* 94–95.

[12] Collins, *Crisis and Catharsis,* 56.

4.38; Pliny, *Paneg.* 53.3-4; Martial, *Epig.* 11.33). This characterization of Domitian, along with his reputation as a persecutor of Christians, eventually became church tradition. The argument against Irenaeus is that he may have followed Melito's line of reasoning and dated the book under Domitian's reign.[13]

Collins argues persuasively against Melito's alleged influence on Irenaeus by pointing out that the context of Irenaeus' remark concerning the date of the Apocalypse lacks any reference to Nero, any alleged persecution under Domitian or even any mention of John's exile. Irenaeus' testimony, in fact, falls within the context of his discussion of the identity of the apocalyptic beast and, therefore, is quite incidental, betraying no influence from Melito. She argues that Irenaeus simply appears to have some source that persuades him to date the Apocalypse under Domitian, perhaps due to the testimony of Christians in Asia Minor.[14]

Marshall, who opts for an early date, acknowledges that this argument from silence is persuasive but responds by positing that Irenaeus' lack of detail concerning Domitian's alleged persecution does not necessarily imply that he has an independent source or that he was not influenced by Melito. Since the context of his discussion is not Domitian's reign or even the dating of the Apocalypse, one would not naturally anticipate a detailed excursus on these matters.[15]

Both Collins and Marshall are arguing from silence; however, as Marshall acknowledges, Collins's argument is persuasive since Irenaeus' comment is not contrived but incidental and straightforward. Given this fact and Irenaeus' contacts in Asia Minor, the weight of the evidence seems to be in favor of the reliability of his testimony. As for Irenaeus' reputation for inaccuracies with regard to first-century personages, this fact does not necessarily imply his testimony to the dating of the Apocalypse is also inaccurate. Collins offers the solution that Irenaeus' claim that John the apostle lived until Trajan is the result of his confusing the apostle with John the prophet, in addition, the fact that Irenaeus dates the Apocalypse late in spite of the incongruity with John's age may imply that he had an independent source from which he was drawing his information.[16]

---

[13] Ibid.

[14] Collins, *Crisis and Catharsis*, 56; cf. G. K. Beale, *The Book of Revelation: A Commentary on the Greek Text*, NIGTC (Grand Rapids: Eerdmans, 1999) 19–20.

[15] Marshall, *Parables of War*, 94–95.

[16] Collins, *Crisis and Catharsis*, 56.

As can be observed from the preceding discussion, the debate over the reliability of Irenaeus' testimony is on-going and not easily resolved. As one considers each of the arguments, however, it seems reasonable to accept the validity of Irenaeus' testimony. His inaccuracies with regard to other first-century matters do not necessarily invalidate all of his testimony. The standard applied seems too high when one is required to be accurate on every point in order to be accepted on one. Each remark of Irenaeus should be judged based on its own merit. The incidental nature of his testimony to the dating of the Apocalypse and his connection both with Asia Minor and Polycarp are powerful arguments in favor of the veracity of his testimony. Even Hort, who argued for an early date, acknowledges the power of Irenaeus' witness,

> On the one hand the tradition as to Domitian is not unanimous; on the other it is the prevalent tradition, and it goes back to an author likely to be the recipient of a true tradition on the matter . . . . If external tradition alone could decide [the date of the Apocalypse], there would be a clear preponderance for Domitian.[17]

This being the case, however, as most commentators acknowledge, even if the external evidence argues for a late date, the internal evidence must also support such a supposition.

The Seven Kings and the Nero Redivivus/Redux Myth

While the external evidence favors a late date, those who argue for an early date for the Apocalypse find the strength of their argument in a discussion of the internal evidence. Although both sides point to several indicators within the Apocalypse to bolster their positions, much of the discussion concerning the date of composition centers on Rev 17.9-11. In this passage, John appears to give a clear indicator of the time in which he is writing. He writes,

> This calls for a mind that has wisdom: the seven heads [of the beast] are seven mountains on which the woman is seated; also, they are seven kings, of whom five have fallen, one is living, and the other has not yet come; and when he comes, he must remain only a little while. As for the beast that was and is not, it is an eighth but it belongs to the seven, and it goes to destruction.

John's vision seems to move in this passage from the metaphorical to the historical. The harlot, who sits upon the beast, is here identified by John's

---

[17] F. J. A. Hort, *The Apocalypse of St. John I–III* (London: Macmillan, 1908) xx.

visionary messenger with historical Rome and the seven heads with the seven hills upon which Rome was built.[18] In addition, the heads of the beast are identified with seven kings, and given the identity of the woman as Rome; these seven kings are likely seven Roman emperors. Five have fallen, the sixth is still living and presumably reigning during the writing of John's apocalypse and the seventh is yet to come but will remain only a short time. John then identifies an eighth as the beast who mysteriously belongs to the seven. This king "was and is not"[19] but belongs to the seven, and he will arise only to go to his destruction. This latter king no doubt represents for John some eschatological figure that will embody all of the evil represented in the beast and to some degree already exhibited by the previous rulers. His identity as one of the seven affirms this assessment and leads many scholars to see here an allusion to the Nero *redivivus* or *redux* myth.[20]

Those who argue for an early date for the Apocalypse make much of this passage, believing it to be the most important internal evidence and the

---

[18] Rome was commonly identified and celebrated in the ancient world as the city that was built on seven hills (Suetonius, *Dom.* 4.5).

[19] The beast has been previously identified as one "that was, is not, and is about to ascend from the bottomless pit and go to its destruction" (17.8). This tripartite description is a negative reprise of a similar positive portrayal of God and the Lamb in the opening of the Apocalypse (1.8; cf. 4.8). This description solidifies John's intent to portray the beast as the enemy and anti-type of God. The unholy trinity of the dragon, the beast and the false prophet stand in contrast to God, the Lamb, and the godly prophetic tradition in which John stands (Bauckham, *Climax*, 431–36).

[20] For a lengthy discussion of John's use of the Nero *redivivus/redux* myth see Bauckham, *Climax*, 384–452; cf. Charles, *Revelation*, 1:349–50; Adela Yarbro Collins, *The Combat Myth in the Book of Revelation*, HDR 9 (Missoula, Mont.: Scholars, 1976) 174–76; Beasley-Murray, *Revelation*, 210; Jürgen Roloff, *The Revelation of John*, trans. John E. Alsup, CC (Minneapolis: Fortress, 1993) 156–57; David Aune, *Revelation 6–16*, WBC 52B (Nashville: Thomas Nelson, 1998) 737–38, 770; idem, *Revelation 17–22*, WBC 52C (Nashville: Thomas Nelson, 1998) 950; Pierre Prigent, *L'Apocalypse de Saint Jean*, rev. ed., CNT 14 (Geneva: Labor et Fedes, 2000) 313–14; (Due to the unavailability of the English translation of Prigent's commentary at the inception of this study, all citations in the present work are from the French edition.) contra Beale, *Revelation*, 719–20. Some minority opinions are expressed by J. M. Ford, *Revelation*, AB 38 (New York: Doubleday, 1975) 221, who suggests that it is a reference to Vespasian returning after his exile under Nero; and Robert H. Mounce, *The Book of Revelation*, rev. ed., NICNT (Grand Rapids: Eerdmans, 1998) 252–53, who proposes that it is Caligula who had been seriously ill but recovered. Caligula's propagation of the imperial cult throughout the empire and his attempt to set up his statue in the temple at Jerusalem are further arguments for this position (Josephus, *Ant.* 8.257-61; cf. 19.4).

most significant in support of an early date.[21] Many scholars have assumed that the historical tone of this passage must indicate that the five kings who have fallen are five previous historic emperors who reigned before the writing of John's apocalypse and that the sixth, who is still reigning, is the emperor under whom John sees his apocalyptic visions. The simplest solution may be to begin counting with the first Roman emperor in order to arrive at the emperor contemporaneous with John's apocalypse.

Unfortunately, interpreting this passage is not quite so simple since there is no consensus on where to begin the count of emperors and whom to include. Augustus was the first official emperor of Rome so it would seem natural to begin the count with him and not with Julius Caesar who was technically the last monarch of Rome. Tacitus, a contemporary of John, seems to affirm such an assessment since he begins his Roman history with Augustus as the first emperor (*Hist.*1.1; *Ann.*1.1). Others, however, counter that there is no reason to omit Julius Caesar since other ancient writers include Julius as the first emperor (Suetonius, *Lives of the Caesars*; Josephus, *Ant.* 2.2; *Sib.Or.*5.12; *4 Ezra* 11-12).

If one begins the count with Julius or Augustus then the sixth and reigning emperor would be Nero or Galba, which at first glance appears to favor an early date for the Apocalypse. Indeed, those who defend an early date point to this evidence as nearly conclusive for their argument. Marshall, who favors a date "between the summer of 68 CE and the late spring of 70 CE," trivializes the debate over whether to begin the count with Julius or Augustus, arguing that either count results in an acceptable timeframe.[22] This solution, however, is not as convenient as it first appears. A dating of the Apocalypse under Nero has the advantage of perhaps providing a reason for the persecution motif of the Apocalypse but creates difficulty for explaining what appears to be John's extensive use of the Nero *redivivus/redux* myth.

The Nero *redivivus/redux* myth was a widespread rumor circulating after Nero's death that he was actually not dead but would return to retake the imperial throne. Many in the populace believed that he would return from the east with the Parthian army and take vengeance on Rome. There were in actuality at least three imposters that arose between 69 CE and 89 CE who claimed to be Nero and attempted to lead a revolt against Rome. The first appeared in Greece, the second in Asia Minor, and the third, who

---

[21] So Wilson, *Problem*, 597–99.
[22] Marshall, *Parables of War*, 97; cf. Wilson, *Problem*, 599, who takes a similar position arguing for a date between June 68 and January 69.

gained the support of the Parthian king, seemed a viable threat (Tacitus, *Hist.* 1.2.1; 2.8-9; Dio Cassius, *Rom. Hist.* 63.9.3; 66.19.3; Suetonius, *Nero* 57.2). All three were eventually put down by the Romans. This rumor, which was well-established in Asia, is used to John's advantage in chapters 13 and 17 to benefit his characterization of the beast. John's assertion that one of the seven heads of the beast had suffered a mortal wound from which it had recovered (a characteristic that later becomes part of the entire beast's description, 13.12, 14), his description of the beast as one that "was, and is not, and is about to ascend" (17.8) and as an eighth emperor that belongs to the seven (17.11) point to his own creative use of this mythic tradition.

John's use of this tradition implies that Nero is already dead by the time of the writing of John's apocalypse and therefore could not be the sixth or reigning emperor. This is a problem that both Marshall and Wilson fail adequately to resolve.[23] Robinson sees the inherent difficulty in a count that begins with Julius and ends with Nero and thus postulates that the count must begin with Augustus and conclude with Galba since "one thing is certain it is that Nero is dead and not 'now reigning.'"[24] However, a count that ends with Galba as the sixth emperor also carries certain challenges. If the Apocalypse dates to the reign of Galba, then the question arises as to whether the Nero *redivivus/redux* myth would have had enough time to develop in such a short time span. Early daters would argue that it would have had enough time to develop, noting that the first Nero pretender appeared in 69 CE. While this may seem a valid argument, Bauckham, who has done extensive research into the use of the myth in Jewish apocalyptic, demonstrates persuasively that John uses two forms of the myth which were late first-century developments. Bauckham's examination of the myth tradition makes a date under Galba difficult to defend.[25]

In addition, there is some disagreement as to whether Galba, Otho, and Vitellius, the three military emperors of the turbulent year and a half (68–69 CE) following Nero's death, should be included at all in John's count of the seven kings. Since these three so-called pretenders to the

---

[23] Marshall glosses over the difficulty of a date under Nero by suggesting that John has resorted to ex eventu prophecy and that the "historical present" for the writing is under Galba or Otho (*Parables of War*, 91). Wilson, *Problem*, 603–4, argues against John using ex eventu prophecy, as is typical of many apocalyptic pseudepigraphic works, but fails to deal adequately with a date for the Apocalypse under Nero.

[24] Robinson, *Redating*, 243.

[25] Bauckham, *Climax*, 407–31.

throne never actually established their reigns, some argue that John would not have counted them in his list of emperors, while others argue that there is no valid reason to omit them.²⁶ The omission of the three pretenders is favored by those who argue for a late date as part of a solution to the difficulties this passage poses. Their omission, however, does not completely resolve all of the relevant issues. For example, if one begins the count with Augustus and omits the three pretenders, then the sixth emperor is Vespasian, the seventh who reigns only a little while is Titus, and the eighth, which is identified with the beast, is Domitian. The idea that Domitian is represented by the beast fits nicely with church tradition that he was a second Nero; however, it does not adhere well to the text. The text states that the currently reigning emperor is the sixth and the eighth, which was one of the seven, is not yet but will soon arise. Attempts to resolve this dilemma by arguing here that John is employing *ex eventu* prophecy are not persuasive in this atypical apocalyptic work.²⁷

Collins argues that the assumption that the starting point for John's list is Julius or Augustus heads the discussion in the wrong direction.²⁸ She posits instead that John has adopted a text from the late 60s CE written by anti-Roman Jews but adapts it for his own purpose as is indicated by his addition of an eighth emperor. The count of seven kings reflects Jewish "sabbatical eschatology" and fits well within John's symbolic use of this number, but Collins does not believe that the number of kings is purely symbolic.²⁹ She argues that the count is also historically important to John because of the care with which he takes to calculate them. The count she proposes incorporates the Jewish provenance of John's source, to some degree John's penchant for symbolism, and the apparent implication within the text for historical accuracy. She begins her count with Gaius Caligula, for he is the first to reign after Christ and to cause the Jews difficulty in the manner of Antiochus Epiphanies. John's Jewish background may have influenced him to begin with this anti-Jewish emperor, but he adapts the material for his Christian purpose. He omits Galba, Otho, and

---

²⁶ Some observe (e.g., Marshall, *Parables of War*, 91, n.5) that these three military emperors are included in other ancient accounts of the caesars such as Suetonius, *Lives of the Caesars*, Tacitus, *Roman History* and the eagle vision of *4 Ezra* 11–12. Yarbro Collins, *Crisis and Catharsis*, 60, contends that these comparisons are not valid when one factors in the issues of genre and purpose.

²⁷ Contra André Feuillet, "Les 144,000 Israélites Marqués d'un Sceau," *NovT* 9 (1967) 219.

²⁸ Collins, *Crisis and Catharsis*, 64.

²⁹ Ibid., 63.

Vitellius on the grounds that they caused the Christians no difficulty and thus Domitian becomes the sixth emperor who is presently reigning.

Collins's solution appears to resolve the inherent difficulties posed by 17.9-11 to a late date for the Apocalypse. The fact that Caligula is the first emperor to begin his reign with the advent of the church age and his attempt in beast-like fashion (Rev 13.14-15) to place his image in the temple in Jerusalem argue persuasively for her position. Yet her criterion for omitting Galba, Otho, and Vitellius on the grounds that they exhibited no anti-Christian behavior seems somewhat arbitrary. What anti-Christian behavior did Vespasian or Titus exhibit? They presumably remain in the count because of their involvement in the Jewish war, and, thus one may appeal to John's Jewish background and source. However, the inherent weakness in this solution at this point seems to be that appeal is made to John's Jewish and Christian allegiances when convenient. Marshall also criticizes Collins's solution for its reliance on a hypothetical pre-70 source to resolve perceived inconsistencies between the Apocalypse and a late date.[30]

As one can see, there are a number of solutions that have been proposed in order to decipher John's list of seven kings in 17.9-11, most of which have inherent weaknesses.[31] The best solution, however, may be one that avoids the difficulties of a chronological count altogether. A view that has been gaining some ground in contemporary scholarship is that John did not intend to imply any particular chronological count of emperors but rather intended a more symbolic message.[32] The number seven is clearly a number around which the Apocalypse is structured (e.g., seven lampstands, seven seals, seven trumpets, seven bowls)[33] and denotes the idea of completion or totality.[34] The seven heads of John's beast fits within this motif and is likely a combination of the beasts of Dan 7.3-7. John freely combines characteristics of Daniel's four beasts, suggesting that his

---

[30] Marshall, *Parables of War*, 91.

[31] See Collins, *Crisis and Catharsis*, 58–64, for an overview of the current proposals.

[32] Beckwith, *Apocalypse*, 706–8; J. P. M. Sweet, *Revelation*, PNTC (London: SCM, 1979) 25–27; Beasley-Murray, *Revelation*, 256–57; Bauckham, *Climax*, 405–7; Mounce, *Revelation*, 317; Aune, *Revelation 17–22*, 948; cf. Beale, *Revelation*, 21–24, who acknowledges the difficulties with numbering the emperors and in the final analysis suggests that the best solution may be the symbolic interpretation, although he does not appear completely convinced.

[33] Note also Collins, *Combat Myth*, 19, where she presents a structural outline that is based on a series of seven-fold visions in the Apocalypse.

[34] Bauckham, *Climax*, 405.

beast "sums up and surpasses the evil empires of history in itself."[35] These seven heads also provide the symbolic transfer to seven mountains upon which Rome was built and thus point to the present evil empire. This symbolic imagery John then develops into seven kings with an eighth that is about to appear. Bauckham argues that John does not wish to point to seven consecutive figures but merely to locate his hearers within his eschatological timeframe.[36] He does not try to tell them where to start counting but only that the sixth king is presently reigning, and they are aware of who that is. A seventh must yet come and reign a little while, and then the end will come. The final ruler is an eighth, perhaps because he represents a "final excess of evil"[37] and because the numerological value of eight carries eschatological implications. The message behind the image of the seven kings is not intended to communicate a chronological count of emperors, but it is the message of the entire Apocalypse that the end is near but not yet. Although the symbolic interpretation is not immune to criticism, it does appear to provide the most viable interpretation of 17.9-11. It is consistent with the symbolic message of the Apocalypse, avoids the complications involved with a chronological count, and maintains the possibility of a late date.

Revelation 11.1-2

In addition to Rev 17.9-11, early daters also point to Rev 11.1-2 as a further internal indicator of a pre-70 date for the composition of the Apocalypse. The implication of this passage, in which John is instructed to measure the temple, is that the temple was still standing at the time of John's writing. The solution for some late-date scholars is to propose that John has adopted a pre-70 CE text of Jewish origin from a tradition that the temple would not be destroyed and has adapted it for his own purpose.[38] Of course, the criticism leveled at this solution is that such a hypothetical source is only a convenient way to avoid the implications of a straightforward and literal reading of the text which argues for a pre-70 date.[39] However, those who argue for an early date based on a historical

---

[35] Ibid., 404.
[36] Ibid., 406.
[37] Ibid., 405.
[38] Beckwith, *Apocalypse*, 586–87; Charles, *Revelation*, 1:269–73, 285-86; Beasley-Murray, *Revelation*, 176–78; Collins, *Crisis and Catharsis*, 65–68; Aune, *Revelation 17–22*, 588–93.
[39] Marshall, *Parables of War*, 96; cf. Wilson, *Problem*, 601–3.

reading of this text have failed to account adequately for the implications of the symbolic meaning developed within the details of the text that seem to remove it from a historical interpretation.

For instance, the Ezekiel-like (40–48) measuring of the temple in which John is commanded to engage is more than likely a symbolic act and is intended to communicate a message of preservation and purity, particularly since the measuring never actually takes place.[40] Moreover, John's use of the numerical designation forty-two months is also clearly symbolic[41] and is based on Daniel's similar symbolic timeframe (7.25; 12.7) as is confirmed in the following visions of 11.3-13 and 12.1-17. In addition, Collins contends that John would never call earthly Jerusalem the Holy City (11.2), since he reserves this designation for the heavenly Jerusalem (21.8); instead earthly Jerusalem is called Sodom and Egypt (11.8).[42]

The overwhelming symbolic nature of the text, along with the strong allusions to both Daniel's visions (7.25; 8.11-14; 12.7; cf. Zech 12.3) and Ezekiel's measuring of the temple, argue for an interpretation that is essentially divorced from the historical setting and, thus unreliable for dating the Apocalypse.[43] The allusion to Ezekiel's measuring of the temple (40-48) is particularly instructive since Ezekiel envisions the measuring of an earthly temple, yet, at the time of his writing the temple is in ruins. This may also be the case for John. It is not necessary to argue that John has adopted a pre-70 Jewish text for he has clearly adapted the vision to fit within his apocalyptic framework, making any attempt to glean any historical information from it virtually impossible.

Rome as Babylon

Both 17.9-11 and 11.1-2 are the most common passages used to argue for a pre-70 date for the Apocalypse and yet, as has been demonstrated by the proposed solutions, neither creates a serious obstacle to positing a late

---

[40] So Collins, *Crisis and Catharsis*, 66; cf. Marshall, *Parables of War*, 96, who also finds the argument for a symbolic meaning behind the measuring convincing but still believes the text indicates an early date. For a fuller discussion of the symbolic meaning of measuring as well as the entire vision of 11.1-2, see chapter 3 below.

[41] Some early daters acknowledge the symbolism behind the forty-two months (e.g., Robinson, *Redating*, 238–42) while others do not (e.g., Wilson, *Problem*, 604).

[42] Collins, *Crisis and Catharsis*, 65–68. The interpretation of the city to which John refers in 11.8 is debated and will be discussed in more detail below (chapter 3). Marshall, for example, argues that the city in 11.8 is not earthly Jerusalem but Rome (*Parables of War*, 92–93).

[43] Beale, *Revelation*, 20–21; cf. Bauckham, *Climax*, 266–73.

date. There is, however, a powerful internal argument for a post-70 date and that is John's metaphorical use of Babylon for Rome. Beale believes this to be perhaps the most significant evidence for a late date, observing, as do Collins and others, that Babylon as a metaphor for Rome appears in Jewish literature roughly contemporary with John's apocalypse only *after* 70 CE (4 Ezra 3.1-2, 28-31; *2 Bar.* 10.1-3; 11.1; 67.7; *Sib. Or.* 5.143, 159).[44] Rome's destruction of Jerusalem clearly recalled for many Jews its previous destruction centuries before at the hands of the Babylonians. While it is true that Babylon was not the only name used for Rome by first-century Jewish writers,[45] Babylon carried the greatest significance after 70 CE, and John's use of it implies that he borrowed from his Jewish contemporaries a name that had quickly become traditional by the time of his writing.[46] This scenario would best fit a date late in the first century.

Domitian and the Christians

There are some more minor internal arguments offered for a late dating of the Apocalypse, such as the poor spiritual condition of the churches, the fact that the Laodicean message gives no indication of the city's devastation after the 60/61 CE earthquake,[47] and a possible allusion to Domitian's vineyard edict (92 CE) in Rev 6.6;[48] but each of these provides little to no convincing evidence. Late-date proponents had also traditionally pointed to the connection between an alleged Christian persecution under Domitian and the numerous allusions to persecution and the imperial cult within the Apocalypse. However, many recent late-date scholars have retreated from this position.[49] It is now generally recognized that there is little evidence for a wide-spread systematic persecution of Christians under Domitian, although local confrontations were still likely. In addi-

---

[44] Beale, *Revelation*, 18–19; cf. Collins, *Crisis and Catharsis*, 57–58; Aune, *Revelation 1–5*, lxi. Marshall acknowledges that Babylon appears in post-70 Jewish literature but argues that this does not have to be the case for the Apocalypse (*Parables of War*, 92–93). He postulates that such a designation could as easily fit a date after the start of the Jewish war which, of course, accommodates his argument for the setting of the Apocalypse.

[45] Rome was also called Kittim, Egypt, and Edom with Edom being the most common in rabbinic literature. Collins, *Crisis and Catharsis*, 57.

[46] Ibid., 58.

[47] For these see Beale, *Revelation*, 16–17.

[48] See Aune, *Revelation 1–5*, lxiii.

[49] Collins, *Crisis and Catharsis*, 69–73; Leonard L. Thompson, *The Book of Revelation: Apocalypse and Empire* (New York: Oxford University Press, 1990) 95–109; Aune, *Revelation 1–5*, lxvii–lxx.

tion, the traditional portrayal of Domitian's aggressive promotion of the imperial cult and his insistence on divine recognition, particularly the title *Dominus et Deus* (Suetunius, *Dom.* 8.13), has also been questioned although not entirely ruled out. Collins and others have argued that divine titles were used less at the insistence of Domitian and more by others to curry his favor.[50] It must be acknowledged, however, that the imperial cult was prevalent and well established in the province of Asia and may have provided a setting in which local Christians felt threatened and may have been often challenged due to their "atheistic" stance.[51] The Apocalypse certainly anticipates imminent persecution which may be a response to increasing societal pressures.

The scope of this work does not allow a thorough overview of all the issues affecting the debate over the date of the Apocalypse; however, many of the major points have been outlined briefly. The external evidence favors a late date. There seems to be no solid reason to reject the veracity of Irenaeus' testimony to a date near the end of Domitian's reign. The context of his remark communicates neither bias nor undue influence impugning the genuineness of his testimony, and his connections with Asia Minor and Polycarp permit the possibility of a pure line of tradition. Revelation 17.9-11 appears to be the greatest obstacle to agreement on a late date; however, the difficulty in determining a correct chronology for John's seven kings is not an actual threat to a late date but rather an indication that a symbolic interpretation of this passage is the best solution. John's metaphorical use of Babylon for Rome is the strongest internal evidence for a post-70 date and is consistent with a Domitianic date. In addition, John's use of the Nero *redivivus/redux* myth reflects a tradition that developed later in the first century, also confirming a late first-century date. The evidence, there-

---

[50] Collins, *Crisis and Catharsis*, 72; Thompson, *Book of Revelation*, 105–6; cf. Beale, *Revelation*, 9–11, who agrees with Thomspon's assessment that there was bias on the part of early Roman historians (Tacitus, Suetonius, Dio Chrysostom, and Dio Cassius) who wrote of Domitian's cruelty and desire for divine recognition; however, he feels Thompson overstates the case and argues that these writers' testimonies cannot be dismissed completely. Beale correctly points out that Thompson fails to account adequately for the bias on the part of those writers (e.g., Statius, Juvenal, Quintilian, Martial) who wrote favorably of Domitian during his reign.

[51] S. R. F. Price has demonstrated well the pervasiveness of the imperial cult in Asia, particularly at the end of the first century (*Rituals and Power: The Roman Imperial Cult in Asia Minor* [Cambridge: Cambridge University Press, 1984]). See also Beale, *Revelation*, 12–15. Collins, *Crisis and Catharsis*, 72–73, acknowledges that the Apocalypse could have been written at least in part in response to the imperial cult to bolster Christian exclusivity.

fore, favors a late date for the Apocalypse likely at the end of Domitian's reign around 95–96 CE.

An Overview of Recent Scholarship

In the last twenty years scholars have written some brief articles and essays that attempted to address the Apocalypse's place in the Jewish-Christian debate, but none seems to approach the topic in the comprehensive manner proposed here. Recent commentaries on the Apocalypse of John by David Aune, Gregory Beale, and Grant Osborne do not take up the issue in any depth. All three acknowledge that Rev 2.9 and 3.9 suggest conflict between Jews and the church, but they do not pursue the issue beyond these passages.[52]

Christopher Rowland, who has written extensively on the origins of Christianity and its relationship to Judaism,[53] has also written two commentaries on the Apocalypse of John.[54] He also fails to examine the place of John's apocalypse in the study of Jewish-Christian relations. Moreover, his interpretation of Rev 2.9 and 3.9 seems ambivalent and somewhat contradictory. In his 1993 Epworth Commentary on John's apocalypse, Rowland interprets these two passages as references to conflict between the church and "rival Jewish congregations." He suggests that Jewish Christians who continued to worship in the synagogue may have been persecuted (2.10) or challenged to deny Jesus' name (3.8).[55] Later, however, in his 1998 commentary for the *New Interpreter's Bible*, he softens his interpretation and in some ways seems to contradict his previous position. Although he does not rule out the possibility, he cautions against assuming these passages portray some kind of anti-Jewish polemic and suggests that they could refer to conflict with Jewish Christians or Gentile Judaizers much like Paul's opponents in Galatia or Colossae.[56] This seems to suggest

---

[52] Aune, *Revelation 1–5*, 164–65; cf. Beale, *Revelation*, 239–45, 283–92; Grant R. Osborne, *Revelation*, BECNT (Grand Rapids: Baker, 2002) 129–32, 190–91.

[53] Christopher Rowland, *Christian Origins: From Messianic Movement to Christian Religion* (Minneapolis: Augsburg, 1985); idem, "Moses and Patmos: Reflections on the Jewish Background of Early Christianity," in *Words Remembered, Texts Renewed: Essays in Honour of John F. A. Sawyer*, ed. Jon Davies et al., JSOTSup 195 (Sheffield: Sheffield Academic, 1995) 280–99.

[54] Christopher Rowland, *Revelation*, EC (London: Epworth, 1993); idem, "The Book of Revelation: Introduction, Commentary and Reflections," in *Hebrews, James, 1 & 2 Peter, 1, 2, &3 John, Jude, Revelation*, NIB 12 (Nashville: Abingdon, 1998) 503–744.

[55] Rowland, *Revelation*, 68.

[56] Rowland, "Book of Revelation," 577, 585, 588.

that the church's conflict was internal rather than with the Jewish community, as Rowland had proposed earlier. Beyond these remarks, Rowland does not pursue the topic of Jewish-Christian relations throughout the rest of his study of John's apocalypse.

Adela Yarbro Collins, Peder Borgen, and Michal Wojciechowski, however, have written articles that attempt to address this topic in a more in-depth manner. Wojciechowski in his article, "Church as Israel According to the Revelation of St. John,"[57] makes an analysis of pertinent passages in John's apocalypse (Revelation 7; 14; 11; 12; and 21) with regard to John's view of the church and Judaism. His article, however, is quite brief and lacks the depth of research needed to treat adequately this issue. He also surprisingly excludes Rev 2.9 and 3.9 from his discussion. Wojciechowski's reason for excluding these important passages is due to his desire to focus on John's theological and eschatological view of the church and Israel but not on the implication of his view for the study of Jewish-Christian relations. He asserts that a study of Jewish-Christian relations in John's apocalypse would be limited to Rev 2.9 and 3.9.

Unlike Wojciechowski, Collins[58] and Borgen[59] focus on the issue of Jewish-Christian relations from the perspective of John's apocalypse. Therefore, contrary to Wojciechowski, they concentrate on relational issues that arise from 2.9 and 3.9. For example, Collins identifies 2.9 and 3.9 as passages that show there was conflict between the Jewish and Christian communities of Smyrna and Philadelphia. She finds confirmation in 2.10 that this conflict reached the level of Christian persecution by Jews.[60]

Unfortunately, Collins's analysis stops short of a thorough examination of the rest of John's apocalypse and how it might add to an understanding of John's position on the issue of Jewish-Christian relations. This is perhaps because she believes that John's position toward Judaism is too "ambivalent" and thus is not as clearly discernable in the rest of his apocalypse. For example, she remarks in *Crisis and Catharsis: the Power of the*

---

[57] Michal Wojciechowski, "Church as Israel According to the Revelation of St. John," *ColT* 64 (1994) 33–40.

[58] Adela Yarbro Collins, "Vilification and Self-Definition in the Book of Revelation," in *Christians Among Jews and Gentiles: Essays in Honor of Krister Stendahl on His Sixty-fifth Birthday*, ed. George W. E. Nickelsburg and George W. MacRae (Philadelphia: Fortress, 1986) 308–20.

[59] Peder Borgen, "Polemic in the Book of Revelation," in *Anti-Semitism and Early Christianity: Issues of Polemic and Faith*, ed. Craig A. Evans and Donald A. Hagner (Minneapolis: Fortress, 1993) 199–211.

[60] Collins, *Crisis and Catharsis*, 85–86.

Apocalypse that, although John calls earthly Jerusalem "Sodom and Egypt" (11.8), he seems to hold out some hope of Jewish conversion (11.13) and also equally uses Jerusalem elsewhere as a salvific image (3.12; 21.2, 10).[61] She seems shortsighted here, however, and is missing an opportunity to strengthen her conclusions through the information that John provides in the rest of his apocalypse.

Peder Borgen essentially agrees with Collins's interpretation of Rev 2.9 and 3.9. He too sees behind these passages a conflict between the Jewish and Christian communities of Smyrna and Philadelphia. His interests, however, are more narrowly focused on the exact nature of the conflict. Should this conflict be characterized as extramural, which might be further characterized as anti-Jewish or anti-Semitic, or is it intramural, in which the church as a Jewish sect is struggling theologically with the rest of Judaism? Borgen chooses the latter characterization. He believes that, although the early believers were probably already being pushed out of the synagogues, they still saw themselves as a "distinct group within a Jewish context" who believed themselves to be the true Jews.[62] More than Collins, however, Borgen does venture beyond Rev 2.9 and 3.9. He considers a number of other passages (e.g., Jerusalem passages 3.12; 11.8; 21.2; the 144,000 in chapter 7) where John makes use of Jewish imagery, but he does this primarily with the intention of bolstering his own thesis that the Jewish-Christian conflict portrayed in John's apocalypse is an intramural one.

Eduard Lohse[63] and Alan J. Beagley[64] offer a different perspective on the subject of Jewish-Christian relations in John's apocalypse. Lohse diminishes the role of a Jewish-Christian conflict in the Apocalypse while Beagley makes it the foundation of his thesis. Although Lohse interprets 2.9 and 3.9 as clearly directed against ethnic Jews, he does not feel that this conflict holds a central place in John's apocalypse. He believes that John does identify the church as the true Israel but that he is careful in his presentation because he is attempting to appeal both to a Christian and a Jewish audience. Lohse's conclusions head the discussion in the right direction but need more development. His assertion that John wishes to appeal to a Jewish audience is tenuous.

---

[61] Ibid., 86–87.

[62] Borgen, "Polemic," 200.

[63] Eduard Lohse, "Synagogue of Satan and Church of God: Jews and Christians in the Book of Revelation," *SEÅ* 58 (1993) 105–23.

[64] Alan James Beagley, *The 'Sitz im Leben' of the Apocalypse with Particular Reference to the Role of the Church's Enemies*, BZNW 50 (Berlin: de Gruyter, 1987).

Beagley, on the other hand, takes a different hermeneutical approach. He does not agree with the traditional interpretation that John's apocalypse is primarily concerned with a Domitianic persecution of Christians. He argues instead that it is concerned with God's judgment of Israel. John reinterprets the common identification of Rome with Babylon and its prophesied destruction as references to Jerusalem. Beagley believes this interpretation to be more consistent with a theme of judgment upon Israel, which he traces from the OT prophets through the NT literature. It is John's apocalypse that reveals the completion of this judgment. The Jews, he argues, are being judged for their obduracy of heart, their rejection of the Messiah, and their persecution of the Christians.[65] Rome's role in the Apocalypse is in forming an evil alliance with Jerusalem against the Christians.

Beagley's thesis is not widely supported and is difficult to defend. Evidence for Jewish collusion with Rome is lacking as is John's concern with God's judgment on Israel. Babylon is more clearly identified with Rome than with Jerusalem. The vision of the harlot in chapter 17 makes this identity nearly absolute. The seven heads of the beast on which the harlot is seated are identified as both seven hills and seven kings (17.9). In addition, the waters on which the harlot is seated are identified with the peoples and nations of the earth over which, no doubt, the harlot has power (17.15; cf. 13.7b). These are clearly symbolic references to Rome and Roman power. For John, Rome is the incarnation of evil in the world. It has been corrupted by its lust for power, its greed, and its arrogant idolatry which has reached its height in the emperor cult (13.1-18). It is Rome not Jerusalem that is "drunk with the blood of the saints" (17.6). John's concern in the Apocalypse, therefore, is with the spiritual—and to some degree the physical—threat that this pagan culture poses to God's people. Thus the overarching theme of the Apocalypse is not the judgment of Israel but a call to perseverance and uncompromising spirituality. What condemnation of the Jews that might be intimated in the Apocalypse (e.g., 2.9; 3.9; 11.8) is certainly not a major theme, nor does it indicate an indiscriminate rejection of the Jewish people.[66]

John W. Marshall's recent work, *Parables of War: Reading John's Jewish Apocalypse*, stands on the opposite end of the spectrum from Beagley's

---

[65] Beagley, '*Sitz im Leben*,' 113.

[66] Beagley is careful in the final paragraph of his work to state that he does not wish his work to be used "as the basis for anti-Semitism"; however, his very next statement betrays a supersessionist theology that has historically led to such bigotry. He writes, "The rejection [by God] of which we have spoken is a rejection of Israel as a nation."

work. Marshall argues for a relinquishing of the common portrayal of tripartite conflict within the Apocalypse among Jews, Christians, and pagans and instead postulates that the Apocalypse should not be interpreted as a Christian document, but rather as a Jewish text within a Jewish context. The context for John's apocalypse, Marshall posits, is Asian Diaspora Judaism during the early part of the First Jewish Revolt (68–69 CE) with Rome. He argues that John, who is a devoted Jew, is writing to his fellow Jews to warn them against compromise with the culture and to offer hope in the face of the Jewish-Roman conflict transpiring in Judea. It is not Jerusalem and Rome that have formed an evil alliance against Christians, but rather Rome that will be judged for its persecution of Jerusalem.

Marshall's unusual hypothesis requires that he devote nearly the entire first half of his work parsing out a position that attempts to undermine the traditional scholarly approach to the Apocalypse as a Christian document through a critique of recent scholarship on the Apocalypse, through proposing a broader definition of terms (e.g., synagogue, church, Christianity, Judaism), and through a reexamination of the historical, semantic and theological implications of the use of these terms in the study of the Apocalypse. Marshall then embarks on an exegesis of passages with particularly Jewish overtones (7.4-8; 14.1-5; 11.1-13) from the perspective of his proposed new context for the Apocalypse which, he observes, have often caused interpretive difficulty from a Christian hermeneutical perspective. He criticizes the source critical solutions often used to explain these passages (e.g., by Charles and Collins) and proposes that they be read not as Jewish texts adopted for a Christian context, but rather as responses to the Judean conflict of the late 60s CE.

Within Marshall's approach is an attempt to debunk the notion that there is any possibility to discern conflict between Jews and Christians within the Apocalypse. He argues that John's "synagogue of Satan" accusations are not indictments of a Jewish-Christian writer against ethnic Jews, but rather a harsh criticism of his fellow Jews who have compromised with the pagan culture. John rather calls his fellow Asian Jews to "keep the commandments of God and hold the testimony of Jesus" (12.17). Marshall emphasizes what he perceives as the often neglected first half of this phrase as a call to faithfulness to God's covenant with Israel. The call to "hold the testimony of Jesus" poses little threat to Marshall's proposed Jewish context, for he reads "testimony of Jesus" as a subjective genitive and argues that John is presenting Jesus as a model of faithfulness to Israel's covenant with God.[67]

While Marshall's approach is novel and intriguing, he fails to defend adequately his thesis. His attempt to establish the premise that the Judean conflict was a credible concern for Asian Jews and thus an impetus for the writing of the Apocalypse lacks adequate evidence and is tenuous at best. He also believes that his hermeneutical approach offers a more straightforward interpretation of the passages under consideration which have been notoriously difficult to interpret from a Christian perspective. However, Marshall's approach is plagued with an inverse set of problems. While the traditional approach appears to have difficulty interpreting seemingly Jewish texts within a Christian context, Marshall's approach has difficulty interpreting clearly Christian rhetoric within a Jewish context. His interpretation of John's repeated references to the "testimony of Jesus" as subjective rather than objective is speculative and not supported by the context. Even if one accepts his interpretation, Marshall does not explain of what significance Jesus' model of covenant obedience would be to Asian Jews.[68]

Marshall's interpretation of 11.1-13 equally presents problems for his thesis. While he is able to adapt these vision narratives fairly easily to the context of the Judean war, Marshall must deal with the identity of the "great city" as the place "where also their [the two witnesses] Lord was crucified" (11.8). In keeping with John's usual use of the nomenclature "great city," Marshall contends that the city is not Jerusalem but Rome. However, since Jesus was not crucified in Rome, Marshall postulates that John prophesies in part the condemnation of Rome "surprisingly, for its crucifixion of Jesus *in Rome*" (italics original).[69] This is of course a "spiritual" (πνευματικῶς) interpretation on the part of John. Marshall's interpretation, however, strains credibility as does his assertion that 11.8 "makes it possible to recognize the only literature in the Christian canon that places the blame for the crucifixion of Jesus squarely on Rome."[70]

The reinterpretation of the Apocalypse as a completely Jewish rather than a Christian document is a problematic task and one at which Marshall does not succeed. Even when Marshall attempts to accommodate texts with traditionally Christian interpretations, his explanation is

---

[67] Marshall, *Parables of War*, 145.
[68] Ibid., 148.
[69] Ibid., 165.
[70] Ibid., 172.

not convincing. Not only does he have difficulty establishing an entirely Jewish context for the passages he does address, he fails to address the implications of other pertinent passages within the Apocalypse. For example, noticeably missing from Marshall's work is an in-depth consideration of John's very Jewish vision of the new Jerusalem. Marshall offers little analysis of either how the vision of the new Jerusalem fits within his schema or the implications of John's portrayal of the city as founded on the twelve apostles of the Lamb.[71] The latter characteristic is a decidedly Christian interpolation for a Jewish writer. His compromising conclusion that John's Judaism is one that "honours Jesus"[72] only raises more complicated issues than it resolves. The awkwardness of Marshall's position is betrayed when he acknowledges, "Though John does envision the lamb and the crucified Lord as central forces in the resolution of the conflicts he addresses, he speaks in these parables as a Jew moving within Judaism and fully loyal to Judaism."[73]

A final work to consider is Peter Hirschberg's, *Das eschatologische Israel*,[74] which is perhaps the most comprehensive consideration to date of John's theological perspective on the relationship between the church and Israel in the Apocalypse. Hirschberg recognizes the ill effects that a history of anti-Jewish theology, particularly supersessionism, has had in the church leading up to the Holocaust and questions whether there can be found any incipient elements of this doctrine in the NT, particularly the Apocalypse of John. Hirschberg focuses his study on the Apocalypse due not only to its frequent neglect in the study of Jewish-Christian relations but particularly due to the often held notion that the theology of John's apocalypse appears to promote supersessionism. It is this latter concern which Hirschberg attempts to investigate by examining key passages within John's apocalypse (2.9, 3.9, 7.1-17 and 21.1-22.5).

Hirschberg's conclusion is that John does not promote a supersessionist view but that he sees the church as the fulfillment of Judaism accomplished through the redemptive work of the Lamb. As the eschatological Israel, the church is Israel open to the nations. Therefore for John, the church has not lost continuity with Judaism. Hence, John can speak of the

---

[71] Marshall refers briefly to the vision as "Jerusalem Vindicated" within his structural analysis of the Apocalypse but offers no in-depth critical analysis (ibid., 181). On 186 he notes that 21.12 contains a reference to Israel but completely ignores the Christian context.

[72] Ibid., 175.

[73] Ibid., 173.

[74] Peter Hirschberg, *Das eschatologische Israel: Untersuchungen zum Gottesvolkverständnis der Johannesoffenbarung*, WMANT 84 (Neukirchen-Vluyn: Neukirchener, 1999).

people of God in both Jewish terms (e.g., 144,000) and as a people from all nations (5.9; 7.9).

Hirschberg's study is an important step in recognizing the contribution the Apocalypse has to offer to the discussion of early Jewish-Christian relations. His discussion is balanced and his conclusions plausible. His study, however, neglects some important passages in developing John's perspective on the church's relationship to Judaism. Although he mentions these passages at times throughout his discussion, Hirschberg could have devoted more space to Rev 11.1-13[75] and in particular 12.1-17. The latter vision offers a blending of both Israel and the church into one significant metaphorical symbol which speaks volumes concerning John's view of the church in relationship to Israel. Although Hirschberg's goal is to demonstrate that John is not and should not be a source for supersessionist theology, a greater consideration of John's perspective in relationship to the increasingly Christian anti-Jewish rhetoric of his era would also have served his study well.

The Implications of the Proposed Project

Although opinions vary, it seems clear that John's apocalypse provides some evidence for understanding the nature of Jewish-Christian relations at the end of the first century—even if one limits the evidence to Rev 2.9 and 3.9. Beyond these latter two passages, however, there is considerable debate as to whether the remaining passages and images of John's apocalypse contribute significantly to the study of Jewish-Christian relations. This writer proposes, however, that a study of the entire Apocalypse would show that John displays a consistent and identifiable position concerning the relationship between Israel and the church. Such a study would have as its goal to respond to a key historical question: How does the Apocalypse help to advance an understanding of Jewish-Christian relations at the end of the first century?

John's use of Jewish imagery for the church and his Christianizing of the Jewish scriptures suggests that his understanding of Jewish-Christian relations is in some ways consistent with that evidenced by other late first-century and early second-century Christian writers. This is not to propose, as Beagley implies, that John's apocalypse is an anti-Jewish tract. Borgen is probably correct that John, a Jewish-Christian himself, saw the conflict as intramural. John's perspective is certainly not anti-Semitic and not

---

[75] His lengthiest discussion of this passage appears on 216–22 under his discussion of the new Jerusalem.

even anti-Jewish. One might be able to say, however, that he or she sees within John's apocalypse a perspective that later developed into a more anti-Jewish stance in some segments of the church. For example, this anti-Jewish stance can be seen in the epistles of Ignatius of Antioch just ten to fifteen years later.

One could also argue that John views the church as God's "new spiritual Israel." While it must be acknowledged that John never directly refers to the church in this manner, such an implication is possible. Such an argument, however, does not imply that John would have used this terminology or that if he had, he would have used it to espouse a supersessionist view. John clearly envisions continuity between Israel and the church and never subordinates one to the other. For John, the church is subsumed in, and the full extension of, God's covenant people Israel.

The church is God's *Israel* in that it represents God's covenant people, both Jews and Gentiles, who are heirs of the covenant promises first given to Israel and realized in the redemptive work of the Lamb. It is God's *spiritual* Israel because the "true Jew" is no longer based on ethnicity but on allegiance to God's redemptive plan. For John, covenant loyalty and eventual eschatological reward is a matter of uncompromising spiritual faithfulness. The church, God's spiritual Israel, is comprised of those who "keep the commandments of God and hold the testimony of Jesus" (Rev 12.17; cf. 19.10). The church is God's *new* spiritual Israel not because it has replaced ethnic Israel but because it represents a new covenant people comprised of people from all nations (Rev 5.9; 7.9). It is in one sense the fulfillment of the Jewish prophetic hope for the ingathering of the nations in a manner not completely anticipated even by the Hebrew prophets. John recognizes this continuity through his extensive use of OT prophetic language while often altering this language to reflect a christological perspective.

Unlike the Hebrew prophets, John never makes a distinction between ethnic Israel and the nations. Rather, the redeemed of the nations *are* Israel, but in a spiritual rather than an ethnic sense. This perspective is reflected in John's use of Jewish symbols for the church. The saints are those sealed from the twelve tribes of Israel (7.1-8), yet also the innumerable multitude from every nation (7.9). They are the temple (11.1-2) and the two witnesses (reminiscent of Moses and Elijah), who suffer the same fate as "their Lord" (11.3-13). They are also the heavenly woman, who is at once the mother of the Messiah but also of the saints (12.1-17), and they are the bride of the Lamb, the new Jerusalem (21.1-22.5). The church is redeemed Israel, both Jews and Gentiles, which follows the paschal Lamb and has accepted his redemptive work. Those who do not follow the Lamb follow the beast to their eternal destruction. It is to this end that the Apocalypse is written, to encourage the faithful to persevere and to warn the unfaithful of certain judgment.

The value of this study rests in its potential to provide further literary evidence of the nature of Jewish-Christian relations during this early period. Traditionally the Apocalypse of John has been given a small voice among the meager evidence that can be collected. If a thorough study of the entire Apocalypse—one not limited to 2.9 and 3.9—can reveal that John has a clearly definable perspective with regard to Israel and the church, then John's apocalypse would have to be given a greater voice in understanding Jewish-Christian relations during the sub-apostolic period. John's position could then be plotted on the grid of Jewish-Christian relations between 70 and 150 CE. Such a study would, at a minimum, enlarge the pool of evidence for the study of Jewish-Christian relations and, at a maximum, yield new insight.

1

An Overview of Jewish-Christian Relations (70–150 CE):
Factors in the Developing Schism

Early Conflict

THE church was a completely Jewish institution at its inception, which reflected the ethnicity and cultural focus of its founder. The induction of its first Gentile converts in Antioch (Acts 11.19-21), however, changed the complexion of the church forever and brought about one of the most divisive controversies the emerging church would have to face. How would a primarily Jewish movement relate to these non-Jewish members—people from whom they had all of their lives separated themselves? What would be the place of the Jewish law and circumcision? Should Gentiles be required to become Jews in order to follow Jesus the Messiah? Although the writer of Acts records that these questions were answered at a Jerusalem council (Acts 15; cf. 11.1-18), these issues by no means disappeared from the church. Jews and Gentiles may have become members of the same body, but hostilities still flared. For decades after the birth of the church there were Christian Jews and Gentile Judaizers who argued that the church needed to be more Jewish and that observance of Jewish regulations was necessary to this new movement. The Apostle Paul argued aggressively against such a position in his letters to the Galatians, Philippians, and Colossians. The Church Fathers, such as Ignatius of Antioch and the writer of the *Epistle of Barnabas*, aggressively continued this line of argumentation into the second century.

The conflicts with Judaism, however, were not only internal. Although the church had begun as a Jewish sect, it became increasingly aware of its rejection by Judaism as evidenced in the NT. Acts, which purports to recount the church's first missionary activity, illustrates that the Jewish response to Christian evangelism was often violent.[1] Even Paul refers to the hostility that the Palestinian church experienced at the hands of the Jews and pronounces a harsh judgment upon them (1 Thess 2.14-16; cf. Paul's own testimony, Gal 1.13; 2 Cor 11.24-25). Jewish-Christian relations only continued to deteriorate in the post-apostolic period. An examination of the literature reveals an anti-Judaic stance even more aggressive than that of Paul or the other NT writers. The hope of salvation for the Jews, which is found particularly in the writings of Paul (Rom 1.16; 9–11, particularly 11.26), seems to have all but disappeared by the end of the second century. Generally, there is a detectable progression in the separation between Judaism and the church throughout the second century.[2] By the latter half of the second century, the church has clearly replaced Israel as the people of God, and the Jews are condemned as God-killers (Justin, *Dial.* 11.5; Melito, *Peri Pascha* 55).

Was it for completely theological reasons that the church began to reject the Jewish people or were there also social and political factors? The theological reasons, of course, are spelled out in much of the second-century literature. The church criticizes the Jews for rejecting Jesus as their Messiah, which was due to their obduracy of heart and blindness to the scriptures. God, therefore, has judged them by rejecting them and their ritualism. The church has replaced them as the people of God with the result that their scriptures now belong to the Christians who interpret them properly.[3] It would be overly simplistic, however, to point solely to theological reasons for Christian hostility toward the Jews. Theological arguments were certainly at the heart of increased hostilities on both sides, but history reveals that there were also social and political factors that contributed to the overall relational deterioration.

The evidence for the period of Jewish-Christian relations between 70 and 150 CE is extremely limited, immensely one-sided, and much has to be inferred. The writings of Josephus conclude coverage around 70 CE, and the Jewish sources that date beyond this period contain little concerning the Christians. What few remarks that are found in these sources are difficult to interpret. The Christian movement, which was not well known

---

[1] Although Acts records that Jews (as well as Gentiles) were responsible for instigating trouble against the Christians, not all Jews rejected the message.

[2] Peter Richardson, *Israel in the Apostolic Church*, SNTSMS 10 (Cambridge: Cambridge University Press, 1969) 32.

[3] Lee M. McDonald, "Anti-Judaism in the Early Church Fathers," in *Anti-Semitism and Early Christianity: Issues of Polemic and Faith*, ed. Craig A. Evans and Donald A. Hagner (Minneapolis: Fortress, 1993) 229.

at the time, did not leave much of a mark on pagan sources either. This results in the majority of written evidence coming from Christian literature. It is, of course, only one viewpoint and is generally characterized by ad hoc responses to internal church problems, which is true of the Apostolic Fathers whose writings largely fill this time period. Nevertheless, one may make inferences and draw some conclusions from this limited evidence.

Emerging Christian Identity

Christianity shared with Judaism the same God, the same scriptures and, therefore, the same religious roots. Judaism was already an ancient and recognized religion in the world that generally enjoyed legal protection as an established religion in the Roman Empire. Christianity, however, found itself being pushed out from under the umbrella of Jewish recognition quite early in its history, largely because of hostility toward and Jewish rejection of the Jesus followers and their message. A majority of Jews considered a gospel of a crucified messiah to be not only offensive but also heretical. Christian claims to the divinity of Jesus directly challenged Jewish monotheism, and for Jews who were expecting a political messiah that would usher in the kingdom of God, Jesus was a complete failure.[4] Such strong feelings arguably led to a synagogue ban[5] against Jewish-Christians and the practice of openly cursing Christians as heretics.[6]

This orphaning of Christianity placed on it increased pressure to define itself within Greco-Roman society, and this self-identity came at the expense of Judaism. The second-century Christian apologists betray this need to defend Christianity to a pagan society while simultaneously differentiating it from Judaism (e.g., *Diogn.* 1; 3–5).[7] Christians, who also laid claim to the Jewish scriptures, had to show that they were the legitimate heirs of the old covenant and had replaced the Jews as the true

---

[4] See the discussion in Craig Evans, "Root Causes of the Jewish-Christian Rift from Jesus to Justin," in *Christian-Jewish Relations through the Centuries*, JSNTSup 192 (Sheffield: Sheffield Academic, 2000) 20–35. Evans argues that the root cause for the Jewish-Christian split was the incongruity between Jewish messianic expectation and the crucified Jesus.

[5] Jack T. Sanders, *Schismatics, Sectarians, Dissidents, Deviants: The First One Hundred Years of Jewish-Christian Relations* (Valley Forge, Pa.: Trinity, 1993) 42–43, suggests that this is what is being indicated in John 9.22; 12.42; 16.2; cf. Richardson, *Israel*, 43–44.

[6] This is known as the *birkath haminim* or the twelfth of the Eighteen Benedictions (*Shemoneh Esreh*) of the Jewish *Tefillah*, recited three times daily by devout Jews. This is discussed in more detail below, 42–49.

[7] Chapter 11 also suggests a rejection of the Jews and an attempt to make the church Gentile. On this last point, see Richardson, *Israel*, 20.

people of God. They tackled this problem in two ways. They Christianized the Jewish scriptures while subordinating them to the developing New Testament canon.[8] This kind of rhetoric can be detected early in the second century. Ignatius of Antioch, for example, in his letter to the Magnesians proclaimed the superiority of Christianity over Judaism and adopted the ancient prophets exclusively for Christianity. He wrote, "Christianity did not believe in Judaism, but Judaism in Christianity" (*Magn.* 10.3). He further declared that the "most godly prophets lived according to Christ Jesus," and this is why they were persecuted (presumably by their fellow Jews; *Magn.* 8.2; cf. *Phld.* 9.1-2). *Barnabas*, written sometime near the end of the first century or the beginning of the second, goes so far as to suggest that the old covenant never actually belonged to the Jews arguing that it was lost to them when Moses smashed the tablets on Mount Sinai (4.6-8; 14.1-4; cf. 9.4.). In addition, the writer makes extensive use of allegory to interpret the Jewish scriptures Christologically.

There were other factors as well that contributed to this growing schism between Christianity and Judaism. There were the problems of Judaizers within the church and Jewish missionary activity outside the church. There was also, as Lee McDonald terms it, the "intimidation factor."[9] Jews not only enjoyed political and religious status in the empire, they also far outnumbered the Christians. Jews probably numbered around six to seven million or 7%–10% of the imperial population. On the other hand, Christians perhaps numbered less than 100,000 by the end of the first century.[10]

Roman persecution of Christians caused an increased desire on the part of the Jews to distinguish themselves from this emerging sect. It is not clear when the Roman political or social establishment began to distinguish Christians from Jews. Judge argues that the Romans never confused the Christians with the Jews and from their earliest contact saw a

---

[8] Lloyd Gaston, "Judaism of the Uncircumcised in Ignatius and Related Writers," in *Anti-Judaism in Early Christianity: Separation and Polemic,* ed. Stephen G. Wilson, Anti-Judaism in Early Christianity 2, SSCJ 2 (Waterloo, Ont.: Wilfrid Laurier University Press, 1986) 33–44.

[9] McDonald, "Anti-Judaism," 242–45.

[10] McDonald, "Anti-Judaism," 242; cf. Stephen G. Wilson, *Related Strangers: Jews and Christians, 70–170 C.E.* (Minneapolis: Fortress, 1995) 25. For various other scholarly estimates see Marcel Simon, *Verus Israel: A Study of the Relations between Christians and Jews in the Roman Empire (AD 135–425),* LLJC (London: Vallentine Mitchell, 1996); ET of: *Verus Israel: Étude sur les relations entre Chrétiens et Juifs dans l'Empire Romain (135–425)* (Paris: de Boccard, 1964) 33–34. The estimates cited by Simon fall within this 7%–10% range.

distinction between them.[11] He says that the very name "Christian," first introduced in Acts 11.26, was coined not by Jews but by Romans since the name implies the messiahship of Jesus and its suffix (*-ianus*) is of Latin origin.[12] According to Richardson, the Jews themselves were making a distinction as early as Paul's ministry; yet he does not believe that the Romans made a distinction this early, arguing that this lack of distinction resulted in the Jews being expelled from Rome by Claudius (49 CE) as a result of Christian activity. This, he believes, is one of the factors that led to the Jews pressing for a distinction between themselves and Christians. The Jewish desire to avoid persecution coupled with well-placed Jews in the imperial court brought about an eventual political distinction.[13]

Judge counters, however, that the Roman expulsion of the Jews was more likely a result of agitation within the Roman Jewish community itself. He finds no credence in the argument based on Suetonius (*Claud.* 25.4)[14] that the Jews were expelled because of conflict with the Christian community. He further observes that there is no NT evidence that conflict existed between the Jewish and Christian communities of Rome; in fact, the Jewish leadership seems to have little knowledge of controversy over the gospel (Acts 28.21-22). Judge, however, would agree that the Jews used their political standing to differentiate themselves from the Christians.[15]

The foregoing debate reveals just how inconclusive the evidence is for an early Roman discrimination between Jews and Christians, but such a distinction seems to have taken shape at least by the time of the Neronian persecution of Christians in 64 CE; however, whether this distinction extended beyond Rome or held firm in successive administrations is unclear. Wilson postulates that there may have still been some confusion between the two groups as late as the reign of Domitian when one takes into con-

---

[11] E. A. Judge, "Judaism and the Rise of Christianity: A Roman Perspective," *TynBul* 45 (1994) 359–62, 368.

[12] Ibid., 363.

[13] Richardson, *Israel*, 42–43; cf. Paul R. Trebilco, *Jewish Communities in Asia Minor* (Cambridge: Cambridge University Press, 1991) 24–25, whose analysis of Acts 19.23-41 posits that this incident may be an example of a Jewish attempt to avoid persecution by making a distinction between themselves and the Christians, which a hostile Ephesian crowd failed to do.

[14] Suetonius writes, "Since the Jews constantly made disturbances at the instigation of Chrestus, he [Claudius] expelled them from Rome" (Rolfe, LCL). Many scholars believe that *Chrestus* is a misspelling of *Christus*.

[15] Judge, "Judaism," 361–62, 364; cf. Stanley E. Porter and Brook W. R. Pearson, "Ancient Understandings of the Christian-Jewish Split," in *Christian-Jewish Relations through the Centuries*, JSNTSup 192 (Sheffield: Sheffield Academic, 2000) 50–51.

sideration, for example, Suetonius' testimony concerning the collection of the Jewish tax (*Dom.* 12.2).[16] Judge calls into question this traditional interpretation as well.[17] Whatever lack of clarity there may have been, however, disappeared by the reign of Trajan[18] where, according to Pliny's letters (*Ep. Tra.* 10.96), the Roman authorities were taking legal action against Christians as outlaws.

Jewish Persecution of Christians

While Roman persecution of the Christians is certain, the extent of this persecution is not; even less certain is the extent of Jewish persecution of Christians. It has been traditionally suggested that Jewish persecution of Christians was indeed a factor in the deterioration of relations. Richardson believes that it played a significant roll and sees an unbroken line of Jewish persecution beginning with the crucifixion of Jesus.[19] All four Gospels blame Jewish instigation for the death of Jesus. The Fourth Gospel particularly highlights Jewish animosity with Jesus often seen in long discourses that highlight this opposition (e.g., 5.16-47; 6.22-59; 8.12-59). In John 8.44, Jesus even tells a Jewish crowd that they are of their father, the devil—a passage reminiscent of the Apocalypse's "synagogue of Satan" accusation (Rev 2.9; 3.9). The book of Acts records frequent opposition from Jews to the spread of the church beginning in Palestine and continuing in the Diaspora regions of Asia Minor and the Greek peninsula (Acts 4.21; 5.40; 13.49; 14.4-5, 19; 17.5-9, 13; 18.6, 12-17; cf. 1 Thess 2.14-16).[20]

In recent scholarship, there has been a move away from the traditional view that Jews consistently and aggressively persecuted Christians, recognizing the meager and one-sided nature of the evidence. This trend is partly the result of a post-World War 2 desire to re-evaluate the historical evidence while attempting to avoid the church's traditionally anti-Semitic posture. This trend toward objectivity is to be applauded; however, the proverbial baby should not be thrown out with the bath water. Although nearly all of the evidence comes from Christian sources, it cannot be com-

---

[16] Wilson, *Related Strangers*, 16. Suetonius writes, "Besides other taxes, that on the Jews was levied with the utmost rigour, and those were prosecuted *who without publicly acknowledging that faith yet lived as Jews*, as well as those who concealed their origin and did not pay the tribute levied upon their people" (Rolfe, LCL; emphasis mine).

[17] Judge, "Judaism," 367–68.

[18] So Wilson, *Related Strangers*, 16; Richardson, *Israel*, 43.

[19] Richardson, *Israel*, 43–46.

[20] See the analysis of the NT evidence in Trebilco, *Jewish Communities*, 20–27.

pletely dismissed as exaggerated, fabricated, baseless theological rhetoric[21] or merely the reflection of an intra-sect squabble.[22]

Sanders, for example, downplays any idea of Jewish persecution and vigorously opposes the idea of Jewish execution of Christians. He does not deny a possible synagogue ban or that spontaneous stonings may have taken place, but few, he argues, were deadly. He suggests they were merely a means by which Christians were chased out of town. He further postulates that it is very unlikely that Jews even had the authority to execute anyone and does not believe that the evidence supports such executions.[23]

Sanders may be correct that Jewish authority did not include execution—at least not outside of Palestine.[24] This, of course, did not preclude spontaneous mob violence by both Jews and Gentiles. Within Palestine, however, the author of Acts testifies that the Jews exercised the authority not only to punish but to execute as well.[25] The historicity of Acts, however, is sometimes questioned as Sanders does when he rejects most of Acts as unreliable and anti-Semitic.[26] He even questions Paul's own testimony of persecution at the hands of the Jews (2 Cor 11.24-25), not on the grounds of its historicity, but its timing. He argues that there is no certainty when Paul received these lashings—before or after he became a Christian.[27]

---

[21] See, for example, the discussion in Judith M. Lieu, "Accusations of Jewish Persecution in Early Christian Sources, with Particular Reference to Justin Martyr and the *Martyrdom of Polycarp*," in *Tolerance and Intolerance in Early Judaism and Christianity*, ed. Graham N. Stanton and Guy G. Stroumsa (Cambridge: Cambridge University Press, 1998) 279–95. Lieu discusses the possibility that the Christian accusations of Jewish persecution are based partly on theological rhetoric that creates a perceived reality; however, Lieu tries to maintain an appropriate balance between rhetoric and historical possibility.

[22] See, for example, David Frankfurter, "Jews or Not? Reconstructing the 'Other' in Rev 2:9 and 3:9," *HTR* 94 (2001) 406-7, who argues that the gospels (Matthew and John) reflect intramural squabbles rather than external threats, dismisses the *M. of Polycarp* as historically insufficient, and relegates Rev 2.9; 3.9 to an unhistorical portion of an apocalyptic "tribulation scenario."

[23] Sanders, *Schismatics*, 47–48, 91.

[24] Shimon Applebaum, "The Legal Status of the Jewish Communities in the Diaspora," in *The Jewish People in the First Century*, ed. S. Safrai et al., CRINT 1 (Philadelphia: Fortress, 1974) 461, however, postulates that Diaspora Jewish communities had the authority to make arrests outside of Palestine.

[25] However, the Jews may not have been exercising an authority to execute but perhaps the executions were more acts of mob violence since the Fourth Gospel indicates that Jesus was brought to Pilate because of the Jewish authorities' lack of judicial power to execute (John 18.31).

[26] Sanders, *Schismatics*, 1–4.

[27] Sanders, *Schismatics*, 5–10.

Sanders raises some valid points but is too extreme in his conclusions. It is unlikely that a Pharisee of the Pharisees and a blameless law-keeper (Phil 3.5-6; cf. Gal 1.14) like the pre-Christian Paul would have received the most severe punishment Jewish law allowed short of stoning—not to mention five times; indeed, Paul even testifies to having been once stoned (2 Cor 11.25; cf. Acts 14.19b). Paul is listing for the Corinthians those trials that validate his apostleship; it would only seem logical, therefore, that they are his experiences as a Christian missionary. Persecution by the Jews is part of that claim.

As for the historicity of the Acts accounts, a more moderate approach seems prudent. Trebilco, through an analysis of the textual evidence and the corroboration of Paul's epistles, makes a strong case for the historicity of at least some of the Acts accounts of Jewish persecution in Asia Minor.[28] Wilson rightly observes that even if the Acts accounts are exaggerated, they still provide some proof of Jewish opposition to Christians.[29] Luke is ostensibly writing about events that have occurred in the past, but he gives no indication that Jewish opposition has changed at the time of his writing.

The Apocalypse of John also alludes to difficult relations between Christians and Jews in the cities of Smyrna and Philadelphia that may have involved persecution (2.9-10; 3.9).[30] The evidence is inconclusive, but it seems to reveal some sort of hostility between Jews and Christians that at least involved a war of words (2.9, τὴν βλασφημίαν) and at most Jewish persecution of Christians (2.10). John charges that these persons slandering the church call themselves Jews but really are not; they are instead a "synagogue of Satan." This charge, coupled with a general tendency in Revelation to appropriate Jewish images for the church, suggests that John has in mind the local Jewish communities of Smyrna and Philadelphia; though they claim to be Jews, it is in fact the Christians, John argues, who are the "true Jews."[31]

If John is referring to the Jews of Smyrna and Philadelphia, then what can be inferred from what he says? It seems unlikely that his remarks are exaggerated or fabricated since his mention of the "Jews" in these two cities seems in no way contrived or gratuitous. This hostility in

---

[28] Trebilco, *Jewish Communities*, 20–27.
[29] Wilson, *Related Strangers*, 174.
[30] This argument will be developed more fully in the following chapter.
[31] John never actually uses this terminology, but this seems to be the implication of his "synagogue of Satan" accusations.

relations is only one among several difficulties all seven churches are facing. It is also doubtful that he intends to be anti-Semitic. John himself is a Jewish Christian and the term "Jew" in these passages is not being used in a pejorative way. His remarks certainly suggest a level of hostility that is extremely disconcerting to these two churches and requires words of encouragement. Whether these hostilities have reached the level of Jewish instigation of persecution against Christians is unclear; Rev 2.10 suggests that possibility. The mention of impending persecution and imprisonment instigated by the "devil" implies a connection with the "synagogue of Satan" in the preceding verse. It insinuates that certain members of the Jewish community in Smyrna and possibly Philadelphia were instigating public action against the Christians.

The *Martyrdom of Polycarp*, dated a half century later, also contains some controversial passages that implicate the Jews as regular participants in Christian persecution in the city of Smyrna. Although the Jews are not responsible for this execution, they are portrayed as eagerly participating (13.1). The major question that arises is how reliable this information is. The account purports to have been written shortly after the event (18.2-3) from the observations of eyewitnesses (9.1; 15.1). Chapter 21, which was perhaps added later, gives specific information concerning the date of the martyrdom. All of these factors seem to contribute to the veracity and historicity of the account; however, it is the details of the account that impugn its authenticity and reliability. The account appears to have been altered to conform to the Gospels' accounts of Jesus' death (1.1). This fact alone offers a plausible explanation for the author's interest in highlighting Jewish participation in the execution. For example, the Jews are specifically singled out of the crowd as participating in an angry cry for Polycarp's death (12.2-3), which is a scene reminiscent of the Gospels' accounts of Jesus' own trial before his death (Luke 23.18-21 and parallels).

This literary *Tendenz* throws into question the reliability of these references to the Jews. In fact, a closer analysis of this example might even suggest that these references to the Jews are either exaggerated or even fabricated. For example, the cry of the crowd, which the writer specifically notes includes Jews, does not seem suited for this mixed audience. "This is the teacher of Asia," the crowd cries out, "the father of Christians, the destroyer of *our gods*, who teaches many not *to sacrifice or worship*" (12.2, emphasis mine). Judith Lieu correctly notes that this cry is unlikely to be found on Jewish lips since most Jews did not participate in pagan worship. On the contrary, she also observes that this is not the real issue for the writer. What is at issue in the *M. of Polycarp* is that the world, comprised of both Jews and Gentiles, is against the Christians.[32] There are other observations, which space will not allow to be treated here, that would raise serious concerns about how Jews are portrayed in the *M. of Polycarp*.[33] All of these objections demand serious consideration. Lieu, however, makes an important summarizing observation: "The recognition of the theological significance of the presentation of the Jewish role in the martyrdom of Polycarp, whether or not it is helpfully labeled 'antisemitic', demands rather than replaces a historical interpretation."[34]

What then does this evidence reflect concerning the historical situation? From the Christian perspective, there is a consistent perception of persecution and Jewish opposition from the inception of the church.[35] How much this Christian evidence reflects theological rhetoric or historical reality is impossible to determine precisely.[36] The consistency of the evidence over a long period of time argues for at least some historical veracity. Paul's testimony stands out in this regard in that he testifies to his own Jewish zeal in persecuting the church and to the opposition he received from his people following his Damascus road experience (Gal 1.13; 2 Cor 11.24-25; 1 Thess 2.14-16). Although mid to late first-century Christian testimony may reflect mainly an intra-sect conflict, the *M. of Polycarp* and also Justin Martyr's *Dialogue with Trypho*, both written about mid-second century, indicate that this conflict continued even after the Jewish-Christian schism had developed significantly. Justin, like the *M. of Polycarp*, implicates the Jews in Christian persecution (*Dial.* 16.4; 17.1; 133.6; *1 Apol.* 31.6). Although it can be argued that Justin's remarks are extreme, they too carry some historical validity.[37]

As for the situation in Smyrna and possibly Philadelphia, the implication of the Jews in the martyrdom of Polycarp, though perhaps exaggerated, at the very least reflects a competition between Christianity and Judaism in Smyrna and, placed alongside other evidence, may reflect a competition not limited to this one setting. How far this competition

---

[32] Judith Lieu, *Image and Reality: The Jews in the World of the Christians in the Second Century* (Edinburgh: T. & T. Clark, 1996) 60; idem, "Jewish Persecution," 285–86.

[33] For a fuller discussion see Lieu, *Image and Reality*, 57–94.

[34] Lieu, *Image and Reality*, 70; cf. idem, "Jewish Persecution," 291, where she makes a similar concluding statement.

[35] Although the present discussion has reflected on literature from the first 100 years of the church, testimony to Jewish opposition exists beyond this period (e.g., *Martyrdom of Pionius* 3.6; Origen, *Cels.* 6.27; Eusebius, *Hist. eccl.* 5.16).

[36] So Lieu, "Jewish Persecution," 290–91.

[37] For a fuller discussion see Lieu, *Image and Reality*, 103–48.

moved beyond a war of words or claims of theological supremacy is difficult to say with certainty. Though these charges are one-sided and possibly inflated, they cannot be dismissed too quickly. John's implication of Jewish opposition to the Smyrnean church coupled with the testimony of the *M. of Polycarp* may signal an on-going hostility between the Christian and Jewish communities in Smyrna for many years—a hostility that may have at times involved physical persecution.

The Jewish Wars

Two major political events that made a considerable contribution to the ever widening split between Jews and Christians are the Jewish Wars of 66–74 CE and 132–135 CE.[38] There has been some debate over which of these wars was the most significant in its effects on Jewish-Christian relations. Recent scholarship has tended to favor the Second Jewish Revolt, also known as the Bar Kokhba revolt, as the most decisive event of the two,[39] but the destruction of the temple in 70 CE had its ramifications.

It is difficult to know exactly the impact the destruction of the temple had on Jewish-Christian relations. Scholarly opinion tends to envision a Diaspora Judaism that had little concern with the events of the First Jewish Revolt, and the church too by this time had already recognized that its future lay with the Gentile churches. Trebilco, on the other hand, believes that Diaspora Jews (particularly the Jews of Asia Minor) had "a strong attachment to the historic land of Israel and to the centrality of the temple and its worship." His conclusion is based on evidence that Jews of Asia Minor and elsewhere considered the payment of the temple tax a sacred duty. However, he does not directly state what impact the destruction of the temple might have had on these Jews.[40] Marshall musters evidence from Josephus which he reads "against the grain" in order to suggest the possibility that there was at least some concern among certain elements of Diaspora Judaism over the events of the First Jewish Revolt than is traditionally recognized.[41] The evidence, however, is sketchy and requires considerable speculation. In fact, the lack of preoccupation in Jewish and

---

[38] Wilson, *Related Strangers*, 8, points out that little is known of the effects of the Jewish revolt under Trajan and, therefore, are not usually considered in this discussion.

[39] So Wilson, *Related Strangers*, 8–10; Dunn, *Partings*, 231, 243; G. W. H. Lampe, "A. D. 70 in Christian Reflection," in *Jesus and the Politics of His Day*, ed. Ernst Brummel and C. F. D. Moule (Cambridge: Cambridge University Press, 1984) 155; Richardson, *Israel*, 36–38; cf. Simon, *Verus Israel*, xiv–xv.

[40] Trebilco, *Jewish Communities*, 13–16.

[41] Marshall, *Parables of War*, 98–119.

Christian literature with the destruction of the temple implies that the event had little impact on either group.[42] However, this is not to imply that the temple's destruction did not impact Jewish-Christian relations at least indirectly.

Dunn outlines some effects that the destruction of the temple had on both Palestinian Judaism and Jewish Christians. For the Jews, it meant the loss of a major pillar of Second Temple Judaism; it also brought about the demise of the major sects of pre-70-CE Judaism and the decisive rise of rabbinic Judaism as the one lasting form of Judaism for centuries to come. As for the Jewish Christians, it is uncertain what effects resulted from the destruction of Jerusalem. It certainly provided incentive for the Christians to distance themselves from Jewish nationalism, and Dunn writes that it is "almost certain" that a deathblow was dealt to the base of conservative Jewish Christianity.[43] There is, however, a tradition that the Jerusalem church fled before the Roman siege and Eusebius records a tradition of successive Jewish Christian bishops in Jerusalem through 135 C.E. (*Hist. eccl.* 3.5.2-3; 4.5).

It is uncertain what impact the destruction of the temple had on Diaspora Jews and Christians, and it is equally uncertain what effect it had on Jewish-Christian relations. The loss of the temple may not have been the defining moment in the demise of Jewish-Christian relations, but it certainly helped to accelerate their deterioration. For the Christians, who were beginning to define themselves apart from Judaism, the destruction of the temple was only confirmation of God's rejection of Israel. The temple's destruction and the later failure of the Bar Kokhba revolt eventually became fuel for anti-Jewish polemic.[44] The church had superseded Israel and had become the "new Israel." Although there is no extant reference of the church ever calling itself the new Israel until Justin's *Dialogue with Trypho* (11.5), it is clear that earlier inferences were being made (e.g.,

---

[42] Lampe, "A.D. 70," 153–57; cf. Simon, *Verus Israel*, 35–36, who agrees that Diaspora Judaism was minimally affected by the events of 70 CE. He even suggests that some in the Diaspora may have seen the event in a positive light because it removed the inequality that they felt with Palestinian Judaism. However, he suggests that Palestinian Judaism was impacted to a much greater extent.

[43] Dunn, *Partings*, 232–33.

[44] Wilson, *Related Strangers*, 10, cites in this regard the epistle of *Barnabas*. *Barnabas*, which Wilson dates ca. 98 CE, mentions the destruction of the temple and seems disturbed by its possible reconstruction (16.1-5). From this point on, states Wilson, the destruction of the temple and the later expulsion of the Jews from Jerusalem are never viewed neutrally in Christian literature. They are lumped together as proof of God's condemnation of Jews.

Barn. 4.6-8; *1 Clem.* 17-19; 29-30.1; 32.4; 45; Ign. *Phld.* 9; Ign. *Magn.* 8-10; Ign. *Smyrn.* 1.2; *2 Clem.* 2.3.).

In the intervening years between 70 and 132 CE, Jewish-Christian relations became increasingly strained.[45] It was the Bar Kokhba revolt of 132–135 CE, however, that seems to be the decisive event in relations. Dunn states, "After the second revolt the separation of the main bodies of Christianity and Judaism was clear-cut and final, whatever interaction there continued to be at the margins."[46] It is difficult to say, according to Wilson, if this event merely marked a "radically new stage" in relations or was the final straw in a relationship that was already hanging in the balance.[47] Whichever the case, it is clear that after Bar Kokhba relations took a definitive turn for the worse.

Simon Ben Kosiba, dubbed Bar Kokhba ("son of the star"), was a messianic pretender who, during his revolt, gained brief autonomy from Roman rule. During this time, he allegedly persecuted and even executed Christians for their refusal to deny Jesus and to support Bar Kokhba as messiah (Justin, *1 Apol.* 31.6; cf. *Dial.*, 16). For the Christians, the entire event left bitter lasting memories. What had been a point of contention for decades between Jews and Christians—the messiahship of Jesus—finally came to the fore and became the impetus for Jewish execution of Christians. The Roman response to the rebellion was harsh and decisive. Years of repression followed the revolt (135–138 CE) during which time Jews were banned from Jerusalem and the environs except for one annual visit. The Romans constructed on the site of Jerusalem a pagan city and a temple to Jupiter, which resulted in the displacement of most of the Jews in and around Jerusalem.[48] It was from this point forward that the Jerusalem church came under Gentile leadership (*Hist. eccl.* 4.5) and with this came the demise of Jewish Christianity. The two events—the destruction of the temple in 70 CE and the Jewish banishment from Jerusalem after Bar Kokhba—became further confirmation for the church of God's rejection of the Jews.[49]

---

[45] Dunn, *Partings*, 238, states that this period *"was decisive for the parting of the ways"* (emphasis original).

[46] Dunn, *Partings*, 238.

[47] Wilson, *Related Strangers*, 10; cf. Richardson, *Israel*, 35; Dunn, *Partings*, 243.

[48] Wilson, *Related Strangers*, 7.

[49] Justin, *Dial.* 16, actually asserts that circumcision, once a blessed sign of the covenant, had now become a curse to the Jews. He states this in light of their banishment from Jerusalem by the Romans after Bar Kokhba. Circumcision was now the distinguishing mark by which their enemies denied them access to the Holy City.

Christian Judaizers

An additional factor to consider briefly in this overview of the breakdown in Jewish-Christian relations is the effect of Judaizers in the church. The attractiveness of Judaism to certain elements of the Christian church remained a sore spot for several centuries. The Judaizers, like Jewish Christians, were a group that spanned the divide between Judaism and Christianity. Jewish Christians, whom Gaston defines as those who called themselves Jews even before Christian baptism and who to some extent remained part of that community,[50] do not really enter into the debate between Jews and Christians. As Lieu observes, little is said about them in the extant literature and they do little to inspire the debate.[51] Lee McDonald, however, sympathetically points out that they were the "clear losers" in the debate between Jews and Christians since both sides rejected them as "heretics."[52]

The Judaizers, on the other hand, became a source of contention and a factor that contributed to anti-Jewish sentiment in the church. The use of the term "Judaizer" has become somewhat of a misnomer in scholarship since it has often been used of Christian Jews who tried to push their Jewish practices on Gentile Christians (e.g., Acts 15.5; Gal. 2). Gager argues that it is difficult to make a distinction between Jewish Christians and Gentile Christians who adopted Jewish customs. Both groups saw a commitment to the Mosaic Law as in some way necessary or complimentary to belief in Jesus. Their influence, therefore, is essentially the same. He chooses to view the activity of both groups as Christian Judaizing.[53]

Wilson and Gaston, however, make a finer distinction in their definition of a Judaizer. Gaston chooses to use the term "Judaizer" and "to Judaize" in it original sense as a designation for Gentiles who have adopted Jewish customs.[54] He adds a further caveat for clarity; those who encourage others to Judaize, whether Jews, Christian Jews, or Gentiles, "should never for that reason be called judaizers."[55] Wilson essentially agrees with

---

[50] Gaston, "Judaism of the Uncircumcised," 35.

[51] Lieu, *Image and Reality*, 284.

[52] McDonald, "Anti-Judaism," 219.

[53] John G. Gager, *The Origins of Anti-Semitism: Attitudes toward Judaism in Pagan and Christian Antiquity* (New York: Oxford University Press, 1983) 117–18.

[54] Gaston, "Judaism of the Uncircumcised," 35, notes the ancient use of the term was to refer to the forced conversion of Gentiles to Judaism (Est 8:17 LXX; Josephus, *J.W.* 2.454).

[55] Gaston, "Judaism of the Uncircumcised," 36.

Gaston in that he defines a Judaizer as a Gentile who has adopted certain aspects of Judaism. In the church, they were Christian Gentiles (apart from Christian Jews) who observed certain Jewish practices.[56] This definition does not necessarily imply a deliberate need or attempt on their part "to Judaize" others but that remains a possibility. It is Wilson's slightly broader definition that will be adopted here.

The presence of Judaizers in the church is fairly well attested in the first several centuries of the church. What was thought to have only existed in pre-70-CE Christianity actually remained part of the church much longer. Gager goes as far as to say that Christian Judaizing appears to have been stronger in the fourth century than in the first.[57] The attractiveness of Judaism to Gentile Christians became a major source of anti-Judaism in the early church and a factor in the anti-Jewish polemic found in the writings of the Fathers.[58] In the period under consideration here (70–150 CE), the evidence for Judaizing in the church is perhaps a bit more ambiguous than in other periods. Traces of Judaizing activity, however, can be found in such writings as the epistle of *Barnabas* and the epistles of *Ignatius*.

The epistle of *Barnabas* in its extreme repudiation of any Jewish claim to the old covenant might suggest the strong presence of Judaizing Christians in the intended audience. Wilson takes up this point by suggesting that there were Judaizers among the epistle's recipients who were arguing that the old covenant belonged both to Jews and Christians and it is this idea that the writer specifically refutes.[59] The evidence in the epistles of *Ignatius* is primarily found in his letters to the Magnesians and the Philadelphians. His admonition to the Magnesians that to live according to Judaism is to have forfeited the grace of God (8.1), his contrast between keeping the Sabbath and the Lord's Day (9.1), his calling absurd

---

[56] Wilson, *Related Strangers*, 161.

[57] Gager, *Origins of Anti-Semitism*, 118, cites, for example, John Chrystostom's sermons directed against Judaizing among Christians in fourth-century Antioch, Syria.

[58] Gager, *Origins of Anti-Semitism*, 118, writes, "There can no longer be any doubt that a powerful and persistent factor in generating Christian anti-Judaism is the phenomenon of Judaizing among early Christians." Cf. Gaston, "Judaism of the Uncircumcised," 33–44; Wilson, *Related Strangers*, 160.

[59] Wilson, *Related Strangers*, 136–39, 161. See *Barn.* 3.6: 4.6-8; 13-14. Wilson remarks that 3.6 and 4.6 taken together suggest the presence of Gentile Judaizers in the church. He favors the reading of L with regard to the textual problem in 4.6—"*that the covenant is both theirs and ours. It is ours, but . . .*" (emphasis original). Michael W. Holmes also states that this is the generally preferred reading (Holmes, editor, *The Apostolic Fathers: Greek Texts and English Translations of Their Writings*, rev. ed., ed. and trans. J. B. Lightfoot and J. R. Harmer [Grand Rapids: Baker, 1999] 281).

the idea of professing Jesus Christ and Judaizing (ἰουδαΐζειν; 10.3), and his suggestion in the Philadelphian epistle that it is the uncircumcised who are expounding Judaism (6.1) strongly point to the presence of Gentile Judaizers in these two local congregations.

The Birkath Haminim

What have been introduced so far have been charges leveled against the Jews and Jewish sympathizers in Christian literature, but what does Jewish literature of the period have to offer? Unfortunately, there is little evidence since Jewish literature reflects meager interest or concern with the Christian movement, which is likely a result of Judaism's established and relatively secure position in Greco-Roman society. One particular issue, however, that is a possible factor in Jewish-Christian relations is the *birkath haminim* (BH) or the "blessing against heretics." The existence of the BH, the twelfth of the Eighteen Benedictions (*Shemoneh Esreh*) of the Jewish *Tefillah*[60] recited three times daily by devout Jews (*m. Ber.* 3:3),[61] is perhaps the most substantial but controversial evidence to date that may shed some light on the post-70 Jewish stance toward Christians.

The Babylonian Talmud (*b. Ber.* 28b-29a, cf. *y. Ber.* 4:3) attributes the origin of this "benediction" on heretics to Samuel the Small who constructed it at Yavneh upon the request of Gamaliel II, who was head of the Academy in Yavneh from 80–110 CE. Many scholars date its composition more narrowly to between 85 and 95 CE, although there is little firm evidence for this date.[62] The BH was composed as a way to exclude heretics

---

[60] For a history of the *Tefillah* (or *Amidah*) and its canonization see Solomon Zeitlin, "The Tefillah, the Shemoneh Esreh: An Historical Study of the First Canonization of the Hebrew Liturgy," *JQR* 54 (1964) 208–49. For a presentation of the various versions of the *Tefillah* and its early compositions see Louis Finkelstein, "The Development of the Amidah," *JQR* 16 (1925) 1–43; 127–70.

[61] Although exempted from the obligatory recitation of certain prayers (e.g., the *Shema*), women, slaves, and children along with all Jewish males were required to recite the Eighteen Benedictions.

[62] Stefan J. Joubert, "A Bone of Contention in Recent Scholarship: The 'Birkat ha-Minim' and the Separation of Church and Synagogue in the First Century A.D.," *Neot* 27 (1993) 351; Steven T. Katz, "Issues in the Separation of Judaism and Christianity after 70 CE: A Reconsideration," *JBL* 103 (1984) 43–76; R. Travers Herford, *Christianity in Talmud and Midrash* (1903; reprinted, New York: Ktav, 1989) 125–37. Herford argues for a date shortly after 80 CE. His conjecture is based on a lengthy examination of evidence from Jewish sources and tradition that would suggest that Samuel the Small was an elderly man near the end of his life when he composed the benediction. Herford argues that there is evidence to suggest that while Samuel served under Gamaliel II, he was also a contemporary of pre-70 rabbis.

from being precentors at synagogue worship since it would have been read as part of the synagogue liturgy.

The publication in 1898 by Solomon Schechter of the Cairo Genizah version of the BH stimulated renewed discussion over the past century concerning the role of the BH in the separation of Jews from Christians.[63] The Genizah version, believed to be of Palestinian origin, is of particular interest because it incorporates the *notsrim* in its curse against the *minim*.[64] The term *notsrim* has been traditionally understood to be a Jewish designation for Christians, being transliterated from the Greek text as *Nazoreans* (Ναζωραίων, Acts 24.5; cf. *b. Ta'an.* 27b). A number of scholars have seen in the Genizah text Jewish evidence for the early separation of Judaism and Christianity and, more specifically, a cause for that separation.[65] Its Palestinian origin and its apparent antiquity lend credence to the possibility that it is representative of the original BH first constructed at Yavneh, but the evidence is uncertain.

There is some debate over whether this prayer was directed specifically at (Jewish) Christians or more broadly at other Jewish heretical sects as well. Much of the discussion centers on whether the term *notsrim* was part of the original text, and if not, whether the term *minim* alone could have been used to target (Jewish) Christians. The best evidence for the use of the BH comes from the fourth- and early fifth-century testimonies of Epiphanius and Jerome. It is their testimony that provides the earliest and clearest evidence for the regular use of the BH in a form that is likely represented by the Genizah text. Both Epiphanius and Jerome write that the Nazoreans were cursed regularly by the Jews in their synagogues (*Pan.* 29.9.2; *Comm. Am.* 1.11-12; *Comm. Isa.* 5.18-19; 49.7; 52.4-6). Jerome's testimony is particularly significant, for he states four times that this curse

---

[63] Solomon Schechter, "Genizah Specimens," *JQR* 1/10 (1898) 657.

[64] The text of the BH reads as follows, "And for apostates let there be no hope; and may the insolent kingdom be quickly uprooted, in our days. And may the *notsrim* and the *minim* perish quickly; and may they be erased from the Book of Life and may they not be inscribed with the righteous. Blessed art thou, Lord, who humblest the insolent" (Palestinian recension). This translation is taken from Peter van der Horst, "The Birkat Ha-minim in Recent Research," in *Hellenism-Judaism-Christianity: Essays on Their Interaction*, CBET 8 (Kampen: Kok Pharos, 1994) 99.

[65] See W. D. Davies, *The Setting of the Sermon on the Mount* (Cambridge: Cambridge University Press, 1964) 275–76; R. T. France, *Matthew: Evangelist and Teacher* (Grand Rapids: Zondervan, 1989) 85–86; J. Louis Martyn, *History and Theology in the Fourth Gospel*, 3d ed., NTL (Louisville: Westminster John Knox, 2003) 62–65; John T. Townsend, "The Gospel of John and the Jews: The Story of a Religious Divorce," in *Anti-Semitism and the Foundations of Christianity*, ed. Alan T. Davies (New York: Paulist, 1979) 85, esp. n.89.

of the Nazoreans is actually a curse on all Christians. He writes, "Until today in their synagogues they blaspheme the christian [sic] people under the name Nazoreans" (*Comm. Am.* 1.11-12 [Klijn and Reinink]).

Jerome and Epiphanius provide a fixed historical point at which it is reasonable to assume the BH was in regular use and that the form likely contained the term *notsrim*—a form perhaps representative of the Genizah text. The question still remains, however, as to what evidence exists that might indicate that this version of the BH was in use much earlier or that it represents the original first-century benediction.

The third-century writings of Origen provide some vague references to Jewish anti-Christian rhetoric, but are not much help in determining with any reliability the use and wording of the BH. Origen does state that the Jews curse Christ and blaspheme him in their synagogues, but he makes no reference to a regular cursing of Christians during prayer (*Hom. Ps. 37* 2.8; *Hom. Jer.* 10.8.1; 19.12.3).

Justin Martyr's *Dialogue with Trypho*, which dates to the middle of the second century, provides more precise evidence. Justin states in several instances that the Jews curse Christians (16.4; 47.4; 93.4; 95.4; 96.2; 108.3; 123.6; 133.6; 137.2; cf. 17.1; 35.8; 117.3), and in three instances specifically states that this is done in the synagogues (16.4; 47.4; 96.2; possibly 137.2). However, there is considerable debate over whether these references demonstrate that Justin was aware of the regular use of the BH and in particular that it was used against Christians.[66]

The evidence from Justin is compelling, yet, ambiguous enough to leave an aspect of doubt. The difficulty with Justin's testimony lies in two main areas. First, there is no clear certainty as to how reliable or objective Justin's comments are or if he even has the BH in mind. Second is the more complicated issue of perception. Does Justin's perception that Christians were being cursed necessarily imply that this was the Jewish perspective? This question, of course, addresses the original intent of the BH. Was the BH formulated or used primarily by Jews to target Christians? Justin's multiple accusations of the cursing of Christians coupled with the apparent antiquity of the Genizah version might suggest that at least by the second century the BH had taken on an anti-Christian tone. It is difficult, however, to draw a one-to-one correspondence.

---

[66] See the discussion Reuven Kimelman, "*Birkat Ha-Minim* and the Lack of Evidence for an Anti-Christian Jewish Prayer in Late Antiquity," in *Jewish and Christian Self-definition: Aspects of Judaism in the Graeco-Roman Period*, ed. E. P. Sanders et al. (Philadelphia: Fortress, 1981) 2:226–44, on Justin see particularly 235–36; cf. Katz, "Issues," 43–76; Joubert, "Bone of Contention," 351–63.

The earliest Christian text sometimes connected to the BH is the Gospel of John which makes three references to synagogue expulsion (9.22; 12.42; 16.2). J. L. Martyn argues that these texts probably represent a reference to the BH, which was constructed around the same time period.[67] Most scholars, however, are more cautious than Martyn in their evaluation.[68] While the relative historical proximity of the writing of the BH and the Fourth Gospel makes a correspondence tempting, there are some difficulties with drawing such a conclusion. The Fourth Gospel references may indicate that the Johannine community was experiencing some kind of local Jewish opposition, but these references make no mention of cursing, prayer, or any other element that might imply the BH was at issue.

The evidence is inconclusive, therefore, that the BH was originally constructed to target Christians or that the earliest version contained a reference to the *notsrim*.[69] The earliest indication of the use of the BH containing the term *notsrim*, comes through the testimonies of Jerome and Epiphanius. Although Justin demonstrates an awareness of Jews cursing Christians in their synagogue services by the middle of the second century, he never mentions the term *notsrim* making it impossible to determine if this term was part of the original prayer. The value of Justin's testimony is that it shows a considerable deterioration of Jewish-Christian relations by about 150 CE. Many scholars suggest that it is more likely that *notsrim* was added to the BH sometime between the end of the Bar

---

[67] Martyn, *History and Theology*, 60, n. 69, argues that the "formal nature of the language" in 9.22 and the "remarkable degree of correspondence" between the two elements in John 16.2 (expulsion and execution) and Justin (*Dial.* 16.4, 95.4, 110; "1. curse = cast out and 2. kill") suggest a strong possibility that John 9.22 et al. and the account of the writing of the BH in *b. Ber.* 28b-29a are linked.

[68] See the discussions in Dunn, *Partings*, 222; J. Andrew Overman, *Matthew's Gospel and Formative Judaism: The Social World of the Matthean Community* (Minneapolis: Fortress, 1990) 54; Kimelman, "Birkat," 234–35. Dunn shows a bit more caution than Martyn in his belief that John refers to "something like the BH" even if it was "only a local equivalent." Overman places more distance between John and the BH when he suggests that John 9.22 et al. refer to "an initial stage of banning" but does not agree with J. L. Martyn that there is any formal link with the BH. Kimelman questions even the historicity of these remarks and sees no connection between John and the BH.

[69] W. D. Davies's argument that *notsrim* is an integral part of the original text is not persuasive (276). Kimelman, offers a simple but cogent argument against such a conclusion. He remarks that in all versions of the BH that contain the term *notsrim*, it always precedes *minim* ("Birkat," 233). Therefore, he argues that if *notsrim* were part of the original text, then it would have likely become known as the "*birkath ha-notsrim*."

Kochba revolt (135 CE) and the fourth century.[70] The Bar Kochba revolt seems to have marked a significant downturn in Jewish-Christian relations and, therefore, certainly could be a point after which the BH took a more anti-Christian tone. However, the events surrounding the Bar Kochba revolt likely had a more chilling effect on the Christian attitude toward Jews than vice versa.

Even if the original version of the BH did not contain the term *notsrim*, some argue that it is still possible that its original purpose was to exclude Jewish Christians from the synagogue. Lawrence Schiffman believes that even without *notsrim* the benediction was anti-Christian from the start, arguing that the original purpose of the benediction was to prevent the *minim* from being precentors in the synagogue and that this would naturally only affect Jewish Christians.[71] If *notsrim* was not part of the original text, however, then it is more difficult to argue the BH was anti-Christian. Indeed, one might easily argue that a later addition of *notsrim* implies that the original version did not specifically target Christians.

A study of the term *minim* is not of significant help here either. Whether the rabbis intended for the *minim* to define heretics in general or more specifically Jewish Christians remains debatable. Philip Alexander says that the use of the term may be distinctively rabbinic since it does not appear outside of rabbinic literature, which makes it difficult to determine precisely its meaning.[72] R. T. Herford has done an extensive study of the appearances of the terms *min*, *minim* and *minuth* in rabbinic literature and draws the guarded conclusion that *minim* is a rabbinic term for Jewish Christians.[73] One could argue that in a number of instances *minim* is used as a reference to Jewish Christianity; however, the danger lies in declaring that this the exclusive meaning of the term (e.g., *t. Yad.* 2.13; *t. Šabb.* 13.5; *t. Ḥul.* 2.20-21). Kimelman and Katz more correctly argue for a broader definition of *minim*. Both cite *y. Sanh.* 10:5-6 as proof that the term can

---

[70] See Dunn, *Partings*, 222; William Horbury, "The Benediction of the *Minim* and Jewish-Christian Controversy," *JTS* 33 (1982) 47–48; Katz, 72; Kimelman, "*Birkat*," 238–39; Lawrence H. Schiffman, "At the Crossroads: Tannaitic Perspectives on the Jewish-Christian Schism," in *Jewish and Christian Self-definition: Aspects of Judaism in the Graeco-Roman Period*, ed. E. P. Sanders et al. (Philadelphia: Fortress, 1981) 2:152; Wilson, *Related Strangers*, 183.

[71] Schiffman, "Crossroads," 152.

[72] Philip S. Alexander, "'The Parting of the Ways' from the Perspective of Rabbinic Judaism," in *Jews and Christians: The Parting of the Ways A.D. 70 to 135*, ed. James D. G. Dunn, WUNT 66 (Tübingen: Mohr/Siebeck, 1992; reprinted, Grand Rapids: Eerdmans, 1999) 8–9.

[73] Herford, *Christianity*, 380–81.

refer to other groups besides Christians, but Kimelman acknowledges that Jewish Christians were certainly included under this term.[74]

The evidence discussed thus far presents a composite picture of a benediction that did not originally contain the term *notsrim* and that was likely first constructed against the *minim*, a term that referred to Jewish sects outside of the rabbinic movement. Although *minim* must be ruled out as an exclusive term for Jewish Christians, references in rabbinic literature indicate that Jewish Christians were among this group. The rabbis were aware of the presence of Jewish Christians and Jewish believers would certainly not have perceived the BH as a welcoming gesture. Only later did the BH begin to impact Jewish-Christian relations on a broader scale (perhaps after 135 CE).

What must be avoided here is to overstate the historical situation. The traditional view that the first-century benediction was originally directed against Christians is based primarily on two historically unsupportable assumptions. It has been assumed that rabbinic Judaism had a greater influence over post-70 Judaism than it likely had[75] and that post-70 Christianity posed a more serious threat to rabbinic Judaism than was likely the case. The latter assumption might be conversely stated as an assumption that rabbinic Judaism was disproportionately concerned with post-70 Christianity. Given the inadequacies of these assumptions, a consideration of the purpose of the BH must be undertaken with a renewed understanding of the historical context of post-70 Palestinian Judaism.

Rabbinic Judaism was not de facto the dominant movement in Judaism after 70 CE. The rabbis did not likely begin to gain widespread control over Judaism until the third century and then perhaps only initially in Palestine.[76] Cohen suggests that the rabbis did not gain ultimate control of all of Judaism until the seventh century.[77] The destruction of the

---

[74] Kimelman, "*Birkat*," 231–32; Katz, 72–73. Kimelman writes, "The Palestinian prayer against the *minim* was aimed at Jewish sectarians among whom Jewish Christians figured prominently" (232).

[75] Justin's familiarity with the curse and the charge that emissaries from Jerusalem had been sent to Diaspora Jews in order to spread warnings against Christians suggests widespread and organized rabbinic influence (*Dial.* 17). Lieu, *Image and Reality*, 131, however, points out that the evidence from Justin is not as certain as it first appears. Although he is aware of rabbinic activity and pronouncements, it is not at all apparent from where he gets this knowledge. It is quite possible that he collected his information from a number of different sources and even Palestine itself. In other words, his understanding may not reflect accurately the situation in second-century Ephesus.

[76] Alexander, "Parting," 21.

[77] Shaye J. D. Cohen, *From the Maccabees to the Mishnah*, LEC (Philadelphia: Westmin-

temple in 70 CE created a void in what had been formally a very sectarian Judaism.[78] The virtual disappearance of the Sadducees and the Essenes[79] created a political opportunity for the rabbis, but this does not imply that their dominance came without a struggle. Most Jews were probably indifferent to the rabbis and did not see them as an authority. Philip Alexander believes that the Tannaitic literature shows a struggle with the people of the land that did not dissipate until the third century.[80] At the sectarian level, the Samaritans and Jewish Christians also remained as religious rivals and the surviving priests likely still felt they were the leaders of the people.[81]

Gamaliel's call for a benediction against the *minim* in the 80s CE, therefore, may have been less an attempt to target Christianity and more an attempt to thrust rabbinic Judaism forward as the only orthodox and legitimate form of Judaism. Alexander proposes that the purpose of the BH was "to establish Rabbinism as orthodoxy within the synagogue."[82] Self-definition necessarily encompasses exclusion.[83] The rabbis wanted to define and unify post-70 Judaism according to their own definition, and the BH was a first step in this process that undoubtedly took centuries to complete.[84] After the destruction of the temple, a unified Judaism became paramount to its survival.[85]

Jewish Christianity, as a surviving rival of rabbinic Judaism, felt the impact of this move toward consolidation and definition. The addition of the BH to the Eighteen Benedictions perhaps limited their official involvement in synagogue worship and may have sent rippling effects throughout the larger Christian community. The evidence, however, does not permit a decisive conclusion as to how early and how widespread the effects of the BH were on the Christian movement as a whole. Although Judaism and

---

ster, 1987) 221.

[78] Cohen, *Maccabees to the Mishnah*, 221.

[79] Although not likely a major factor, Dunn, *Partings*, 232, suggests that the Sadducees and Essenes were still present after 70 CE, taking into account Josephus' present tense remarks about them.

[80] Alexander, "Parting," 19–25.

[81] Cohen, *Maccabees to the Mishnah*, 221, 224–26.

[82] Alexander, "Parting," 9.

[83] Overman, *Matthew's Gospel*, 48–56, makes this point in his discussion of post-70 Judaism; cf. Collins, "Vilification," 308–20, who makes a similar argument with regard to emerging Christianity.

[84] See Overman, *Matthew's Gospel*, 51; Joubert, "A Bone of Contention," 355–56.

[85] Schiffman, "At the Crossroads," 147–48.

Christianity were growing apart at the end of the first century as a result of a number of factors and the BH could have been one of them, a significant rupture does not seem clearly discernable until after the Bar Kokhba revolt in 135 CE.[86] Justin's *Dialogue with Trypho* is evidence of the extent of this break and perhaps, to some degree, the extent of the effects of the BH on Jewish-Christian relations. The increasing hostility of the Gentile church and its later dominance in the fourth century likely resulted in the church eventually viewing the BH as a direct threat—an attitude that was only encouraged by the Jewish addition of *notsrim* to the text.

Conclusion

In order to establish the place of the Apocalypse of John in the developing Jewish-Christian schism between 70 and 150 CE, an overview of the available evidence from this period has been undertaken in order to discern the factors that contributed to the ever widening schism. Most of the evidence comes from Christian sources and reveals a trend toward the replacement of the Jews as the people of God. The vilification of the Jews became an important part of Christian self-definition and this strategy took on a two-pronged approach. The extant Christian literature from the period reveals a strategy by which the church Christianized the Jewish scriptures and adopted a replacement theology viewing itself as the true people of God. This latter strategy appears to come to a climax by the mid-second century in the writings of Justin Martyr who is the first in Christian literature to call the church unambiguously the new spiritual Israel (*Dial.* 11.5).[87]

The separation of Christianity from Judaism was more a concern of the church than of Judaism. Little evidence exists in Jewish literature that evinces any preoccupation with an attempt to distance itself from Christianity. The strongest possible Jewish evidence is the *birkath haminim*, but its original form and purpose remain a matter of debate. It was, however, perceived by Christians in the fourth century (Jerome and Epiphanius) and perhaps as early as the second century (Justin) as an anti-Christian prayer.

The two Jewish Wars that resulted in the destruction of the Jerusalem temple in 70 CE and the expulsion of the Jews from Jerusalem in 135 CE also played a role in the separation of Jews and Christians. The destruction

---

[86] See Dunn, *Partings*, 238; Schiffman, "At the Crossroads," 155–56; Wilson, *Related Strangers*, 183.

[87] Galatians 6.16 could arguably be cited as the first reference but the dispute over its interpretation makes any firm conclusion tenuous.

of the temple was later interpreted as God's judgment on unfaithful Israel. In addition, the expulsion in 135 CE assisted in the demise of Jewish Christianity and marks a definitive rupture in Jewish-Christian relations. Moreover, the involvement of the Jews in the persecution of Christians as recorded throughout Christian literature created further animosity between Jews and Christians.

The instigation of persecution may be behind John's visceral denouncement of the Jews in Rev 2.9 and 3.9. It is these two passages and their interpretation that have been pivotal in the discussion of the place of the Apocalypse in the Jewish-Christian debate. Do John's remarks reveal his own rejection of ethnic Israel as the people of God? Is John being anti-Jewish or anti-Judaic? Although he does not use the term "Jew" in a pejorative sense in these two passages, he seems to be drawing some distinction between ethnic Jews and Christians as the people of God. The implication is that a "true Jew" is not determined by ethnicity, but by allegiance to God and the Lamb. To oppose God is to belong to Satan. It would, however, be incongruous to call John an anti-Semite or anti-Jewish. He is himself a Jew. He does, however, interpret the Jewish scriptures from a decidedly Christian point of view and, unlike Paul, offers no clear opinion on the fate of ethnic Judaism. His use of Jewish imagery for the church also strongly suggests that he sees it at minimum as a benefactor of Jewish covenant promises and at a maximum Israel's replacement. How far John moves in this direction, as other segments of the church do, toward a Christianizing of the Jewish scriptures and a supersessionist theology can only be answered through a closer examination of Rev 2.9 and 3.9 as well as other key vision passages of his apocalypse. It is to these first two passages that the discussion will now turn.

2

"Those Who Call Themselves Jews":
Conflict in Smyrna and Philadelphia

JOHN'S apocalypse is written to seven churches in the Roman province of Asia with an aim to call them to patient endurance through faithful discipleship. The main visionary section of the Apocalypse (4.1—22.5) is prefaced with seven messages (2.1—3.22) written to the "angel" or "messenger" (ἀγγέλῳ) of each of these seven Asian churches. The seven messages provide important, yet often ambiguous, evidence for the historical and social setting of these churches and the Apocalypse as a whole. Each of these messages uniquely addresses the spiritual and corporeal threats facing these churches.

The Smyrnean and Philadelphian messages (2.8-11; 3.7-13) are of particular interest as a starting point for deciphering John's view of the relationship between Judaism and Christianity. The two messages are unique among the seven messages in that they are the only two that do not give a negative appraisal of the churches' spiritual state. Further, like the churches of Ephesus, Pergamum and Thyatira that appear to be facing a common internal threat, these two churches appear to be facing a comparable external threat. John uses identical language to reference their opponents whom he identifies as "those who call themselves Jews and are not, but are a synagogue of Satan" (2.9; cf. 3.9, translation mine). The identity of these so-called Jews and their particular threat to the churches is a subject of considerable debate.

The most widely held and most compelling interpretation is that these two churches were in some way in conflict with the Jewish communities of Smyrna and Philadelphia. In this conflict, the Christians appear to be socially and economically disadvantaged (2.9a; 3.8b), and persecution looms as a viable threat if not already a present reality (2.10; 3.8b). If this interpretation is correct, then these two passages provide an initial glimpse into John's view of the relationship between the church and Judaism and perhaps a key to deciphering his perspective in the rest of the Apocalypse.

The Smyrnean Situation

The message to the church in Smyrna begins with the customary opening in which John introduces his visionary messenger. He then offers a brief but unique message of encouragement to this besieged church. Rev 2.9-10 outlines the Smyrnean situation by enumerating three likely interrelated difficulties facing the believers. They are experiencing tribulation (θλῖψις), poverty (πτωχεία), and slander (βλασφημία) from a group who call themselves Jews (Ἰουδαῖοι) but whom John calls a "synagogue of Satan" (συναγωγὴ τοῦ σατανᾶ). More suffering (πάσχειν) and tribulation is looming on the horizon.

The Smyrneans are poor, yet, in spite of their physical poverty, the message assures them that they are truly rich. Their poverty, and certainly their tribulation as well, are only momentary sufferings of this material world. The real reality—a clear theme of John's entire apocalypse—is the spiritual reality, and in that reality the church is rich.[1] Along with their poverty, the Smyrneans are also facing tribulation, but it is difficult to be precise as to its exact nature. Rev 2.10 might suggest that their tribulation would soon take the form of physical persecution (if it had not already), which was not unfamiliar to these churches as the following message to Pergamum indicates (2.13). However, the Smyrnean tribulation may have also involved some form of economic deprivation which would in turn have resulted in their poverty. Although it is possible that the believers are poor because they come primarily from the lower economic stratum of society or perhaps because of their liberal giving, it is more likely that the believers found it difficult to make a living in a pagan society.[2] The believers were probably ostracized from society because of what their neighbors viewed as "anti-social" behavior; this was their unwillingness to participate in the local pagan cults, rituals, and guilds. This anti-social behavior would have prevented them from conducting business freely and likely led to persecution (cf. Heb 10.32-34).

---

[1] The promise of eschatological wealth is a common NT theme (Matt 5.3 = Luke 6.20; Matt 6.19-21 = Luke 12.33-34; Luke 12.21; 2 Cor 6.10; Jas 2.5). This paradoxical use of wealth is also found outside of the NT. For further references and discussion see Aune, *Revelation 6–16*, 389–403; Beale, *Revelation*, 239; Prigent, *L'Apocalypse*, 127.

[2] G. B. Caird, *The Revelation of Saint John*, BNTC (1966; Peabody, Mass.: Hendrickson, n.d.) 35; Colin J. Hemer, *The Letters to the Seven Churches of Asia in Their Local Setting*, (1986; reprinted, BRS; Grand Rapids: Eerdmans; Livonia, Mich.: Dove, 2001) 68; cf. Sanders, *Schismatics*, 170; Aune, *Revelation 1–5*, 161; Mark R. J. Bredin, "The Synagogue of Satan Accusation in Revelation 2:9," *BTB* 28 (1999) 161–63.

Beale suggests that the Neronian persecution of the mid-60s had placed the Christians under increased scrutiny.[3] As long as Christians were seen as a sect of Judaism, they benefited from some of the religious toleration enjoyed by Judaism; however, by the end of the first century, the increasingly Gentile church was finding itself more and more outside the umbrella of Judaism. This was due in part to the church's increased need for self-definition and perhaps Judaism's desire to shed itself of what it perceived to be a heretical sect. Therefore, Christians became more vulnerable to accusations of anti-social behavior from their pagan neighbors that may have been encouraged by the local Jewish community. It may be just such a scenario that John is describing here in the message to Smyrna.

"Those Who Call Themselves Jews"

Along with poverty and tribulation, the Smyrneans are facing opposition from a group that identifies itself as "Jews" (Ἰουδαῖοι). John, however, disputes their claim to this title and rather labels them a "synagogue of Satan." A majority of scholars find in this passage evidence that the Jewish and Christian communities in Smyrna were in conflict and that John is adopting for the church the claim to be the "true Jews."[4] There are, however, some scholars who disagree and argue that John's accusation more accurately reflects an intra-church struggle.

Much has been made in recent scholarship of the fact that first-century Judaism was not monolithic and that the boundary between Christianity and Judaism remained porous for some time. Indeed, some scholars have shied away from the use of terms such as "Christianity" in opposition to "Judaism" as historically anachronistic.[5] The debate over the

---

[3] Beale, *Revelation*, 239–41.

[4] Beckwith, *Apocalypse*, 452–53; Charles, *Revelation*, 1:56–57; Ernst Lohmeyer, *Die Offenbarung des Johannes*, 2d ed., HNT 16 (Tübingen: Mohr/Siebeck, 1953) 24; Caird, *Revelation*, 35; Collins, *Crisis and Catharsis*, 75, 85–86; idem, "Insiders and Outsiders in the Book of Revelation and Its Social Context," in *"To See Ourselves as Others See Us": Christians, Jews, and "Others" in Late Antiquity*, ed. Jacob Neusner and Ernest Frerichs (Chico, Calif.: Scholars, 1985) 205–10; Hemer, *Letters*, 65–67; Aune, *Revelation 1–5*, 162; Beale, *Revelation*, 241; Prigent, *L'Apocalypse*, 127–28, 156; Gregory Stevenson, *Power and Place: Temple and Identity in the Book of Revelation*, BZNW 107 (Berlin: de Gruyter, 2001) 225–27; Osborne, *Revelation*, 131.

[5] So Frankfurter, "Jews or Not?" 407–9; cf. Marshall, *Parables of War*, 1–87 (particularly 68–87) who discusses these terms extensively, particularly the historical, semantic, and theological implications of their use in the study of the Apocalypse, with the goal of re-evaluating the fundamental identification of John's apocalypse as Christian rather than Jewish.

interpretation of Rev 2.9 and 3.9 to some degree centers on the meaning of Ἰουδαῖοι and whether John uses this nomenclature in the traditional sense of ethnic Jews or that the term should be understood more broadly. Bruce Malina and John Pilch, in their recent social-science commentary, argue that "Judeans" is a better translation of Ἰουδαῖοι since the Greeks and Romans identified Israelites with their territory of origin. They suggest that "there were in fact no 'Jews' of the sort that exist today."[6] David Frankfurter, on the other hand, argues that the designation Ἰουδαῖοι cannot be limited to just one ethnic group or geographical region, but can embrace even Gentiles who observe Jewish practices. In fact, it is this perceived imprecise nature of much of the terminology (e.g., Ἰουδαῖοι, συναγωγή, ἐκκλησία) that permits him to establish his interpretation of 2.9 and 3.9 as signifying an intra-church conflict between John and "Pauline Gentile Jesus believers."[7]

Frankfurter argues that John, as a Jewish believer in Jesus and a rigorous sectarian, is "scrupulously concerned with *purity*" and that his concern is with the "*degree of halakhic observance* of people who were also focused upon Jesus" (emphasis original).[8] This rigorous sense of purity is manifested in John's accusation against the "Nicolaitans," "Jezebel," and the "neo-Balaamians" as well as his concern for the sexual purity of the 144,000 (14.4).[9] Frankfurter places the so-called Jews of Smyrna and Philadelphia in a similar category as the other groups against whom John rails. They are all neo-Pauline Gentiles who have failed within what John views as a primarily Jewish movement to adhere strictly to Jewish practices and, thus they are threatening "the cohesion of the Elect in the endtimes."[10] The so-called Jews of the Smyrnean and Philadelphian churches, Frankfurter postulates, are Gentile "God-fearers" who have come into the Jesus movement maintaining some cohesion with Judaism while adopting Paul's view that the "true Jew" is the "inward Jew" (Rom 2.28-29).[11] For a sectarian Jew like John, such a belief deserves strong condemnation. These so-called Jews are denied the name "Jew" because they advocate a brand of Christianity not "kosher" in John's view. According to Frankfurter, John's

---

[6] Bruce J. Malina and John J. Pilch, *Social-Science Commentary on the Book of Revelation* (Minneapolis: Fortress, 2000) 54; cf. Bredin, "Synagogue of Satan," 160–64.
[7] Frankfurter, "Jews or Not?" 421–22.
[8] Ibid., 410, 415.
[9] Ibid., 415–16.
[10] Ibid., 421–22.
[11] Ibid., 419.

argument with the "Nicolaitans," "Jezebel," the "neo-Balaamians," and the Gentile "God-fearers" reflects the continuing conflict between Paul's brand of Christianity and that of a more sectarian Jewish Christianity. It is not a matter of heterodoxy versus orthodoxy, but an intra-sect conflict from an "intra-Jewish perspective."[12]

Although Frankfurter's interpretation differs from Kraft's, he and Kraft share the belief that the so-called Jews of Smyrna and Philadelphia stand on common theological ground with the "Nicolaitans," the "Balaamites" and the followers of "Jezebel" and that this conflict is an intra-church struggle. Kraft, however, postulates that these so-called Jews are a syncretistic Christian group within the church that denied the salvific effects of the death and resurrection of Christ. They were prepared to compromise with the state and the pagan culture and sought refuge from persecution in the shadow of the synagogue. He implicitly identifies these so-called Jews with the Nicolaitans who were threatening the churches in Ephesus (2.6), Pergamum (2.15), and possibly Thyatira (2.20),[13] thus maintaining that these churches along with Smyrna and Philadelphia were all threatened by the same group.[14]

Lloyd Gaston takes a similar position, finding support for his interpretation in the epistles of Ignatius written some fifteen to twenty years after John's apocalypse.[15] As one may argue is the case in Ignatius' epis-

---

[12] Ibid., 415.

[13] There is no explicit reference to the Nicolaitans in the message to Thyatira; however, the similar accusations against "Jezebel" in Thyatira and the "teaching of Balaam" in Pergamum suggests a common problem. Rev 2.15 provides the necessary link to hypothesize that there was a common heretical problem in Ephesus, Pergamum and Thyatira that had its root in the teaching of the Nicolaitans. The language employed, οὕτως . . . καὶ σὺ . . . ὁμοίως, argues for a link between the previously described "teaching of Balaam" and the Nicolaitans. The language also implies a link with the Nicolaitans of the Ephesian church. If it is indeed the Nicolaitans who are teaching believers to eat meat sacrificed to idols and to commit fornication, then their presence, though not stated explicitly, is implied in Thyatira by the similar charge leveled against the heretics troubling that believing community. For a fuller discussion of this connection see Aune, *Revelation 1–5*, 188; cf. Beasley-Murray, *Revelation*, 85–86; Hemer, *Letters*, 90–94; Kenneth A. Fox, "The Nicolaitans, Nicolaus and the Early Church," *SR* 23 (1994) 485–96; Stevenson, *Power and Place*, 228–29.

[14] Heinrich Kraft, *Die Offenbarung des Johannes*, HNT 16a (Tübingen: Mohr/Siebeck, 1974) 60–61.

[15] Gaston, "Judaism of the Uncircumcised," 42–43; cf. C. K. Barrett, "Jews and Judaizers in the Epistles of Ignatius," in *Jews, Greeks and Christians: Essays in Honor of William David Davies*, ed. Robert Hamerton-Kelly and Robin Scroggs (Leiden: Brill, 1976) 230–31, 235, 239, 242.

tles,[16] Gaston suggests that there is a "two-front polemic" being raised in John's apocalypse against what is ostensibly one opponent. Since one may reasonably argue that the Nicolaitans and those who teach eating food sacrificed to idols and sexual immorality are one group, Gaston believes that these so-called Jews of Smyrna and Philadelphia are also of this same heretical group, which he calls "Gentile gnosticizing libertines."[17]

F. W. Horn also postulates that the so-called Jews were a group that compromised with the pagan culture; however, he does not propose that this group was necessarily part of the Christian church.[18] He raises the specter of compromise with the pagan culture as a primary concern of John's throughout the Apocalypse, which causes John to draw a dividing line that runs through the center of both the Jewish and Christian communities. Thus Horn interprets the "synagogue of Satan" in Smyrna as those in the Jewish community who have compromised with pagan society in contrast to the faithful Jews who have not, just as the so-called apostles (2.2) and Nicolaitans (2.6; 2.15; cf. 2.20) have compromised in contrast to the faithful saints. While Horn acknowledges that some Jews of Smyrna are likely involved in instigating Roman persecution of Christians, this is not the overarching issue. John denies them the name "Jew" not because he covets it for the Christians, but because it belongs to the Jews who have not compromised with the pagan culture. Therefore, the struggle over who are the "true Jews" is an intra-Jewish affair.

Other scholars have alternatively suggested that these so-called Jews are a group of Gentile Christian Judaizers.[19] Stephen Wilson postulates that if John's words are "taken at face value," these self-proclaimed Jews are not Jews at all, then it is reasonable to identify them as Gentiles.[20] J.

---

[16] There has been considerable scholarly debate over whether Ignatius was combating one or two heresies in his seven epistles. This writer takes the position, contrary to Gaston, that Ignatius was in fact arguing against two heresies, docetism and Judaizing. For arguments in favor of one Ignatian heresy see L. W. Barnard, *Studies in the Apostolic Fathers and Their Background* (Oxford: Blackwell, 1966) 22–25; Barrett, "Jews and Judaizers," 232–39. For the two heresy argument see Jerry L. Sumney, "Those Who 'Ignorantly Deny Him': The Opponents of Ignatius of Antioch," *JECS* 1 (1993) 346–49; Lieu, *Image and Reality*, 29–35.

[17] Gaston, "Judaism of the Uncircumcised," 42.

[18] Friedrich Wilhelm Horn, "Zwischen der Synagoge des Satans und dem neuen Jerusalem: Die christlich-jüdische Standortbestimmung in der Apokalypse des Johannes," *ZRGG* 46 (1994) 143–62.

[19] Gager, *Origins of Anti-Semitism*, 132; Wilson, *Related Strangers*, 162–63; J. Ramsey Michaels, *Revelation*, IVPNTC (Downers Grove, Ill.: InterVarsity, 1997) 72–75.

[20] Wilson, *Related Strangers*, 163.

Ramsey Michaels would agree and finds it difficult to believe that John, a Jew himself, would accuse other Jews of lying about their own ethnicity (3.9).[21] This group, then, must not be Jews but Christian Judaizers who were likely seeking shelter in the synagogue from local persecution.[22]

Those who argue that the so-called Jews are Christian Judaizers also find support in Ignatius' epistles. In his epistles to the Philadelphian and Magnesian churches, Ignatius appears to be wrestling with a Judaizing group. He tells the Philadelphian believers that "it is better to hear about Christianity from a man who is circumcised than about Judaism from one who is not" (*Phld.* 6.1), and to the Magnesians he writes, "It is utterly absurd to profess Jesus Christ and to practice Judaism" (*Magn.* 10.3). He instead admonishes them "to live according to Christianity. For whoever is called by any other name than this one does not belong to God" (*Magn.* 10.1). This latter reference provides some similarity to John's much stronger accusation against his opponents that they are a "synagogue of Satan." If Judaizers were a menace to the Asian churches only some fifteen to twenty years after the writing of John's apocalypse, then it is arguably possible that this is the true identity of the so-called Jews of Smyrna and Philadelphia.

There are, however, several major weaknesses with the preceding interpretations. The interpretations proposed by Kraft, Gaston, and Wilson rely too much on Ignatius' epistles to provide supporting evidence for identifying John's opponents. As Collins correctly observes, one must be cautious when using Ignatius' epistles to interpret John's apocalypse.[23] She notes, for example, that Ignatius came from Antioch and a church influenced by Paul's thought while John may have originated in Palestine and was influenced by the Jewish apocalyptic tradition and the Sibylline Oracles.[24] Ignatius also seems to have a more developed distinction between Judaism and Christianity than John does—even more than Paul does.[25] Furthermore, there is some debate as to how much Ignatius' rhetoric reflects his experience in Antioch rather than the conditions in Asia.[26]

---

[21] Michaels, *Revelation*, 74. Frankfurter, "Jews or Not?" 407, makes a similar observation.

[22] Wilson, *Related Strangers*, 163.

[23] Collins, "Villification," 312.

[24] Collins, *Crisis and Catharsis*, 46–49.

[25] Collins, "Villification," 312.

[26] See Virginia Corwin, *St. Ignatius and Christianity in Antioch* (New Haven: Yale University Press, 1960); cf. Barnard, *Studies*, 22–25.

In addition, contrary to both Kraft, Gaston, and to some degree Frankfurter, there is no evidence in the text to suggest that these so-called Jews should be identified with the groups John opposes in Ephesus, Pergamum, and Thyatira. Moreover, if opposition groups were syncretistic Christians as Kraft suggests, then they would have little reason to seek shelter in the synagogue since they would not likely be open to persecution.[27]

The argument that the so-called Jews of Smyrna and Philadelphia are Christians does not deal satisfactorily with the context of the Smyrnean message. This group is accused of slander (βλασφημία) against the Smyrnean believers that may have led secondarily to their persecution (2.10). If this were a Christian group, then they would not likely be slandering other Christians and certainly not to the local authorities. There is no hint that any other heretical group John names is guilty of such opposition against their fellow believers. Wilson, perceiving this difficulty, attempts unsuccessfully to surmount this problem by suggesting an alternative perspective on the connection between the so-called Jews and the assumed persecution. He suggests that it was their attempt to avoid persecution through their association with the Jewish synagogue, a source of occasional persecution for the believers, that has earned them (and implicitly the Jews as well) condemnation from John.[28] The context, however, does not support such an inference.

Horn's approach has the advantage of emphasizing a theme that already plays large in the Apocalypse and that is John's concern over the corruption of pagan society and the purity of God's people. On the other hand, Horn's application of this theme to passages such as 2.9 and 3.9 (as well as 7.3-8; 14.1-5; 11.1-13; 21.9–22.5) results in hermeneutical inconsistencies, the development of a false dichotomy between faithful Jews and Gentiles, and the diminishing of an important sub-theme of the merging of the Christian tradition with Jewish motifs. These weaknesses can be seen for example, in Horn's interpretation of the "synagogue of Satan" passage in the Philadelphian message. While the similar language of this message and the Smyrnean message argues for an analogous interpretation, the language of the Philadelphian message forces Horn to adopt a more traditional interpretation, acknowledging that John believes the Jewish synagogue of Philadelphia, in a reversal of Jewish prophetic tradition, will ultimately recognize that the Christians are the true people of

---

[27] So Collins, "Insiders and Outsiders," 206.
[28] Wilson, *Related Strangers*, 163.

God. Further inconsistencies can be seen in Horn's interpretation of the 144,000 sealed (7.3-8) where he argues that this group must be faithful Jews and that the reference to the twelve tribes here has no relationship to that of 21.12. The latter text within its context of the new Jerusalem, argues against this artificial dichotomy that Horn is trying to maintain.

As for Frankfurter's interpretation, he appears to be following a similar historical line as F. C. Baur in promulgating the idea that there is an intra-church conflict in Asia between John's strict sectarian style Jewish Christianity and neo-Pauline theology. This, however, is unlikely the case. While the concern over πορνεία and eating food sacrificed to idols in other messages may be reminiscent of previous Jew/Gentile concerns (e.g., Acts 15; 1 Cor 6.12-20; 8.1-12; 10.14–11.1;), there is no evidence of these issues in the Smyrnean and Philadelphian messages; indeed, the debate's signature issue of circumcision is curiously absent.[29]

Frankfurter is, however, correct when he establishes a cautionary tone with regard to the definition of terms. It is vitally important that contemporary labels are not forced onto first-century movements that might distort the historical picture. As Frankfurter notes, Kraemer and Cohen have both demonstrated the broad definition possible for a term such as Ἰουδαῖοι.[30] This, however, does not imply, as Frankfurter himself demonstrates, that John's precise use of Ἰουδαῖοι cannot be determined.

While it is true that the line between "Judaism" and "Christianity" is still fluid at the end of the first century, there is separation taking place. Early Christian literature indicates that at least some distinction was developing in certain communities among Jesus' followers. Matthew refers to "their synagogues" (4.23; 9.35; 10.17; cf. Mark 1.39; Luke 4.15), the Fourth Gospel often pits Jesus against "the Jews" (*passim*; also consider the synagogue ban of 9.22; 12.42; 16.2), and Acts describes the church and synagogue in separate institutional style language.[31]

---

[29] A point that Frankfurter, "Jews or Not?" 422, n. 81, acknowledges is unusual, but he does not believe that it weakens his argument. See Aune, *Revelation 1–5*, 165, who makes a similar observation.

[30] Frankfurter, "Jews or Not?" 407, n.18. See Ross S. Kraemer, "On the Meaning of the Term 'Jew' in Greco-Roman Inscriptions," *HTR* 82 (1989) 35–53 (reprinted in *Diaspora Jews and Judaism: Essays in Honor of and in Dialogue with A. Thomas Kraabel*, ed. J. Andrew Overman and Robert S. MacLennan [Atlanta: Scholars, 1992] 311–29); Shaye J. D. Cohen, *The Beginnings of Jewishness: Boundaries, Varieties, Uncertainties* (Berkeley: University of California Press, 1999) 25–139.

[31] This list is adapted from a similar list by Greg Carey, "The 'Synagogue of Satan' (Rev 2:9; 3:9)—What's at Stake for Us?" (paper presented at the annual meeting of the SBL, Toronto, Canada, 23 November 2002) 7.

Even though Christianity was still developing as a separate religion, Judaism was already a clearly defined institution and had been for centuries through its customs and certainly by the peculiar Jewish practice of circumcision (e.g., 2 Macc 2.21; 14.38; 4 Macc 4.26; Acts 13.43; Gal 1.13-14; Dio, *R. H.* 65.4.3; cf. 37.17.1).[32] This is not to say that Judaism was monolithic or that the definition of who was Jewish did not vary within Judaism or even among its pagan observers; however, the portrayal in recent scholarship of the vague indefinability of Ἰουδαῖοι sometimes overstates the case.[33] The argument that John is wrestling with fellow Christians in Smyrna and Philadelphia seems to rely too heavily on a broad definition of Ἰουδαῖοι.

It seems reasonable to conjecture that enough separation had occurred between the synagogue and the church in some circles to allow the possibility that John is addressing conflict between the Jewish community and the local Christian believers in Smyrna and Philadelphia. The contexts of the messages to these two churches argue for the traditional use of Ἰουδαῖοι to refer to ethnic Jews who are members of the local synagogue and who are in conflict with the local Christian communities of Smyrna and Philadelphia. This interpretation is substantiated by the allusions to persecution particularly in the Smyrnean message (2.10).

John's concern in the messages to Smyrna and Philadelphia is not with the spiritual state of the churches as in other messages, but with what they are suffering. These churches are not accused of being spiritually tepid, nor do they have members who advocate false teachings. They are instead encouraged to persevere in the face of external opposition. The Philadelphian believers are praised for not having denied the Name (3.8) and the Smyrneans are encouraged to "be faithful unto death" (2.10). It is the divine messenger who recognizes the Smyrneans' poverty and tribulation (2.9a) and the powerlessness of the Philadelphians (3.8). He also knows of the slander (βλασφημία) of the so-called Jews in Smyrna and of similar opposition in Philadelphia (2.9b; 3.9). This slander has earned these "Jews" the title "synagogue of Satan," and it is this slander that may be leading to the persecution of the Smyrnean believers.

The interpretation, then, that these so-called Jews are a faction within the church is out of step with the overall context of these passages as well as the overall tenor of the Apocalypse. These references to persecution and

---

[32] There are, of course, too many references to list here from Paul's epistles in which Paul commonly differentiates between Jews and Gentiles through the use of "the circumcised" or "the circumcision" and "the uncircumcised" or "the uncircumcision."

[33] So Carey, "'Synagogue of Satan'," 7-8; contra Frankfurter, "Jews or Not?" 407-9.

slander are not merely an apocalyptic motif with little historical basis,[34] but indicate real threats encountered by the Asian Christians (cf. 2.13). It is the messages to the seven churches of Asia that provide the historical anchor upon which John builds his persecution motif in later passages (e.g., 6.9-11; 13.7; 17.6; 19.2; 20.4b).

It is true that John is visibly concerned in his apocalypse with drawing a line between "insiders" and "outsiders."[35] This rigid perspective is typical of apocalyptic literature. The insiders and outsiders, however, are not defined in terms of Jewish believers vs. Gentile Pauline believers or Gentile Judaizers but in terms of allegiance—those who ally themselves with God or against him. Those who heed John's call to faithful endurance are those who follow the Lamb (14.4) and "keep the commandments of God and hold the testimony of Jesus" (12.17c; cf. 1.2, 9; 14.12; 19.10; 20.4b). They are assured of their spiritual security (3.12; 7.1-17; 14.1-5) and will reap a final reward (21.7). Those who oppose God and by implication his people are allied with Satan and the pagan culture of the day. They are the "earth-dwellers" (8.13; 11.10; 13.8) who serve the beast empowered by the dragon, Satan (13.4). This beast represents the pagan Roman Empire, its economic wealth, and its ungodly claims to divine prerogatives (13.1-18; 17.1–18.24).

Some of the Jews of Smyrna and Philadelphia are labeled a "synagogue of Satan" because they oppose God's people and have allied themselves by default with God's arch-nemesis. This is not to imply that all Jews are of Satan in John's eyes or that John is intending here to be anti-Semitic or even anti-Jewish. John himself is a Jew. He does not use the appellation "Jew" in any derogatory sense. He wants to claim the title for those who are "true Jews" regardless of ethnicity. The "true Jews" for John are the believers who are suffering on behalf of God and the Lamb. John's comprehension of what it means to be a "Jew" (i.e., to belong to the faithful covenant people of God) has been redefined theologically[36] through the Christ-event and has resulted in a reinterpretation of the original covenant and a more inclusive definition of its heirs.

---

[34] Contra Frankfurter, "Jews or Not?" 407.

[35] So ibid., 413.

[36] Even Cohen, *Beginnings of Jewishness*, 26–27, makes this point while recognizing the complicated nature of defining Jewishness in the first century. He believes that John has cleverly adopted a phrase often used to refer to Gentiles who lived as Jews, "those who call themselves Jews and are not," and has cleverly misapplied it to ethnic Jews. John is claiming that the true Jews are the Christians.

This theological redefining of Jewishness does not end with the Smyrnean and Philadelphian messages, but becomes a sub-theme throughout the Apocalypse. John's extensive use of Jewish motifs and imagery adapted and applied to the church demonstrates this point. The sealing of 144,000 from the twelve tribes of Israel (7.4-8; 14.1-5), the measuring of the temple (11.1-2), the two witnesses (11.3-14), the heavenly woman (12.1-17), and the depiction of the new creation as a new Jerusalem with twelve gates named for the twelve tribes and twelve foundations named for the twelve apostles all reinforce the interpretation that John is laying claim in 2.9 and 3.9 to the term "Jew" as the exclusive right of the followers of the Lamb—the true Jews.[37]

The Jewish Communities of Smyrna and Philadelphia

The indictment against at least certain elements within the Jewish communities of Smyrna and Philadelphia of anti-Christian behavior naturally begs the question of what evidence there is for strong influential Jewish communities in these cities. Although the evidence is limited and much has to be inferred from later evidence, it is reasonable to postulate that both Smyrna and Philadelphia had large Jewish communities in the first century. The largest concentrations of Jewish settlements in the Roman Empire were located in Egypt, Palestine, Syria, and Asia Minor.[38] Philo, referring to the 30s CE, indicates that the Jews were numerous in all of the cities of Asia (*Legat.* 33.245; cf. *Flacc.* 7.45-46). Cecil Cadoux believes that a Jewish community probably existed quite early in Smyrna, which was a leading city in Asia.[39] Trebilco concludes from an examination of Jewish and Christian literature that the Jewish communities of Asia Minor were stable and thriving by the first century and that Smyrna shows evidence of an influential community at least by the second and third centuries.[40] A Hadrianic inscription at Smyrna lists among the city donors Jews who had presumably acquired local citizenship.[41] As for Philadelphia, no external

---

[37] So also Graham Harvey, *The True Israel: Uses of the Names Jew, Hebrew and Israel in Ancient Jewish and Early Christian Literature,* AGJU 35 (Leiden: Brill, 1996) 94.

[38] See the discussion in M. Stern, "The Jewish Diaspora," ed. S. Safrai, et al., CRINT 1 (Philadelphia: Fortress, 1974) 117–22; particularly nn.4, 122.

[39] Cecil John Cadoux, *Ancient Smyrna: A History of the City from the Earliest Times to 324 A.D.* (Oxford: Blackwell, 1938) 304.

[40] Trebilco, *Jewish Communities,* 34–36; cf. 189.

[41] There is some debate over how to translate the phrase, οἱ ποτὲ Ἰουδαῖοι in the Smyr-

evidence has been discovered to confirm that a Jewish community existed there at the end of the first century; however, Ignatius' concern with Judaizers in his Philadelphian epistle may imply the presence of a Jewish community in that city. In addition, the discovery of a large second-century synagogue and adjacent gymnasium in nearby Sardis lends support to the supposition that a long-standing Jewish community likely existed in Philadelphia as well.[42]

The Jews of Smyrna and Philadelphia, much like those in the rest of the Ionian cities, would have enjoyed special legal privileges first bestowed on them by the Seleucid kings and reaffirmed under Roman rule.[43] These privileges included the right to limited self-government, to practice their own religion, and to exemption from the pagan cults. Whether the Jews as a whole ever enjoyed the rights of full citizenship in the cities of the Roman Empire was at one time debated. Some scholars, such as William Ramsay, thought that the Jews did gain citizenship based on Philo's and Josephus' testimonies.[44] Mary Smallwood, however, observes that the scholarly consensus has shifted since the 1924 publication of the papyrus containing Claudius' *Letter to Alexandria*.[45] Most scholars believe that the Jews as a group did not enjoy the rights of citizenship in any city of the Hellenistic or early Roman Empire. This is not to say, however, that some individual Jews did not obtain local or even Roman citizenship.[46]

---

nean inscription. E. Mary Smallwood, *The Jews Under Roman Rule from Pompey to Diocletian: A Study in Political Relations,* 2d ed. (Leiden: Brill, 1981) 507, translates it, "former Jews," suggesting that these Jews had obtained local citizenship at the price of repudiating Judaism since full citizenship usually required recognition of the local pagan cults. Collins, "Insiders and Outsiders," 201, on the other hand, translates the phrase, "former Judeans," preferring rather that these are likely recent immigrants from Palestine following the Bar Kokhba revolt.

[42] Shimon Applebaum, "Legal Status," 447–49; Smallwood, *The Jews,* 507, 509; cf. Trebilco, *Jewish Communities,* 37–54.

[43] Both Julius Caesar and Augustus reaffirmed Jewish rights. See Josephus, *Ant.* 12.3.119-28; 14.10.202-10; 213-16; 16.2.27-30. The only significant change in Jewish rights came after the First Jewish Revolt in 66–72 CE. The half-shekel donation to the temple in Jerusalem was converted to a Jewish tax collected by the Romans for the temple of Jupiter Capitolinus in Rome. Applebaum, "Legal Status," 461; Trebilco, *Jewish Communities,* 34.

[44] W. M. Ramsay, *The Letters to the Seven Churches,* updated ed., edited by Mark W. Wilson (Peabody, Mass.: Hendrickson, 1994) 105–10 (orig. ed., 1904). Cf. Josephus, *Ant.* 12.3.119-28; 14.10.185-89; *Ag. Ap.* 2.33-47; Philo, *Good Person* 1.6-7.

[45] First published by H. Idris Bell, ed., *Jews and Christians in Egypt* (London: Oxford University Press, 1924) 1–37; also found in Victor A. Tcherikover and Alexander Fuks, eds., *Corpus Papyrorum Judaicarum* (Jerusalem: Magnes, 1960) 2:36–55.

[46] Smallwood, *The Jews,* 227–28; cf. Applebaum, "Legal Status," 449, 451; Trebilco, *Jewish*

Although most Jews did not enjoy full citizenship, they did have considerable freedom and relative autonomy. Jews living in major cities of the eastern Mediterranean formed themselves into πολιτεύματα, organizations of aliens with residential rights. Most Greco-Roman cities were comprised of πολιτεύματα formed by various ethnic groups which had their own administrative and judicial powers over their members and were distinct and independent of the local civic body. Each πολίτευμα, however, had to be recognized and authorized by the local civic authorities.[47] This status provided the Jews with the means to retain their own identity as a people and allowed them to conduct meetings in their own facilities.[48] They lived out their own customs and rituals and conducted themselves publicly as distinctly Jewish. However they did not cut themselves off from public life. Some perhaps held local or Roman citizenship and were likely active in the community. Citizenship and community activism may have required acknowledgment of local pagan gods, but it did not necessarily require them to abandon their Jewish lifestyle.[49]

The Jewish Christians enjoyed the religious freedom accorded the Jews as long as they maintained their membership in the Jewish πολιτεύματα. By the end of the first century, the increasingly Gentile church along with Jewish hostility likely led to an increased separation of Jewish Christians and the church as a whole from affiliation with the Jewish community. This separation was by no means decisive or uniform throughout the Christian communities for several centuries, but the increased segregation must have placed some Jesus followers in a precarious legal status. Christian gatherings apart from the πολιτεύματα could have been viewed as social gatherings or *collegia*, which Julius Caesar had outlawed, except those of ancient origin. The Jews, of course, were exempted.[50] How strictly his decree, the *Lex Iulia de Collegiis*, was enforced in first-century CE Asia is uncertain. It seems clear that certain professional associations thrived in spite of the restrictions but the exceptions may have been granted because of their political influence. Trajan's reign, however, brought stricter enforcement to the provinces of Asia Minor.[51]

Communities, 172–73.

[47] Smallwood, *The Jews*, 139, 225–26.

[48] See the discussion in Trebilco, *Jewish Communities*, 12–19.

[49] Wilson, *Related Strangers*, 21.

[50] Shimon Applebaum, "The Organization of the Jewish Communities in the Diaspora," in *The Jewish People in the First Century*, ed. S. Safrai et al. CRINT 1 (Philadelphia: Fortress, 1974) 481; Stern, "Diaspora," 163; Trebilco, *Jewish Communities*, 13.

[51] Applebaum, "Organization," 481.

Consequently, Christian gatherings separate from civic or Jewish associations would have been socially and legally in question. Any unrest that they might have caused could have been brought to the attention of the Roman authorities, and it is possible that the Greeks, Greco-Asiatics, or Jews may have used this legal loophole as an opportunity to bring accusations against the Christians to the local authorities. The Greeks would have viewed the Christians as atheists because of their unwillingness to recognize local gods, and the Jews would have been motivated to bring accusations against the Christians by what they perceived as a heretical transgression of their own laws and customs. The result of such accusations could have been trial and punishment and such punishment might have included beatings, expulsion from the city, banishment (which may have included confiscation of property), or execution.[52]

βλασφημία

This scenario may be just the one John is addressing in his message to the Smyrnean believers. John is particularly concerned with the pressure the Jewish community is placing on the Smyrnean church. Couched between references to tribulation in 2.9a and anticipated trial and possible martyrdom in 2.10 is John's accusation against the Jewish community. They are guilty of βλασφημία. From John's perspective, this ungodly activity has resulted in their rejection as true Jews and their condemnation as a "synagogue of Satan." What exactly is the nature of their βλασφημία is not entirely clear. Βλασφημία can be translated as blasphemy against God or slander against another.[53] In John's apocalypse, βλασφημία is otherwise used of the beast, the prostitute, and the earth-dwellers who blaspheme God (13.1, 5-6; 16.9, 11, 21; 17.3).

Collins offers three possible scenarios for understanding the nature of the Jewish βλασφημία in 2.9. First, John may have viewed the claims of these Jews to be Jews as blasphemous. Since they had rejected the Messiah Jesus, John was calling into question their claim to be true Jews. Second, John may have viewed Jewish claims against Christ in opposition to Christian claims to be blasphemous.[54] Third, he may be referring to Jewish accusations against the Christian community that they were a

---

[52] Collins, "Insiders and Outsiders," 199.
[53] "βλασφημία," 178, *BDAG on CD-ROM*. Version 1.0d. 2000, 2001.
[54] So Leonard L. Thompson, *Revelation,* ANTC (Nashville: Abingdon, 1998) 68.

social or civil threat, which John anticipated would lead to civil action and persecution.[55]

Of the three possibilities, the third seems the most probable. It is unlikely that the struggle with the Jewish community was primarily over their right to call themselves Jews.[56] John, who was a Jew himself, likely did not consider blasphemous their claim to be Jews. What earned them the designation of "synagogue of Satan" was much more serious. It is also unlikely that John has in mind Jewish claims about Jesus over against those of the church. Jewish rejection of the messianic claims of Jesus in the first century was not unusual and would not deserve special mention among the tribulations of the Smyrnean believers. What was taking place in Smyrna between Jews and Christians was worthy of special attention because of its serious nature. If the Jewish community in Smyrna was in some way involved in accusing the Christians to the local authorities, then they would have been seen as the agents of the devil who, John writes, is about to throw the Smyrnean believers in prison (2.10).[57] The close contextual proximity of the "synagogue of Satan" in 2.9 and the activity of the "devil" in 10b argues powerfully that the so-called Jews were instigating civil persecution.[58] For John, Satan and the devil are two names for the one enemy of God and his church.[59] He is "the accuser" of the saints (Rev 12.9-10; cf. 20.2,10) and is ostensibly the power behind the Roman government (Rev 13.4). Any involvement of the Jews with the Romans against the Christians merited mention and serious condemnation.

Given the size, legal status, and religious freedom enjoyed by the Jewish population, it is not surprising that Jewish opposition was at times a serious hardship for the church and in particular for the Jewish Christians. While the Jewish πολίτευμα had certain judicial autonomy to govern itself based on Jewish law, it did not have the liberty to execute anyone. This restriction did not, of course, prevent Jews from accusing Christians to the local authorities. Since Christian groups did not have any real legal foundation and their "atheistic" stance was also not pleasing to

---

[55] Collins, "Insiders and Outsiders," 209.

[56] Contra Bredin, "Synagogue of Satan," 160, who believes the dispute was over who had the right to be called the true Judeans based on payment of the Jewish tax.

[57] Collins, "Insiders and Outsiders," 209.

[58] Jan Lambrecht, "Jewish Slander: A Note on Rev 2,9-10," *ETL* 75 (1999) 425; reprinted as "'Synagogues of Satan' (Rev. 2:9 and 3.9): Anti-Judaism in the Book of Revelation," in *Anti-Judaism and the Fourth Gospel*, ed. R. Bieringer et al. (Louisville: Westminster John Knox, 2001) 281.

[59] See Osborne, *Revelation*, 133, on the use of Satan and devil in this passage.

their Greco-Roman neighbors, the believers found themselves vulnerable to social and political persecution from all sides. This is the likely situation in Smyrna at the time of John's apocalypse.

The prevailing evidence, therefore, argues that Jews were mounting formidable opposition against the church. It is difficult to say precisely what instigated the Jewish hostility against the Christians in Smyrna. Certainly it can be said that the Christian message of a crucified but risen messiah was enough to stir Jewish opposition, but it was likely more than that. It may be that the growth of the church became a threat to the Jewish community, especially if proselytism was successful among the Jews themselves. Some scholars have suggested that Christian mission among the Jews was the major reason for Jewish hostility.[60] Whatever the cause, this opposition brought a virulent condemnation from John, who being a Jewish Christian himself may have felt the sting of their attack. The slander of these Jews had perhaps reached the ears of the local magistrates and John anticipates that the result will be persecution and even death (2.10). The Jews and the Roman authorities have unwittingly become the tools of the archenemy of God and his people, Satan or the devil.

The Philadelphian Message

The opposition in Philadelphia appears to be similar to that in Smyrna. Although the word order is slightly different in the Philadelphian message, John equally describes their opponents as a "synagogue of Satan, who say that they are Jews and are not" (3.9a). It seems reasonable to assume, then, that the Philadelphian church is similarly in conflict with the local Jewish community. Unlike the Smyrnean message where the Jews are accused of βλασφημία, John does not say what opposition the Jews are mounting against the Philadelphian church, however, it is serious enough to warrant a word of perseverance to the church and a scathing rebuke of the Jews.

It is not clear whether the Jewish community was accusing the Christians to the local authorities as has been suggested in Smyrna. Unlike the Smyrnean message, there is no direct reference to tribulation or impending persecution; the only direct reference to a future "trial" (ὥρας τοῦ πειρασμοῦ) comes in 3.10 where the faithful believers are promised deliverance while the earth-dwellers are tested. In 3.8, however, the

---

[60] Ramsay, *Letters*, 198–99; Caird, *Revelation*, 35; Trebilco, *Jewish Communities*, 20–21; Mounce, *Revelation*, 75; cf. Hirschberg, *Das eschatologische Israel*, 109–10, who says that the dispute between Christians and Jews likely had both a social and a theological component. The Jews may not have feared as much the loss in numbers of proselytes to the Christians but the loss of socially influential members and thus the loss of prestige.

church's present situation is not yet one of deliverance or triumph. The church is said to have "little power" and is praised for not having denied the Name. Their lack of power, like the Smyrneans' poverty, may be an indication that they were already socially and economically disadvantaged as a result of their Christian faith, and the praise for not having denied the Name may further imply that persecution had already begun.

While persecution from the local authorities may be a genuine threat for the Philadelphian believers, it is difficult to say what role the Jewish community played. It seems reasonable to suggest that at least some Jews were fomenting opposition to the believing community, which is John's primary concern in the Philadelphian message. The content and overall Jewish tone of the message affirms this conclusion. While it is admittedly difficult to ascertain the exact nature of the Jewish-Christian conflict, the message does yield some clues that suggest a possible solution.

Christian missionary activity among the Jews was offered above as a possible reason for Jewish opposition in Smyrna and this reason is possible here in Philadelphia as well. Some scholars have suggested that the promise of an "open door" for the Smyrneans is a promise of a continued successful Christian mission among the Jewish community of Philadelphia in spite of Jewish opposition.[61] In addition, the literal translation of the phrase, διδῶ ἐκ τῆς συναγωγῆς τοῦ σατανᾶ, as "I give [those] of the synagogue of Satan (as your converts)" might give the allusion of a missionary sense to this passage.[62] After all, the believers are told that those of the "synagogue of Satan" will be made to come and bow down at the feet of the Philadelphian believers and *learn* (γνῶσιν) that Christ has loved them (3.9). If one interprets γνῶσιν as indicating a conversion experience rather than an acknowledgment or recognition of the favored position of the believers, then the passage could suggest the eventual conversion of the opposing Jews. While this is one possible interpretation, it does not seem to be the one that best fits the Philadelphian context. The primary issue in the Philadelphian message is not Christian evangelism, but it is a question of who the legitimate people of God are. John seeks to establish in this message not only who the true Jews are but also who has the right of access to God.[63]

---

[61] Ramsay, *Letters*, 296–97; Caird, *Revelation*, 53; Beale, *Revelation*, 286.

[62] This is one interpretation among three possible solutions Hemer, *Letters*, 163, offers for understanding this passage. It is, however, not the solution favored by Hemer (*Letters*). Cf. Charles, *Revelation*, 1:88.

[63] So Stevenson, *Power and Place*, 241–43.

As is usual in each of the seven messages, John offers a clue to the pressing need of each believing community in his description of the divine messenger. In the Philadelphian message, John departs from his usual practice of borrowing his description directly from his vision of the messenger in chapter 1 and offers a somewhat unique description to open this message. The divine messenger is described as "the holy one, the true one, who has the key of David, who opens and no one will shut, who shuts and no one opens" (3.7). This description is probably an allusion to Isa 22.22, in which Isaiah prophesies the calling forth of Eliakim to assume the throne of David. It is on his shoulders that the key of David is placed and thusly his authority is established over Jerusalem and Judah. John perceives this historical prophecy as also having messianic implications.[64] Whereas God called Eliakim and gave him authority to "be a father to the inhabitants of Jerusalem and to the house of Judah" (Isa 22.21), Jesus has been given spiritual authority over God's true people, the church. He is the one who grants access to God's kingdom as symbolized by the house of David (3.7) and the eschatological temple (3.12).[65] John, through the use of Jewish prophecy and cultic imagery, establishes Jesus as the fulfillment of Jewish messianic hope. In addition, as the holy and true one, Jesus' authority is divine and therefore eternal (cf. Rev 6.10).

The Philadelphian church is apparently in need of this assurance of Christ's authority over God's kingdom. The first promise made to them is that of an "open door that no one is able to shut" (3.8). While it is true that an open door has been used in the NT as a metaphor for missions (1 Cor 16.9; 2 Cor 2.12; Col 4.3), this is unlikely the case here.[66] The open door is more accurately a promise of certain access to God's eschatological kingdom (Rev 3.20; 4.1; John 10.7, 9; Acts 14.27).[67] John is raising a polemic against the Jewish opposition addressed in 3.9 and this opposition may be in the form of a synagogue ban.[68] Such a synagogue ban would primarily affect the Jewish Christians and secondarily the entire church. The result would be the expulsion of the believers from the religious protection

---

[64] Beale, *Revelation*, 284–85.

[65] Ibid., 285.

[66] See Stevenson, *Power and Place*, 242, for a linguistic argument against such an interpretation; cf. Hirschberg, *Das eschatologische Israel*, 116; Prigent, *L'Apocalypse*, 155.

[67] Beckwith, *Apocalypse*, 480; Beasley-Murray, *Revelation*, 101; Michaels, *Revelation*, 83–84; Mounce, *Revelation*, 101–2; Stevenson, *Power and Place*, 241; cf. Hirschberg, *Das eschatologische Israel*, 116, who believes it is access to the new Jerusalem.

[68] See Collins, *Crisis and Catharsis*, 86–87.

of the Jewish πολίτευμα and it would be the first step in exposing them to legal action and persecution.

A second promise follows in 3.9 through which John disputes any special claim that the Philadelphian Jews may have to be the true people of God over against the Philadelphian believers. The Holy One promises,

> I will make (διδῶ)[69] those of the synagogue of Satan who say that they are Jews and are not, but are lying—I will make (ποιήσω) them come and bow down before your feet, and they will learn that I have loved you.

Rather than a promise of Jewish conversion, this passage contains a twofold rebuke of the Jewish opposition. Similar to the Smyrnean message (2.9), John first denies the Jewish opposition any claim to be Jews and, instead, calls them liars and a synagogue of Satan. John is not disputing their ethnic right to be called Jews but their spiritual right.

A second challenge follows in 3.9b with a promised eschatological role reversal. In an allusion to Jewish prophecy, John usurps Israel's place as heir of God's promises by declaring that it is the Philadelphian believers that will one day be acknowledged as the ones truly loved by the divine Christ (Isa 43.4; 45.14; 49.22-23; 60.11-2, 14; cf. Ps 86.9).[70] John once again challenges the Philadelphian Jews' claim to be the true Jews by adopting Jewish prophetic hope and applying it to the believing community. If this is indeed John's intention, then this passage provides further evidence for the earlier contention that John has redefined "Jew" theologically and has broadened his definition of the heirs of Israel's covenant promises. This assertion is consistent with his theme throughout both the Smyrnean and Philadelphian messages that the true Jews are not those who oppose the believing community (i.e., the synagogue of Satan) but those who acknowledge God's plan as revealed in Jesus Christ.

The last promise given to the believers in Philadelphia reinforces this interpretation as it returns to the issue of the right of access. The promise is emphatic and telling. The Holy One promises,

---

[69] A literal translation of διδῶ as, "I give," while possible, is not the best translation here. As Hemer, *Letters,* 163, points out, it is better to understand this as a Hebraism and translate it in parallel with the following ποιήσω. Cf. Charles, *Revelation,* 1:88.

[70] See Beale, *Revelation,* 287–88; Charles, *Revelation,* 1:88–89; Hemer, *Letters,* 160–61. Stevenson, *Power and Place,* 243, believes this is a promise that the Jews "will recognize the rightful claim of the Christian community to the title of 'Jew' and to the messianic kingdom."

> I will make you a pillar in the temple of my God; you will never go out of it. I will write on you the name of my God, and the name of the city of my God, the new Jerusalem that comes down from my God out of heaven, and my own new name (3.12).

If the believers are being denied access to the synagogue and in turn denied their rights as the people of God, it is this promise that assures them a permanent eschatological place in the presence of God (cf. Rev 7.15; 22.3-4) as the people of God (i.e., the new Jerusalem; Rev 21.9-10).

John opened this message by establishing Christ's authority over access to the kingdom of God and he closes it in a similar fashion. Jesus' followers, who are opposed by elements of the local Jewish synagogue, are promised an eternal place in God's eschatological temple. Stevenson observes that the Philadelphian message noticeably progresses from synagogue language to temple language, suggesting that John associates the local Jewish community with the synagogue while the Christian community is associated with the temple. The significance of this observation is that the temple is historically and traditionally a broader Jewish symbol and implies that John wishes to subtly make "the claim that the church is heir to this [Jewish] history and tradition."[71] John's symbolic use of both the temple and Jerusalem as sacred places for the believers once again reinforces the conclusion that the believers in Jesus, both Jews and Gentiles, are the true people of God, the "true Jews," and that they hold a primary place in God's eschatological plan. This symbolic relationship between the temple/Jerusalem and the believers becomes particularly evident at the end of the Apocalypse when John merges these symbols in his final eschatological vision of the new Jerusalem.

The "Synagogue of Satan" Accusation

John's rebuke of the Smyrnean and Philadelphian Jews is a two-fold condemnation that strips them of their right to be called Jews and condemns them as belonging to Satan.[72] John denies them their right to be called Jews not only because of their opposition to the believing community but because, in his view, they are not acting like "true" Jews, who are those who follow God and do his will. This implies that John understands the true Jews to be those who acknowledge Jesus as the Messiah—that is,

---

[71] Stevenson, *Power and Place*, 243.

[72] For an in-depth discussion of the common practice in Christian literature to equate the ultimate source of persecution with the devil/Satan see Lieu, "Jewish Persecution," 287–90.

those who belong to the believing communities of Smyrna, Philadelphia and elsewhere. Jesus is God's full revelation of his plan and those who oppose Jesus and his followers automatically fall into Satan's camp. The Jewish synagogues in Smyrna and Philadelphia have therefore ceased to be a "synagogue of the Lord" (τὴν συναγωγὴν Κυρίου, Num 16.3; 20.4 LXX) and have become a "synagogue of Satan."[73]

It is important to observe at this point that John is not using the term "Jew" in a pejorative sense. Indeed, Kraft believes the term "Jew" is never used in a negative way in the NT.[74] Some scholars, however, have tried to draw a contrast between the portrayal of the Jews in the Apocalypse and the Fourth Gospel, arguing that the writer of the Fourth Gospel in contrast to the Apocalypse vilifies the Jews as Christ's enemies. Beckwith disputes such a comparison, citing the gospel writer's ability to distinguish between a "true Jew" (John 1.47; 8.31) and those who oppose Christ (John 8.37-44; this passage agreeing essentially with the Apocalypse).[75] It could be argued, therefore, that both authors fundamentally understand "Jew" as an honorable term worthy only of those who act like "true Jews" (i.e., those Jews who recognize God's messiah and follow him).[76]

John is not condemning the Jews as a race of people or even as a religion. John himself is a Jew. It would be anachronistic to suggest that he is being anti-Semitic or even anti-Jewish. He is condemning those Jews who are opposing God and his people, for a true Jew would not act in such a manner. John's definition of a "Jew" has broadened as it had for the Apostle Paul (Rom 2.28-29). God's people, the "true Jews," now constitute both Jews and Gentiles who have accepted Jesus as the Messiah.

Some scholars liken John's condemnation of his fellow Jews to that of the Qumran community.[77] The Qumran community, which had withdrawn itself from the rest of Palestinian Judaism around the second century BCE, viewed the Jewish leadership in Jerusalem as corrupt. Adherents to the community were called to "separate from the congregation of the men of injustice" (1QS 5.1-2, 10-12)[78] and to adhere fully to the Mosaic

---

[73] Beckwith, *Apocalypse*, 454.
[74] Kraft, *Offenbarung*, 61.
[75] Beckwith, *Apocalypse*, 453–54.
[76] So Aune, *Revelation 1–5*, 162; cf. Stevenson, *Power and Place*, 227.
[77] Beale, *Revelation*, 241; Borgen, "Polemic in the Book of Revelation," 209; Borgen, *Early Christianity and Hellenistic Judaism* (Edinburgh: T. & T. Clark, 1996) 282–83; Bredin, "Synagogue of Satan," 163–64.
[78] All citations from the Dead Sea Scrolls are cited from Geza Vermes, *The Complete Dead Sea Scrolls in English* (New York: Penguin, 1997).

Law as has been revealed to the "Seekers of [God's] will" (5.9). The Jews outside of the community were condemned as "the congregation of traitors" (CD 1.12), "a horde of Satan," and an "assembly of deceit" (1QH 2.22); but the community was called "the Congregation of God" and "the Assembly of God" (1QM 4.9-10). The similarity between John's language and that of the Qumran community is striking.

There are, however, some differences between the Qumran community and the early church. The church was less separatistic and it did, at least at first, hold out some hope for the salvation of the Jewish people (Rom 1.16; 11.26). The Qumran community based its differences on the interpretation of the oral and written law, while John based his distinction on who accepted Jesus as the fulfillment of the Jewish messianic hope. Peder Borgen remarks that even though the early believers were probably already being pushed out of the synagogues and were under threat of Jewish persecution, the two groups were still closely related.[79] John does not wish to abandon the title "Jew" but merely to condemn those within Judaism who do not accept God's revelation, Jesus.

Conclusion

At the outset of this discussion of the messages to the Smyrnean and Philadelphian churches, it was stated that "the most widely held and most compelling interpretation is that these two churches were in some way in conflict with the Jewish communities of Smyrna and Philadelphia,"[80] and a thorough investigation of the evidence has affirmed this position. The similar condemnatory language and contextual cues of these two messages argue powerfully that the believing communities in Smyrna and Philadelphia were facing like opposition from similar groups. Neither of these churches is facing false teaching as in Ephesus, Pergamum, and Thyatira, nor is their spiritual state criticized as in Sardis and Laodicea. They are rather encouraged to persevere, praised for their faithfulness, and assured of future reward. They are communities under duress from outside pressures. The Smyrneans are facing poverty, tribulation, and impending persecution, while the Philadelphians have "little power" and are praised for not having denied the Name. Both are facing opposition from a group or groups whom John condemns as a "synagogue of Satan."

This chapter has argued from both internal and external evidence that it is reasonable to conclude that these opposition groups are comprised of

---

[79] Borgen, "Polemic," 209.
[80] See above, 51.

elements from the local Jewish communities. To propose that these opponents are in reality a Christian sect within these local bodies is inconsistent with the contextual evidence. Although the external evidence is sometimes difficult to date and often comes from later centuries, it is reasonable to infer that Smyrna and Philadelphia had significant Jewish communities at the end of the first century that could have raised formidable opposition to the Jesus followers. John's words to the Smyrnean Christians may indicate that Jewish opposition had led to persecution by the local authorities and the same may be true in Philadelphia, although in this latter case it is more difficult to draw such a conclusion. It is possible that John's primary concern in Philadelphia is with a Jewish synagogue ban. Of course, it is also possible that a synagogue ban was part of the Jewish opposition in Smyrna.[81]

If the opponents in both Smyrna and Philadelphia are indeed the Jewish communities in these two cities, then it may be possible to begin to discern from these two messages John's perception of the relationship between the church and Judaism. John levels a virulent condemnation against these Jews in both messages. In both instances he denies them the right to be called Jews and condemns them as no longer a congregation of the Lord but a synagogue of Satan. Like their Roman counterparts, they have become agents of Satan. Not only are they no longer a congregation of the Lord, but they have lost their place as the heir to God's prophetic promises. It is the Jews in Philadelphia, like the pagan nations of OT prophetic tradition, who will come and acknowledge that the Philadelphian believers are loved of God. This can only be interpreted as a promise of vindication for the church and, along with the synagogue of Satan accusation, a redefinition of who are the true people of God. Those who belong to God are no longer determined by ethnicity but by faithfulness to God. It is Jesus who stands in the Davidic line and who provides authoritative access to God's kingdom. Those who oppose him and his church are agents of Satan.

What is of particular interest is the two-pronged attack discernable in these two messages. John usurps for the church the Jewish right to be

---

[81] Hirschberg, *Das eschatologische Israel*, 112–17, proposes that a synagogue ban was a possible cause of the conflict in both locales. Part of his evidence for this possibility is based on a comparison with John 9.22, 11.42, and 16.2. He believes that the latter texts reflect a situation in Asia Minor in the late first century that allows him to extrapolate a similar context for Rev 2.9; 3.9. This comparison, however, seems based too much on conjecture. Hirschberg is correctly cautious in not seeing either in the Apocalypse or the Fourth Gospel an indication of the *birkath haminim*.

called the people of God and designates the church as the heir of Jewish covenant promise. It is at this point that John is on common ground with later Christian writers. The view that the church is the "new Israel" and is the rightful heir to Israel's promises becomes part of the church's offensive as it seeks to defend both and to define itself in the second century. The epistle of *Barnabas* denies the Jews their right to the old covenant (4.6-8; 14.1-4; cf. 9.4.) and Ignatius proclaims that the Jewish prophets were in reality followers of Christ (*Magn.* 9.2). This offensive perhaps finds its climax in the middle of the second century with Justin Martyr's claim for the church to be "the true and spiritual Israelitish nation" (*Dial.* 11.5 [Williams]).

Does John, however, carry the argument as far as Ignatius or Justin? The evidence is insufficient to argue that John has abandoned or condemned the Jews as God's covenant people. Given John's almost certain Jewish heritage, it would be unrealistic to infer such a strong conclusion. John's virulent condemnation of certain Jews in Smyrna and Philadelphia is not to be understood as anti-Jewish or anti-Semitic, even though subsequent generations of the church may have understood it that way. One may be able to infer that John is anti-Judaic—that he does not see Judaism as a means to salvation—but even this would not be completely accurate. John does not have a clearly developed line of demarcation between Judaism and Christianity, for he sees an unbroken continuity between the Abrahamic covenant and the one inaugurated through Jesus Christ, the Lamb. While he does not see Torah observance as a means to salvation—for it is the sacrifice of the Lamb that has brought redemption (5.9-10)—he has not completely abandoned his faith. It is his Jewish faith that finds completion in the redemptive work of Jesus. It is those "who keep the commandments of God *and* hold the testimony of Jesus" (12.17 emphasis mine) that comprise the new people of God. John's denunciation of the Jewish opposition, therefore, is not directed against the Jews or Judaism as an entity, but it falls within the broader scope of the condemnation of all ungodly opposition throughout the Apocalypse. This condemnation is not just targeted against the Jewish opposition, but it also encompasses rogue elements within the Asian churches who are equally condemned as followers of Balaam and Jezebel.[82] John's condemnation, therefore, is consistent throughout; it is not based on ethnicity or religious heritage, but on one's allegiance either to God or to Satan. In this manner John is consistent and unbiased in developing an apocalyptic dichotomy between good and evil.

---

[82] Hirschberg, *Das eschatological Israel*, 123, makes a similar observation.

What can be observed as very significant in John's condemnation of the Jewish opposition is a redefinition of the people of God and thus who the "true Jews" are. To be a "Jew," or perhaps more accurately an Israelite, has always implied privileged membership in the covenant people of God. John now redefines what it means to be a Jew in more theological terms. It is the faithful of God, both Jews and Gentiles, who comprise God's covenant people. The faithful are those who have not compromised with the pagan culture and who follow the Lamb. They have not aligned themselves with Satan and his cohorts.

In light of the advent of Jesus, John reinterprets his Jewish scriptures through a christological lens, seeing them fulfilled on behalf of God's eschatological people, both Jews and Gentiles, the church. Those who are followers of the Lamb are heirs of God's covenant both past and present. It is for this reason that John can speak of Jesus as the "Lion of the tribe of Judah" (5.5) and the saints as the sealed of the twelve tribes of Israel (7.1-17) or the heirs of the new Jerusalem (21.7). The realities that once defined the corporal people of God have now become the symbols with which God's eschatological people are identified. This is an inclusive people comprised of "saints from every tribe and language and people and nation" (5.9; cf. 7).

3

The 144,000:
Israel or Spiritual Israel?

JOHN'S enumeration of the 144,000 sealed from the twelve tribes of Israel in 7.4-8 and their subsequent reappearance in 14.1-5 is one of the best known images from the Apocalypse and one whose meaning is certainly among the most debated. Who John intends the 144,000 to represent has puzzled commentators for some time and a ready answer is not easily discerned. However, in order to understand John's use of Jewish imagery and subsequently his view of the relationship between the church and Judaism, one must grapple with their identity. The following discussion, therefore, will be primarily concerned with sifting through the prevailing evidence in order to discern a defensible answer to the question, "Who are the 144,000?" The response to this question will contribute to the overall pursuit of understanding John's view of the relationship between the church and Judaism. It is the contention here that the 144,000 represent the spiritually faithful, both Jews and Gentiles, who follow the Lamb as the true Messiah and are sealed as protection from the wrath of God coming upon those who dwell on the earth. This protection from the eschatological judgments of God, however, does not guarantee their protection from physical persecution. It will be argued, as well, that the vision of the 144,000 (7.1-8) and the subsequent vision of the innumerable multitude (7.9-17) are visions of the same group from different perspectives. John's vision of the 144,000 on Mount Zion in the company of the Lamb (14.1-5) will provide corroborating evidence in support of these conclusions. These interpretations, as will be shown, are consistent with the narrative context of the Apocalypse and with John's understanding of the church as God's new spiritual Israel (cf. 2.9; 3.9, 11.1-13; 12.1-17; 21.9-10).

The visions of chapter 7 form part of a larger visionary context that has its beginning in Rev 4.1. Revelation 4.1—8.5 comprises the second in a series of sevenfold visions that form the heart of the Apocalypse.[1] In chapter 4, John sees a stunning vision of what is presumably the throne of God described in dramatic detail. In chapter 5, the focal point of the vision shifts with the revelation of a seven-sealed scroll which is held in the right hand of "the one who sits on the throne" (5.1). This scroll takes on immediate importance because no one is found worthy to open its seven seals. John himself begins to weep at this apparent loss, but is soon comforted with the knowledge that there is indeed someone who is worthy to take the scroll and to open its seals. John is told that "the Lion of the tribe of Judah, the Root of David" has conquered and is able to open the seals (5.5). John then sees not a lion, but a lamb that looks as if it has been slain standing in the midst of the throne of God (5.6). The lamb takes the scroll from the one seated on the throne which results in universal adoration of the lamb. The metaphorical imagery and the worship hymn of chapter 5 leave John's readers without any doubt that the conquering hero is Jesus the Messiah.

Chapter 6 begins with the opening of the first seal followed in sequence by the next five. The first four seals unleash the four horsemen of the Apocalypse who dispense common eschatological judgments (i.e., war, famine, death, and plague).[2] The fifth seal introduces the souls of Christian martyrs who cry out for vindication, but instead are given white robes, which typically represent the purity of the redeemed (cf. 3.15, 18; 4.4; 7.9, 14; 19.14); and they are told to rest until the full number of their fellow believers who will be killed has been completed (6.11). After the comforting of the persecuted comes the opening of the sixth seal and the outpouring of the wrath of "the one who sits on the throne" and the Lamb (6.16). In classic apocalyptic language, John speaks of the horrors that come upon those who dwell on the earth (6.12-15; cf. Joel 2.31; Acts 2.20). The wrath is so great that everyone on earth, from the least to the greatest, seeks to hide as they exclaim in despair, "The great day of their wrath has come, and who is able to stand?"

The opening of chapter 7 brings an interlude between the sixth and seventh seals and provides a response to the closing question of chapter

---

[1] This division follows the structural outline suggested in Collins, *Combat Myth*, 19. There are at least four visions of seven: seven messages, seven seals, seven trumpets and seven bowls/plagues. Collins in her structural outline of Revelation identifies two other sets of seven-fold visions which she calls "seven unnumbered visions" (12.1—15.4; 19.11—21.8).

[2] For a discussion of the possible interpretations of the four horsemen see Aune, *Revelation 6–16*, 389–403; Beale, *Revelation*, 372–89.

6. Chapter 7 is comprised of two distinct but not unrelated visions. Both visions are introduced with John's customary vision formula, μετὰ τοῦτο [ταῦτα] εἶδον (7.1, 9; cf. 4.1; 18.1; 15.5). Revelation 7.1-8 contains a vision in which John sees four angels standing at the four corners of the earth holding back the four winds. A fifth angel ascends from the east with instructions to the others not to "damage the earth or the sea or the trees, until we have marked the servants of our God with a seal on their foreheads" (7.3). John then hears the number of those marked. They are 144,000 "out of every tribe of the people of Israel" (7.4); 12,000 from each of the twelve tribes. In the second vision of chapter 7, John sees an innumerable multitude from every nation standing before the throne of God clad in white (cf. 6.11) and worshiping God and the Lamb. It is a scene of eschatological bliss laced with promises of eternal comfort for those who persevere through the "great tribulation" (7.14).

There are a number of interpretive questions that arise when confronted with these two visions not the least of which is, Whom do the 144,000 represent? The identity of the 144,000 is so intriguing because John has paused in the midst of this otherwise Christian apocalypse to relate to his readers a vision of 12,000 being sealed from each of the twelve tribes of Israel.[3] In order to arrive at some reasonable understanding as to the identity of the 144,000, some more fundamental exegetical questions must initially be addressed. First, What source lies behind this vision narrative, and how might one account for the list's anomalies? Second, What role does this vision play in this interlude and in the apocalyptic narrative as a whole? Third, What is John's intention behind his use of this very 'Jewish' vision?" Fourth, What relationship does it have to the subsequent visions of the innumerable multitude and the 144,000 on Mount Zion in 14.1-5?

The Origin of John's Tribal List (7.5-8)

The original source of John's tribal list in 7.5-8 is unclear. The numbering of 12,000 from each of the twelve tribes of Israel gives this vision a clearly

---

[3] There are only three occurrences of Ἰσραήλ in the Apocalypse (2.14; 7.4; 21.12). The first occurrence is clearly historical while the latter two are of particular interest in the present discussion because they occur in visions that arguably refer to the followers of the Lamb, that is, the church. In both of these instances, John refers to the υἱῶν Ἰσραήλ and their division into twelve tribes. As will be observed in the subsequent discussion, the number twelve plays a symbolic role in the Apocalypse as the number of the people of God and figures prominently not only in the vision of the 144,000 but also in the vision of the new Jerusalem.

Jewish tone and in turn suggests to a number of scholars that a Jewish source stands behind the text.[4] If this is the case, it seems clear that John has adapted this source for his own unique purpose, making the identity of the original source difficult to determine. Richard Bauckham believes that the list is patterned after a Jewish military census like that found in the OT (Num 1.3, 18-46; 26.2, 4; 1 Chron 21.5; 27.23), citing the phrase ἐκ φυλῆς . . . δώδεκα χιλιάδες as modeled on the Num 1.21, 23 (LXX) formula.[5] John may have adopted a Jewish apocalyptic text that looked to the reunion of the Israelite tribes for a final eschatological battle.[6] The inclusion of Levi in the census, however, complicates this conclusion since Levi was not usually included in a military census (Num 1.47-49). The task of finding a solution to the origin of John's list is made even more complex by the presence of anomalies that are difficult to explain. The ordering of the list is peculiar as Judah is listed first, the tribe of Dan is excluded, and Ephraim is replaced with Joseph while Manasseh is retained.

There have been several solutions offered to explain the origin of John's list and the source of its anomalies. Many of these explanations are quite intricate and are not at all points satisfactory. Most scholars interpret the placement of Judah at the head of the list as indicative of John's "Christianizing" of the list in favor of this messianic tribe (cf. 5.5).[7] Others, however, call for caution, theorizing that a Christianizing of the list need not be the reason for the disorder. While acknowledging that many commentators agree that the primacy of Judah is due to a messianic emphasis, David Aune advises prudence, noting that Judah is listed first in OT geographical lists that proceed from south to north (Num 34.19-28;

---

[4] So Beckwith, *Apocalypse*, 535; Beasley-Murray, *Revelation*, 141; Richard Bauckham, "The List of the Tribes in Revelation 7 Again," *JSNT* 42 (1991) 99-115; Charles, *Revelation*, 1:192–93 also believes that there is a Jewish or Jewish Christian source behind this vision, although he posits a separate tradition for 7.1-3.

[5] Bauckham, *Climax*, 217. The description of the 144,000 in Rev 14.1-5 as holy and chaste males may provide further support that John had in mind a Jewish military census in 7.5-8. A military census usually included all Israelite males twenty years and older and it was sometimes the case that soldiers practiced sexual abstinence while on a mission (e.g., 1 Sam 21.5).

[6] The hope of the restoration of the ten lost tribes of Israel after the exile is well documented in Jewish tradition (*Pss. Sol.* 17.26-46; *T. Mos.* 4.6-9; *Sib. Or.* 2.165-73; *4 Ezra* 13.40-48; *2 Bar.* 78; 84.3-10; 85.4; cf. *b. Sanh.* 110b). John, however, is not likely using this text to express a hope for a reunited Israel. See the discussion in Beale, *Revelation*, 419–20.

[7] So Charles, *Revelation*, 1:208; Kraft, 127; Beasley-Murray, *Revelation*, 143; Christopher R. Smith, "The Portrayal of the Church as the new Israel in the Names and Order of the Tribes in Revelation 7.5-8," *JSNT* 39 (1990): 114; Mounce, *Revelation*, 169; Beale, *Revelation*, 417–18; Stevenson, *Power and Place*, 252.

Josh 21.4-7; 1 Chron 12.23-37) and in the order of the tribes' military encampment (Num 2.3; 7.12; 10.14).[8]

Richard Bauckham does not believe that one must posit a Christianizing of the list and argues extensively that the origin and order of John's list rests squarely on Jewish sources.[9] Although Bauckham does believe that John uses this Jewish text ultimately for a Christian purpose, he postulates that this interpretation is imposed onto the list by the succeeding vision of the great multitude in 7.9-17 and not by John's Christian reordering of the list.[10] He believes that John's tribal list follows a widely accepted first-century matriological order (e. g., Pseudo-Philo, *L.A.B.* 8.6; 8.11-14; 26.10-11; cf. Josephus, *Ant.* 2.177-183) with some variation. The listing of the tribe of Judah first finds precedence not in Christian but in Jewish messianic expectation. This is particularly suggested by *L.A.B.* 25.4 and 25.9-13 where Judah, the tribe of Kenaz, is listed first.

Bauckham argues that Kenaz is depicted here by Pseudo-Philo as a "kind of forerunner of David (cf. 21.4-5; 49.1) and probably as a prototype of the future messianic deliverer."[11] His argument, therefore, is that John's list reflects "Jewish Davidic messianism," with which John's own belief in Jesus found resonance. In spite of its intricacies, however, Bauckham's argument is unable to account adequately for the other anomalies in John's list, and he is forced to conclude that some of the peculiarities are perhaps the result of John's "faulty memory."[12]

Like Bauckham, Ross Winkle also postulates a Jewish source for John's list.[13] While Bauckham looks to contemporary lists such as Josephus and Pseudo-Philo, Winkle argues that John's list is patterned after Ezek 48.30-34 with some rather elaborate revisions. Ezekiel's restored Jerusalem, like John's new Jerusalem (21.12), is bounded on four sides by walls that each bear three gates named for the twelve sons of Israel. According to Ezekiel's vision, each set of gates and their tribal name's sake face in one of the four directions of the geographical compass beginning with Reuben, Judah, and Levi in the north and ending with Gad, Asher, and Naphtali in the

---

[8] Aune, *Revelation 6–16*, 462.

[9] Richard Bauckham, "Tribes Again," 99–115. For an opposing response to Bauckham's article see Christopher R. Smith, "The Tribes of Revelation 7 and the Literary Competence of John the Seer," *JETS* 38 (1995) 213–18.

[10] Bauckham, "Tribes Again," 105–6.

[11] Ibid., 111–12.

[12] Ibid., 112.

[13] Ross E. Winkle, "Another Look at the List of Tribes in Revelation 7," *AUSS* 27 (1989) 53–67.

west. Winkle proposes that the tribal list in 7.5-8 follows Ezekiel's list but in a counterclockwise rotation.[14] A comparison of Ezekiel's reversed list with John's list creates, for Winkle, enough similarities to justify the conclusion that Ezekiel's list is the source behind John's list.[15]

This solution to the origin and anomalies of John's list is, however, far from convincing. As Winkle himself observes, a comparison of the reversed Ezekiel list with John's list results in each tribe of Rev 7.5-8—with the exception of Levi and Manasseh—being one position out-of-step with Ezekiel's list. In addition, a true reversal of Ezekiel's tribal order would result in Judah, which Ezekiel locates in the north, being placed at the end of John's list. In order to resolve this problem, Winkle believes that John does not adopt a complete reversal of Ezekiel's list in order to maintain Judah near the top. Winkle postulates two reasons for the purposeful prioritizing of Judah. He believes that John places Judah at the top of his list not only for messianic reasons but also because of what Winkle sees as an "implicit significance given to the north in the book of Revelation."[16]

The messianic promotion of Judah is an easily defensible explanation for John's reordering of the list, but the evidence that Winkle offers for the "regal symbolism associated with the north" is based more on conjecture than on explicit fact.[17] Winkle's explanation for this latter conjecture appears to be more an attempt to maintain a fragile link between Rev 7.5-8 and Ezek 48.30-34. Indeed, if one considers other Jewish texts, this favorable association of Judah with the north seems to be quite limited in its application. Even within Ezekiel this association begins to break down; in Ezek 9.1-4, a passage with which John's vision of 7.1-8 has apparent associations, the messengers from God who carry out his judgment upon unfaithful Israel approach from the north. The geographical encampment of the tribes in Num 2 (cf. 11QT 39:10-14) finds Judah in the east rather than the north, and Dan instead encamps in the north about which *Rab. Gen.* 2.10 [Slotki] states,

> The north is the region whence darkness issues forth into the world, and on that side shall be the tribe of Dan. Why? For it was that tribe which darkened the world with idolatry, when Jeroboam made the two golden calves.

---

[14] Ibid., 56–57.
[15] Ibid., 57.
[16] Ibid., 59.
[17] Ibid., 60.

In Rabbinic tradition, Dan became associated with the north, and it is this passage that has also become a suggested proof text for explaining another anomaly associated with John's list, namely the absence of the tribe of Dan.

One could as easily make a case for the east as the favored compass direction. In Num 2, Judah is encamped on the east, and it is from the direction of the "rising of the sun" that John sees the angel ascend who will seal the servants of God (7.2). The east is the direction from which the glory of God arises (Ezek 43.2) and the direction in which Ezekiel's eschatological temple faces (Ezek 47.1)—a model for John's new Jerusalem. In fact, in his description of the new Jerusalem, John conspicuously begins in the east when detailing the compass directions in which the twelve gates face (Rev 21.13). In addition, the east is also the direction of Messianic expectation (*Sib. Or.* 3.652). Jesus spoke of his own return as lightning that comes form the "east and flashes as far as the west" (Matt 24.27). In the end, however, compass directions were probably of little concern to John in ordering his list, and it is more likely that there are better explanations that lie behind John's unusual tribal list.

For Winkle, the reversal of Ezekiel's list only begins to explain John's unusual list order, but it does not fully account for all of the list's anomalies. He proposes that Ezekiel's list passes through five successive modifications before reaching its present form in Rev 7.5-8.[18] To some extent, Winkle succumbs to the same difficulties as Bauckham. If one proposes that John's list is founded on a particular ancient or contemporary tribal list, then one must find a way to explain how John arrived at his very different final list. The intricate proposals that result are difficult to accept and lead one to the conclusion that John's list is his own creation, the source of which—if any one source—is lost.

In the final analysis, a definitive response to this question of origin is tangential to finding an explanation of the peculiarities of John's list or even to finding a solution to the mysterious identity of the 144,000. It seems a reasonable inference, regardless of the source material behind Rev 7.5-8, that Judah heads John's list for messianic reasons. John has already been careful to specify Judah's place as the messianic tribe in his description of the Lamb as "the Lion of the tribe of Judah, the root of David" (5.5). Whether John reordered an existing list or developed his own to achieve this purpose is not certain, but given the literary context of Rev 7.1-8 and the other anomalies associated with the list, the weight of the

---

[18] See the chart in Winkle, "Another Look," 59.

evidence suggests that John created the present list to achieve his own literary goals in this Christian document.

The absence of Dan and the replacement of Ephraim with Joseph are more difficult to explain and are less clearly seen as changes of Christian origin. Bauckham's suggestion that Dan was simply omitted in order to keep the list at twelve tribes may be the most appealing solution due to its simplicity.[19] This solution, however, begs the question, "Why Dan?" Israel actually was comprised of thirteen tribes with Joseph being separated into Ephraim and Manasseh. This number did not usually present a problem since Levi was exempted from the military census and also did not receive a land inheritance along with the other tribes. It would seem more logical, then, for John to have omitted Levi from the list, or better yet to have listed only Joseph rather than (as he oddly did) both Joseph and Manasseh in order to keep the list at twelve.

A more common argument for the exclusion of Dan has been to attribute its absence to its general reputation for idolatry. Both the Old Testament (Judg 18.16-19; 1 Kgs 12.28-30) and later Jewish tradition[20] associate Dan with idolatry, against which Revelation contains a strong polemic (2.14, 20; 13.14-15; 14.9, 10; 19.20; 21.8; 22.15).[21] Indeed, later church tradition appears to associate the tribe of Dan with the antichrist.[22] The speculation that scribal error mistaking Dan for the abbreviation Μάν[νασσῆ] resulted in the omission of Dan is unlikely and has no evidential support.[23]

Both Smith and Winkle offer another possible explanation for the omission of Dan, attributing it to John's association of the twelve tribes with the twelve apostles.[24] This association is suggested by John's description of the new Jerusalem (21.12-14) where the twelve gates are named for the twelve tribes while the twelve foundations represent the twelve apos-

---

[19] Bauckham, "Tribes Again," 113; cf. Aune, *Revelation 6–16*, 463.

[20] E.g., *Tg. Yer. I* Exod 17.8; *Tg. Yer. I* Num 11.1; *Tg.* Jer 8.16; *Gen. Rab.* 43.2; *Num Rab* 2.10; *b. Sanh.* 96a; *Pesiq Rab Kah* 3.12; *Sifre* Deut 357 on Deut 34.1.

[21] See the discussion in Beale, *Revelation*, 420–21; cf. Winkle, "Another Look," 60.

[22] Irenaeus is the first to make this conjecture although the tradition may be older than he. However, it is difficult to say whether the tradition is pre-Christian or had any influence on John (Irenaeus, *Haer.* 5.30.2). For further discussion see C. E. Hill, "Antichrist from the Tribe of Dan," *JTS* 46 (1995) 99–117.

[23] Proposed by G. V. Sanderson, "In Defence of Dan," *Scr* 3/4 (1948) 114–15; cf. Beale, *Revelation*, 421; Kraft, *Offenbarung*, 127.

[24] Smith, "The Church as the New Israel," 115; Winkle, "Another Look," 61–66.

tles.²⁵ Dan would, then, correspond to Judas, who lost his place among the twelve apostles (Acts 1.25). Winkle develops this correspondence between Dan and Judas by comparing a counterclockwise version of Ezekiel's geographical list to a list of the apostles derived from several NT texts (Matt 10.2-4; Mark 3.16-19; Luke 6.13-16; Acts 1.13), and he finds a one-to-one correspondence between Dan and Judas, both being placed last in the lists.²⁶ This association, as Winkle notes, is "nothing more than implicit, for there is no evidence prior to Revelation that Dan and Judas were associated together."²⁷ He does, however, argue that there is evidence in later church tradition for this association.²⁸ While Winkle's proposal is interesting, it is highly speculative. It is not at all clear that John's list is derived from a reversal of Ezekiel's list and there is no evidence, as Winkle admits, that there was an association between Dan and Judas prior to Revelation. As one can see, it is difficult to arrive at an explanation for the absence of Dan.

The order of John's tribal list is unlike any other extant list, which implies that the list is probably a result of his own design. His placement of Judah first in the tribal list reinforces what he has already begun and will continue to show throughout the Apocalypse; the Lamb is the "Lion of the tribe of Judah, the Root of David," who has conquered (5.5; cf. 7.10; 17.14). John's list, therefore, through this one variance already makes a statement that clearly fits within the narrative context of the Apocalypse and is beginning to reveal John's purpose behind the inclusion of this vision of the 144,000. This list of tribes, unusual as it may be, is not intended to record faithfully a census of Israelites. Rather it is intended to accomplish a literary goal that is much more important. This vision of 12,000 from each of the tribes of Israel is offered in part to respond to the preceding question of chapter 6; who is able to stand before the wrath of God and the Lamb?²⁹ Building on Ezek 9.4-7, John sees in this vision and the subsequent vision of the great multitude (7.9-17) the protection and

---

[25] Winkle, "Another Look," 61–62.

[26] See the diagram in ibid., 62.

[27] Ibid., 61.

[28] As Winkle acknowledges, there is also later tradition that associates Judas with the tribe of Gad. He argues, however, that this tradition diminished in favor of the Danite association. See ibid., 63, for a full discussion and for primary source references.

[29] See the discussion in Hirschberg, *Das eschatologische Israel*, 137–40, who argues that both visions of chapter 7 relate to the preceding six seals of chapter 6. Chapter 7, verses 1-8 is a response to the final question of chapter 6 and 7.9-17 is a response to the cry of the martyrs of seal five.

triumph of those who belong to God. Through the vision of the 144,000, John makes a connection with the present believers to whom he writes and their Jewish spiritual heritage. In short, John sees the church as God's new spiritual Israel.

This view of the 144,000, of course, is debated and will be discussed in more detail below; however, the introduction of this interpretation here allows one to gain a clearer perspective in understanding the oddities of John's tribal list. If John understands this group as representing all believers regardless of ethnicity, which certainly seems to be reinforced by 14.1-5 (particularly 14.4: ἀπὸ τῶν ἀνθρώπων), then his adaptation of this list may be motivated by such intent. The prioritizing of Judah begins to suggest this conclusion and the absence of Dan may share the same purpose.

Dan's association with idolatry in Jewish tradition provides the best explanation for its absence in order to keep the list untainted by a questionable member. The overall tenor of the Apocalypse centers, at least partly, on the question of worship; indeed, whom one chooses to worship determines one's eschatological destiny (7.9-17; 14.1-5, 9-11; cf. 13.8, 15; 20.4, 5; 22.3-4). If the 144,000 represent all faithful believers (as in 14.4-5 where faithfulness is explicit), then any association with idolatry would be unacceptable.

The replacement of Ephraim with Joseph is the most difficult anomaly to explain but it may share this same motivation. Ephraim has also been associated with idolatry in biblical tradition, as can be most clearly seen in Hosea. It is difficult to be certain if this is John's reason for excluding Ephraim and if, in fact, a more innocuous solution could provide the answer. Bauckham observes that in both Num 1.32 and Ezek 37.16, 19 Ephraim and Joseph are closely associated as nearly interchangeable.[30] Numbers 1.32 reads, "The descendants of Joseph, namely, the descendants of Ephraim"; and Ezek 37.16, 19, reads, "For Joseph (the stick of Ephraim) and all the house of Israel associated with it . . . I am about to take the stick of Joseph (which is in the hand of Ephraim)." The example in Num 1.32 seems less apparent since, as Bauckham notes, the name Joseph is being used as a rubric for Ephraim and Manasseh. Ezekiel provides the more interesting passage since this is an account of the eschatological reunion of the tribes where Joseph *appears* to be used as a substitute for Ephraim. Neither passage, however, suggests any strong conclusion with regard to

---

[30] For the Num 1.32 discussion see Bauckham, "Tribes Again," 113–14. For a discussion of Ezek 37.16,19 see Richard Bauckham, "Revelation as a Christian War Scroll," *Neot* 22 (1988) 24. This discussion can also be found in Bauckham, *Climax*, 221–22.

the exclusion of Ephraim, so this anomaly remains the more enigmatic of John's list.

The discussion must now come full circle to state once again that John's tribal list is unique in its order and enumeration. The anomalies found in the list are not easily explained but are probably the result of John's own purpose. If John wishes to portray the church as God's new spiritual Israel, then the peculiarities of the list can be shown to fit within that pattern. These peculiarities, however, only begin to hint at a solution to the larger question of the identity of the 144,000. The weightiest evidence lies in the literary context in which the passage is found.

The Purpose of the Chapter 7 Interlude

As stated above, the vision of the 144,000 is set within the context of the opening of the seven seals begun in chapter 6. The interlude of chapter 7, of which this vision forms the initial part (7.1-8), is placed between the opening of the sixth and seventh seals (8.1). The placing of an interlude at this point in the vision sequence is not unusual for John as can be most obviously seen in the vision of the seven trumpets (8.6-11.19) in which there is an interlude between the sixth and seventh trumpets (10.1–11.14). These visionary interludes not only serve to postpone the final suspense of the concluding seal or trumpet but they also perform a number of literary functions not the least of which is to highlight their own importance. Clearly John wishes his readers to pay close attention to the content of these visionary interludes and what more effective way than to interrupt the vision sequence in this manner. As to the present discussion, the question naturally arises as to what is the significance of the interlude of chapter 7 and its place in the literary plan of the Apocalypse. A clear understanding of the literary purpose of the interlude will help establish a foundation for the identity of the 144,000.

At least three observations can be made with regard to the literary importance of the chapter 7 interlude. First, in its position following the sixth seal it offers a response to the query at the end of chapter 6 from the earth-dwellers as to who can stand before the wrath of God. John's response is twofold. The first vision shows God's sovereign protection of his faithful servants who must endure the tribulation to come (7.1-8). The second vision warps forward in time to show their ultimate eschatological triumphant and reward (7.9-17).

Second, the interlude establishes an apocalyptic dualism that John will maintain throughout the Apocalypse between the faithful servants of

God and those who worship the beast. The earth-dwellers, who curse God and refuse to give him glory (16.9), choose to worship the beast (13.4), to receive his mark (13.16-17), and ultimately share his fate (14.9-11; 16.2; 19.19-21). On the contrary, the servants of God are those who persevere in faith (13.10; 14.12), who refuse the mark of the beast and are sealed by God ultimately to rule and reign with him (3.12; 20.4). John contrasts these two groups for the first time in this interlude and will develop this dichotomy in more detail as the Apocalypse unfolds. After the introduction of the beast and false prophet of chapter 13, John reminds his readers of this dichotomy in similar terms through the imagery of 14.1-13. Once again a vision of the 144,000 sealed is re-introduced, this time on Mount Zion under the watchful care of the Lamb as the followers of the beast are condemned to suffer God's wrath and eternal judgment. This stark contrast between the fear and despair of the earth-dwellers and the sealed and triumphant saints communicates once again the refrain that John sounded repeatedly in the seven messages of chapters 2–3; in the end the faithful of God will be vindicated and will be triumphant. Judgment is not for the people of God but for their enemies.

Third, the interlude of chapter 7 plays a key role in the structural design of the Apocalypse. If one adopts the recapitulation theory as an explanation for the visionary development of the Apocalypse, then chapter 7 fits well within this structure.[31] Adela Yarbro Collins identifies five series of visions in the Apocalypse in which the principle of recapitulation seems to be at work.[32] In each series, one finds a repetition of three basic elements behind the visionary message: persecution of the saints, judgment on the nations, and the victory of God, the Lamb, and/or the saints. Collins points out that recapitulation does not begin in the Apocalypse until chapter 6 with the opening of the seven seals. Here can be seen the first three-fold repetition of the aforementioned themes. The opening of seal five reveals the souls of martyred saints under the altar, seal six unleashes the wrath of God and the Lamb on the inhabitants of the earth, and the interlude of chapter 7 provides the third element—a visionary rendering of the triumph of the saints before God and the Lamb.[33]

---

[31] See Collins, *Combat Myth*, 5–44. Collins provides an excellent discussion of the overall structure of the Apocalypse, including a historical overview and contemporary application of the recapitulation theory.

[32] Ibid., 32.

[33] Ibid., 33–34.

Who are the 144,000?

If the preceding proposals are correct concerning the literary function of the chapter 7 interlude, then the identity of the 144,000 begins to take shape. The two-vision interlude provides assurance to the Asian saints that God will see to the spiritual security of those who belong to him and that their eschatological triumph is secured. Only those who bear the seal of God will be able to stand before the wrath of God and the Lamb. Therefore, the 144,000 must represent the universal people of God since spiritual protection is a guarantee offered to all the saints (7.3; 11.1-13; 12.1-17; 14.1-5; 22.3-4; cf. 2 Cor 1.22; Eph 1.13, 14; 4.30). To interpret this passage in any other way only weakens the purpose of John's interlude. These 144,000 represent the new spiritual Israel of God: the elect on earth who are sealed until the day of redemption and who will enjoy eschatological rest in the presence of the Lamb and of God (7.9-17; 14.1-5). These triumphant saints include people from all nations who have remained faithful in the face of great suffering (7.9, 14; cf. 5.9).

Ethnic Israel

While the evidence suggests thus far that the 144,000 represent the church universal, such a conclusion is not accepted by all. The imagery John uses to communicate his message is the greatest hindrance to arriving at an interpretive consensus. If John chooses to underscore God's protection of all believers, then why has he chosen to communicate it through a vision of sealed Israelites? In fact, one might argue that since John hears a specific number sealed from the twelve tribes of Israel, then the vision must be taken literally; the 144,000 are a remnant of Jews God reserves before the end. This interpretation is reinforced by the contrast between this precisely numbered group and the innumerable multitude of the second vision who are more clearly identified as the church since they are a group "from every nation, from all tribes and peoples and languages" (7.9; cf. 5.9).

Feuillet, for example, dismisses what he calls the "current" interpretation that the 144,000 represent the church in favor of their interpretation as ethnic Jews.[34] While he sees the strength in interpreting the 144,000 as the church, since he believes the early church saw itself as spiritual Israel, he does not believe this is the message of Rev 7.1-8.[35] Feuillet recognizes that interpreting the 144,000 as ethnic Israel raises the serious problem of

---

[34] Feuillet, "Les 144,000," 197–98, 201–5.
[35] Ibid., 198–200.

discrimination between Jewish and Gentile Christians. Are the Jews the only ones to enjoy God's protection from the coming calamities? Is such an interpretation consistent with both the Apocalypse and the NT as a whole? Certainly it is not, and Feuillet does not try to support any such discrimination.[36] Rather he relies on a historical interpretation to explain his exegesis.

In order to apply his interpretation to this passage, Feuillet first isolates John's vision of 7.1-8 within its literary context. This is an action that sends him down a dangerous hermeneutical path. He first isolates this vision from the vision of 7.9-17, believing that the two visions are distinct.[37] The first represents the remnant of Israel and the second the church comprised of both Jews and Gentiles. Second, he disconnects the 144,000 of chapter 7 from the same group in 14.1-5, whom he believes to be Christians. Feuillet writes, "Il est en outre indiscutable que les 144,000 'vierges' du chapitre xiv ne peuvent absolument pas server à identifier les 144,000 'fils d'Israël' du chapitre vii."[38] Once he has isolated the vision of 7.1-8 from these key passages, then he is free to apply his own interpretation.

Feuillet interprets the 144,000 as ethnic Jews (not Jewish Christians) who have separated themselves from the synagogue and who are not hostile to Christianity.[39] He bases his interpretation on OT prophetic tradition of a remnant to be saved out of Israel. This is a remnant first saved from the sword (Ezek 9.1-4), then returned from captivity, and that eventually becomes a remnant for the Messiah. Feuillet finds NT support for his view in Romans 9-11 where he sees Paul's salvation of "all Israel" contrasted with the "full number of the Gentiles" (Rom 11.25-26) as parallel to John's two visions of Rev 7.1-17. He further argues that all the judgments of Rev 4-11 take their inspiration from Ezekiel because Feuillet believes that John sees the destruction of the temple in 70 CE as a time similar to Ezekiel's day when the judgment of God was upon Israel.[40] Feuillet sees a parallel between the measuring of the temple in Rev 11.1-2 and Ezekiel's temple vision in Ezekiel 40–42. It is in this act of measuring that John symbolizes the separation from the synagogue of the faithful Jewish remnant that

---

[36] Ibid., 197, 220.
[37] Ibid., 198.
[38] Ibid., 203.
[39] Ibid., 207–11, 220.
[40] Ibid., 223–24.

becomes the spiritual temple. This preserved remnant is represented by the 144,000 of chapter 7.[41]

The belief that the destruction of the temple stands behind the visions of Revelation 4–11 requires Feuillet to date the writing of the Apocalypse as close to 70 CE as possible. Based on an interpretation of the beast's seven heads in 17.9-11, he dates the Apocalypse to the reign of Vespasian and invokes the apocalyptic tradition of "fictitious antedating" to explain John's prophetic perspective on the events.[42] Even though he acknowledges that John is not typical of apocalyptic writers who, for example, employ pseudonymity for the purpose of antedating, he does believe that John attempts to fool his readers to give a sense of prophetic oracle in order to draw out the "theological significance" of the temple's destruction.[43]

Feuillet's interpretation is less than convincing and faces a number of obstacles against its acceptance, the most serious of which is his misinterpretation of the literary context of the Apocalypse. Feuillet appears to have missed the purpose of John's vision of the 144,000 and its role in the overall plan of the Apocalypse. As has already been observed, this vision of the sealed serves to establish an apocalyptic dualism that will be maintained throughout the text. The 144,000 are contrasted to the marked of the beast that first appear in chapter 13. It is a contrast between the righteous and the wicked (not ethnic groups) and replicates the struggle between good and evil often played out in Jewish literature.[44] As part of the interlude of chapter 7, it also serves as a message of encouragement for the Asian saints concerning God's watchful care. To make the 144,000 a remnant of ethnic Jews forces onto the text an interpretation difficult to defend. This interpretation not only requires creative dating of the Apocalypse, but it also requires that the 70 CE destruction of the temple become a major concern of John in nearly half of his apocalypse which is untenable. In addition, while one might conceivably argue for a distinction between the 144,000 and the innumerable multitude of chapter 7, it is inconceivable to divorce the 144,000 of chapter 7 from those of chapter 14, whom Feuillet himself

---

[41] Ibid., 221.
[42] Ibid., 219.
[43] Ibid., 219–20.
[44] A number of passages can be cited that show God's sovereign protection of his people as opposed to the destruction of the wicked (e.g., Ezek 9.1-4; Dan 12.1; The War Scroll; *Pss. Sol.* 15.4-9; *4 Ezra* 12.33-34; 13.48). The NT continues this tradition as can be seen in the dualistic use of light and darkness in John's gospel and epistles (cf. Matt 12.30; Luke 11.23).

acknowledges are "virgin" Christians. There is little basis for this interpretive division and Feuillet's reasoning is not persuasive.[45]

It would seem that an interpretation of the 144,000 as ethnic Israel requires that one see either in the plan of God or in the subject matter of the Apocalypse a separate concern for Jews apart from the church. This is not only true for Feuillet, but it is also true for other scholars such as Horn, Geyser, and Walvoord. Horn postulates that the 144,000 are faithful Jews not Christians who have not compromised with pagan culture.[46] Geyser argues that John's use of the number twelve and its multiples throughout the Apocalypse (e.g., 144,000 sealed, twelve tribes, twelve gates, twelve stars) proves that "the books predominant concern is with the restoration of the twelve tribes of Israel, their restoration as a twelve-tribe kingdom, in a renewed and purified city of David."[47] Walvoord's futurist hermeneutical approach also leads him to the conclusion that the 144,000 are literal Israel and indeed that much of Revelation has to do with God's plan for Israel, since the church has been secretly raptured before the events of chapters 4–18.[48]

The proposal that the Apocalypse has a separate concern for the fate of ethnic Israel creates a distinction between the church and Israel that is not consistent with the overall tenor of the Apocalypse. It is inappropriate to interpret John's vision of the 144,000 as a testimony to a hope in a literal restoration of the twelve tribes or the sealing of a remnant from ethnic Israel. The peculiarities of John's list, the evident symbolism found in the multiples of twelve and the literary context all argue against a literal interpretation of this vision. To demand a literal interpretation at this point could lead one to the absurd conclusion that much of the Apocalypse must be interpreted literally. This hermeneutical approach would, of course, end in a rather bizarre interpretation of John's equally bizarre visions and would be contrary to the symbolic nature of apocalyptic literature.

Christian Martyrs

If one rules out an interpretation of the 144,000 as ethnic Israel, then what alternatives remain? Some commentators argue that the 144,000 represent

---

[45] Feuillet, "Les 144,000," 203.
[46] Horn, "Zwischen," 156–57.
[47] Albert Geyser, "The Twelve Tribes in Revelation: Judean and Judeo-Christian Apocalypticism," *NTS* 28 (1982) 389.
[48] John F. Walvoord, *The Revelation of Jesus Christ* (Chicago: Moody, 1966) 21–23; cf.141–43.

a limited group within the church, such as Christian martyrs.[49] The descriptive phrases "servants of our God" (7.3) and "first fruits for God and the Lamb" (14.4) are considered key indicators of John's own understanding of this group as Christian martyrs. The "first fruits" descriptor is borrowed from the Jewish sacrificial system, and it is argued that John's own use of the title "servant is almost synonymous with prophet and prophet with martyr" (e.g., 10.7; 11.3, 18; 19.10).[50]

This one-to-one correspondence between servant, prophet, and martyr, however, seems contrived. Indeed, it can be equally argued that John uses "servant" (δοῦλος) elsewhere as a designation for *all* Christians, not just prophets or martyrs (e.g., 2.20; 19.2, 5; 22.3, 6).[51] The proposed correspondence between servant, prophet, and martyr appears to be based primarily on the two witnesses of chapter 11 who carry out a prophetic mission and die a martyr's death (11.3-14). Two of the proof texts for this association are found in 11.3 and 11.18, but neither of these texts (nor any of the others suggested) offer conclusive evidence that John's use of δοῦλος implies martyrdom. Beale keenly observes in his discussion of 11.3 that the identification of prophets throughout the Apocalypse should not be limited to martyrs since even the angel who refuses John's attempts to worship him (19.10; 22.9) identifies himself as "a fellow servant (σύνδουλος) with you and your comrades who hold the testimony of Jesus . . . the spirit of prophecy" and "a fellow servant (σύνδουλος) with you and of your comrades the prophets."[52] John's use of δούλοις in 11.18 is better understood as a designation for all Christians.[53] In this passage, τοῖς προφήταις καὶ τοῖς ἁγίοις καὶ τοῖς φοβουμένοις τὸ ὄνομά σου, τοὺς μικροὺς καὶ τοὺς μεγάλους is set in apposition to τοῖς δούλοις, suggesting that servants is defined as all those who have been faithful to God through the ages and who are about to be rewarded. Furthermore, the context of this entire passage (11.15-19) celebrates the completion of God's plan and with it his triumph, the reward of *all* the saints and the judgment of God.

---

[49] So Martin Kiddle, *The Revelation of St. John*, MNTC (New York: Harper, 1940) 133; Lohmeyer, *Offenbarung*, 70; Caird, *Revelation*, 95; Frederick J. Murphy, *Fallen is Babylon: The Revelation to John*, NTIC (Harrisburg: Trinity, 1998) 222.

[50] Caird, *Revelation*, 95; cf. Kiddle, *Revelation*, 133.

[51] See Beale, *Revelation*, 413; Beasley-Murray, *Revelation*, 140.

[52] Beale, *Revelation*, 573.

[53] Beasley-Murray cites 11.18 among the list of proof texts for his assertion that "servants" is used in the Apocalypse for all Christians. See Beasley-Murray, *Revelation*, 140.

The proposal that the title "first fruits" (ἀπαρχή) implies martyrdom is equally inconclusive. While this language may be borrowed from the Jewish sacrificial system (e.g., Exod 23.19; 34.26; Deut 18.14), John's use of it in 14.4 does not necessarily imply martyrdom. The appearance of the phrase "first fruits" in several NT texts outside of the Apocalypse (Rom 8.23; 1 Cor 15.20, 23; 2 Thess 2.13; James 1.18) suggests that "first fruits" can designate a representative part of the whole group in the same way that the first fruits of the harvest in the OT represented the entire harvest that followed. For example, Jesus is the "first fruits" guaranteeing the full eschatological resurrection (1 Cor 15.20, 23) and the Holy Spirit is the "first fruits" guaranteeing the full inheritance to come (Rom 8.23). In similar fashion as John, both Paul and James address the believers as "first fruits for salvation" (2 Thess 2.13; cf. James 1.18). Just as Paul's intention is not to speak of a limited group but to express that the Thessalonians are the first representatives of a greater harvest to come, so John understands the 144,000 as a group representative of all of the redeemed (14.4). In apocalyptic fashion, John wishes to assure his recipients in the churches that their protection and salvation is assured as they keep themselves through faithful perseverance. This universal appeal is confirmed through the vision of 7.9-17 in which John leaps ahead from the 144,000 on earth to an eschatological scene in heaven of all Christians triumphant before God and the Lamb. This countless multitude "from every nation, from all tribes and peoples and languages" (7.9; cf. 5.9) represents all saints who have passed through the great ordeal yet have remained faithful. The shared experience of being shepherded by the Lamb makes this connection between the 144,000 and the innumerable multitude complete (7.17; cf. 14.4).

The Church Universal

The objections that have been raised against the preceding interpretations begin to point to a broader definition of the 144,000 that extends beyond ethnic or class distinctions and that is more reasonable in light of the literary evidence. The 144,000 probably represent the faithful elect of the church, both Jews and Gentiles, who have been sealed by divine protection from the coming eschatological judgments (9.4; 18.4) but who are not protected from physical persecution (6.9; 13.7; 20.4). A number of observations may be made in favor of this interpretation.

Revelation 14.1-5 offers one of the most unambiguous proofs for the universal identity of the 144,000. In this context John sees the 144,000 for a second time on Mount Zion in the company of the Lamb. John leaves no doubt that this group is to be identified with the sealed of chapter 7 for he adds the additional description that they "had his [the Lamb's] name and his Father's name written on their foreheads" (14.1). The addition of this participial phrase serves to identify this group with the 144,000 sealed of chapter 7 and continues to weave a thematic thread that was first introduced with a promise to the Philadelphian saints (3.12) and finds its terminus in the vision of the new Jerusalem (22.4). The consistent message is that those who persevere and overcome are those to whom God promises spiritual protection through the coming trials (7.1-8) and ultimate eschatological reward in the presence of the Lamb and of God (7.9-17; 14.1-5; 22.4).

This assurance of protection and reward is woven throughout the Apocalypse and surfaces at key moments in the visionary sequence in order to bolster the faith of the Asian saints in the face of awesome and at times frightening revelations. The promise of eschatological reward in the presence of God first made to the Philadelphian (3.12) believers is a reward that in fact awaits all who keep the commandments of God and bear the testimony of Jesus. Thus John builds upon this promise throughout the Apocalypse as the right of all who belong to God.

The interlude of chapter 7 is the first and primary place where John elaborates on this two-fold promise of protection and reward. John pauses after the sixth seal and the out-pouring of God's wrath to assure the saints of God's keeping power (7.1-8) and of their eschatological reward (7.9-17). This two-fold vision of chapter 7 is an elaboration of the promise of 3.12, both of which are couched in Jewish imagery. At this critical point in the Apocalypse before the terrible revelations of God's judgment to come, John wishes to assure his hearers of God's faithfulness in their perseverance. As if fearful to overwhelm his hearers with revelations too great for them to bear, John reinforces this promise of protection and eschatological hope at other key moments in the Apocalypse. He offers this reassurance again in the midst of the trumpet judgments (9.4), during the trumpet interlude (11.1-13), through his vision of the heavenly woman (12.1-17), and through the second vision of the 144,000 (14.1-5). This latter passage, of course, has the clearest bearing on the 144,000 of chapter 7.

The 144,000 of 14.1-5, who are on Mount Zion with the Lamb, are undoubtedly the same group sealed in chapter 7. John clearly wishes his recipients to make this connection for he identifies them as bearers of the Name (14.1). Although chapter 7 never states explicitly that the seal is the name of God and the Lamb, it does state that the seal is placed on their foreheads, and with the corroboration of 3.12; 14.1; and 22.4 the nature of the seal is indisputable. The sealed 144,000 are reintroduced in 14.1-5, for it is once again a perilous moment in the Apocalypse. John's hearers have been introduced to the unholy trinity of Satan, the beast, and the false prophet of chapters 12 and 13. Chapter 13 is a climactic moment in John's revelation, for it is the moment when the spiritual veil is lifted and John's fellow saints are allowed to understand the true reality behind their present suffering. They come face to face with their archnemisis—Satan. Revelation 14.1-5 changes the somber tone of chapter 13 with a renewed assurance to the saints of their security as followers of the Lamb. Once again the vision of the 144,000 is couched in Jewish metaphor, but the message is laced with Christian overtones. Mount Zion, so important in Jewish prophetic tradition, is the visionary location of the Lamb and his followers. This Lamb, whose image evokes Jewish Passover tradition, is none other than Jesus the Messiah, and those he leads on this eschatological Mount Zion are the redeemed ἀπὸ τῶν ἀνθρώπων. This latter phrase precludes any notion that these are a remnant of Jews or Jewish Christians. They are the eschatological people of God, who hail from every nation (cf. 5.9; 7.9), and it is the Lamb as the new Moses who has placed on their lips a new song (cf. 5.9-14) of exodus redemption.[54] The 144,000 of 14.1-5, therefore, cannot be disassociated from the sealed of chapter 7.[55] They are doubtless the same group, and the context of 14.1-5 assists in their identity as the universal people of God preserved through the trials to come.[56] Their faithfulness is an assurance of this preservation (14.4-5), as John constantly reminds the Asian saints throughout the Apocalypse (e.g., 2.7, 11, 17, 28; 3.5, 12, 21; 13.10; 15.2; 21.7).

---

[54] Stevenson, *Power and Place*, 265–67, provides some of the inspiration for these latter remarks. He has an excellent discussion of John's use of Jewish symbols in 14.1-5 along with 15.1-5 and 11.19. Stevenson argues from his comparison of 14.1-5 and 15.1-5, "This merging of the faithful community and the Lamb with Mt. Zion and Moses further identifies the church with Israel, the covenant people of God."

[55] Contra Feuillet, "Les 144,000," 203.

[56] Hirschberg, *Das eschatologische Israel*, 199–200, makes a much more elaborate and unnecessary argument for equating the 144,000 of 14.1-5 with those of 7.3-8 and their identity as the universal people of God. He builds his thesis on 14.6 proposing that the proclamation of the angel in 14.6 is an offer of repentance to the nations. This proclamation he compares to 11.3-13, suggesting that it is a symbolic indication of the church's responsibility to witness to the world. Thus the 144,000 on Mt. Zion are "first fruits" of others who will repent from the nations (indicated by 14.6) and who will comprise along with the symbolic 144,000 the new universal people of God. Hirschberg proposes that 14.1-5 and 6-7 stand in similar relationship as do 7.1-8 and 9-17. First the 144,000 are symbolically represented and then immediately followed by some indication of a people from all nations. The vision of 7.9-17, however, is more static than that of 14.6-7.

One other passage to consider briefly in parallel to 14.1-5 is Rev 15.1-5. Gregory Stevenson has proposed this passage as additional proof for the universal identity of the 144,000.[57] Although not explicitly, John's vision of Rev 15.1-5, Stevenson argues, portrays the 144,000 once again in eternal bliss in the presence of God. John describes these saints as those who have overcome the beast, who stand before the throne of God (note "sea of glass" 15.2; cf. 4.6), and who have harps and are singing the song of Moses and of the Lamb. This latter musical description, Stevenson argues, provides the link between the redeemed group of saints in 15.1-5 with the 144,000 of 14.1-5 (cf. 14.2-3; 15.2-3). In both instances, the redeemed are singing before the throne of God, being accompanied by the music of harps. In 14.3, the 144,000 are singing a song no one else can sing and in 15.3 the song sung by the saints is described as "the song of Moses, the servant of God, and the song of the Lamb." This reference to the "song of Moses" doubtless derives from the Exodus tradition (14.30—15.21) and its secondary identity as the "song of the Lamb" serves to unite the exodus/Passover tradition of Israel with the motif of redemption achieved through the Lamb, God's Messiah. The song of the 144,000 is exclusive because it is a song of redemption which is revealed in 15.3-4. The saints of 15.1-5, therefore, provide further confirmation that the 144,000 are merely another symbol of the universal redeemed of God—all those who have overcome (τοὺς νικῶντας) the beast and "the number of its name." These are the sealed of God who persevere and inherit eschatological bliss in the presence of God and the Lamb (cf. 7.9-17).

This theme of promised reward for those who overcome, consistently repeated in the seven messages (Revelation 2–3), reverberates throughout the Apocalypse and reaches its height in John's vision of the new Jerusalem (21.1–22.5). Once again John sees a vision replete with metaphor from the Jewish prophetic tradition of the eschatological bliss of the saints in the presence of God. This magnificent vision of eschatological Jerusalem and God's new creation serves as a final incentive to the beleaguered Asian believers to persevere; for, as they are reminded once again, it is those who overcome (ὁ νικῶν) who "will inherit these things" (21.7; cf. 22.4).

The preceding discussion has raised two further points of importance with regard to the identity of the 144,000 and that is the Jewish character

---

[57] Stevenson, *Power and Place*, 265–66; cf. Hirschberg, *Das eschatologische Israel*, 197–98, who not only compares 15.1-5 with 14.1-5 but also follows Bornkamm in linking 19.1-9. Revelation 19 offers a completed picture of the 144,000 as the great multitude of God in heaven and reveals the contents of the new song of 14.1-5. While a comparison of 19.1-9 offers some positive comparisons, 15.1-5 seems a closer parallel with 14.1-5.

of John's visions and the relationship of the new Jerusalem to the identity of the 144,000. As has been observed, John makes extensive use throughout the Apocalypse of Jewish cultic imagery (e.g., 3.12; 11.19; 14.1; 15.5-6) and allusions to the Jewish scriptures.[58] One must interpret the visions of the 144,000 in light of this larger literary context in order to understand that the numbering of 12,000 from each of the tribes of Israel or their subsequent location on Mount Zion does not require a Jewish identity for the 144,000. The imagery is obviously symbolic, and John's merger of Jewish imagery into Christian themes is indicative of his reinterpretation of his cultic heritage in light of the Christ event. His numbering of 144,000 from the twelve tribes of Israel, their presence on Mount Zion, or their heritage in the new Jerusalem are all part of John's assurance to the Asian believers of their certain protection and reward within the plan of God. This is why John can move freely between the sealing of 144,000 from Israel (7.1-8) to an innumerable multitude before the throne of God (7.9-17). For him, there is no distinction. The 144,000 are God's new spiritual Israel—the church.[59] John merely draws upon his own Jewish heritage to communicate to the Asian churches their place in the apocalyptic plan of God.

It is, in fact, this Jewish character of John's visions that gives the Apocalypse such rich meaning and provides continuity between the history of Israel and the emerging church. As will be demonstrated throughout this study, John's use of Jewish symbols (e.g., twelve tribes, Mount Zion, temple, Song of Moses, new Jerusalem) as well as his inventive use of the Jewish scriptures is illuminating for the study of John's theological perception of the relationship between Judaism and Christianity. Even here behind John's vision of the sealing of the 144,000 (7.1-8) can be found traces of the Jewish prophetic and apocalyptic tradition. The holding back of the judgments of God for the preservation of the faithful is a thoroughly Jewish idea and can be found throughout Jewish literature (e.g., Ezek 9.4; *1 En.* 66.1-2; *2 Bar.* 6.4; *Pss. Sol.* 15.4-9).

John's vision of 7.1-8 seems most closely related to the vision of Ezek 9.1-4, and it is this passage that may form the literary basis for his vi-

---

[58] The allusions to the Jewish scriptures are too extensive to list here and any list would be debated. The subsequent discussion of the trumpet interlude (10.1—11.13), the heavenly woman (12.1-17), and the new Jerusalem (21.1—22.5) will provide examples and bear out this point.

[59] So George Eldon Ladd, *A Commentary on the Revelation of John* (Grand Rapids: Eerdmans, 1972) 114; cf. Osborne, *Revelation*, 303.

sion.⁶⁰ In this passage, Ezekiel sees seven men coming from the north, six of whom are armed with swords and are ordered to carry out the judgment of God upon idolatrous Israel. The seventh man, who is dressed in linen and carries a "writing case," is instructed to "mark on their foreheads" those who are grieved by the abominations in Israel for the purpose of preserving them from the impending judgment. John's vision of the sealing of the 144,000 has obvious similarities to Ezekiel's vision in that judgment is delayed for the purpose of marking "on their foreheads" the faithful of God. This preservation is in contrast to the judgment meted out on the unfaithful.

There are two observations that should be made with regard to Ezekiel's vision that may shed some interpretive light on the 144,000. First, the distinction made in Ezekiel's vision is not between ethnic groups or among the faithful themselves, but between the faithful and the faithless—the worshipers of God and the idolaters. A similar distinction can be observed in John's apocalypse between the sealed faithful of the 144,000 and the marked of the beast. This contrast is particularly poignant in 14.1-13 and suggests strongly that the 144,000 must represent all believers. Just as Satan marks all of his followers, so God seals all of his faithful servants.⁶¹

Second, Ezekiel's polemic against idolatry is mirrored in the Apocalypse. John not only develops the thematic contrast between those who worship the beast and those who refuse to do so, but he also borrows a common OT analogy between idolatry and sexual impurity (e.g., 2.14-15, 20-23; 17.1-5; 18.3, 9; 19.2). In the OT, Israel is metaphorically married to God and her idolatry is equated with adultery (e.g., Hos; Jer 2.2, 20). John's description of the 144,000 as chaste (παρθένοι; 14.4) followers of the Lamb extends this analogy⁶² because they "have not defiled themselves with women," as the unfaithful saints have with Jezebel (2.22) or the kings of the earth have with the Harlot (18.3). Just as ancient Israel was metaphorically married to God, so the 144,000 are virgins betrothed to the Lamb, which John's vision of the new Jerusalem affirms (21.2, 9).⁶³

---

⁶⁰ Beale, *Revelation*, 409, believes that the source behind John's vision is likely Ezek 9.1-4, but it could possibly be the Passover since this group will ultimately be protected from the trumpets and bowls which follow and resemble the plagues of the Exodus. The correlation between Ezekiel's and John's visions seems more likely.

⁶¹ Beale, *Revelation*, 413.

⁶² See Charles, *Revelation*, 1:203.

⁶³ See I. A. Muirhead, "The Bride of Christ," *SJT* 5 (1952) 175–87. Muirhead discusses the relationship between the Old and New Testament analogies of being the wife of God

Upon a comparison of John's and Ezekiel's visions, it seems clear that the act of sealing the 144,000 must be interpreted as a sealing of all saints regardless of ethnic origin. This conclusion is further strengthened by John's symbolic use of numbers. Throughout the Apocalypse, John makes a broad use of numbers to communicate a symbolic message. For example, John frequently uses the number seven (e.g., seven lamp stands, seven spirits, seven stars, seven seals, seven trumpets, and seven bowls) to communicate completeness, particularly divine completeness, and the number twelve and its multiples (e.g., twelve stars, twelve gates, and twelve apostles) most often represents the people of God.[64] Thus the enumerating of 12,000 from the twelve tribes of Israel for a total of 144,000 sealed is not intended to be a literal cataloguing of Israelites, but is symbolic of the people of God.[65] As Bauckham writes, "twelve is squared for completeness, multiplied by a thousand to suggest vast numbers (7.4-8; 14.1; 21.17)."[66] Pilchan Lee, citing Boring and Harrington, further postulates that the 144,000 are the twelve patriarchs times the twelve apostles multiplied by one thousand to symbolize "'a very large number.'"[67] Lee's more precise identification has the advantage of uniting the twelve tribes (7.3-8) with the vision of the new Jerusalem (21.9–22.5; particularly 21.12-14). Therefore, this symbolic use of twelve and its multiples argues persuasively that the 144,000 represent the church universal as a vast innumerable multitude in symbolic completion—an interpretation that John affirms in 7.9-17 and reaffirms at the end of his apocalypse through the vision of the new Jerusalem.[68]

In the vision of the new Jerusalem (21.9–22.5), John is taken to a high mountain where he is shown "the bride, the wife of the Lamb" (21.9), the new Jerusalem, descending out of heaven from God. John describes

and the bride of the Lamb. He also highlights the analogous relationship between idolatry and fornication.

[64] See Bauckham, *Climax*, 29–37; cf. Hirschberg, *Das eschatologische Israel*, 185–87; Beale, *Revelation*, 58–64.

[65] So Stevenson, *Power and Place*, 252.

[66] Bauckham, *Climax*, 36.

[67] Pilchan Lee, *The New Jerusalem in the Book of Revelation: A Study of Revelation 21–22 in the Light of Its Background in Jewish Tradition*, WUNT 2/129 (Tübingen: Mohr/Siebeck, 2001) 256.

[68] See Hirschberg, *Das eschatologische Israel*, 186, who similarly sees a link between the visions of the 144,000 and the new Jerusalem through John's use of the number twelve. The new universal people of God are implied in both visions but are particularly apparent through the merging of the twelve tribes with the twelve apostles in the new Jerusalem (21.14).

the bride of the Lamb as a city ringed with twelve gates, which bear the names of the twelve tribes of Israel, and as a city founded on twelve foundations that bear the names of the twelve apostles of the Lamb (21.12, 14). The angel, who shows John the heavenly city, measures the city with a golden rod, and it measures a perfect cube with its length, width, and height measuring equally at 12,000 stadia and its wall measuring 144 stadia (cf. Ezek 48.30-34).[69]

What John describes here is undoubtedly symbolic and is not the description of a literal heavenly city. The city represents the "bride, the wife of the Lamb" (21.9) and its description stands in contrast to that of the Harlot in chapter 17.[70] The cubic measurement of the city is perhaps symbolic of the original holy of holies which also measured a cube (1 Kgs 6.20; cf. Ezek 48.35),[71] particularly in view of the fact that John's new Jerusalem has no temple "for its temple is the Lord God the Almighty and the Lamb" (21.22). God now dwells among his people (21.2-4) and they dwell in his presence for eternity (22.3-5).

The city clearly represents the people of God, the church, which as spiritual Israel represents the fulfillment of God's salvific plan.[72] The city is not only described as the bride of the Lamb but its vast measurements, which come in multiples of twelve, are symbolic of the innumerable multitude of saints whom it represents. Indeed, it is these measurements themselves that provide an important interpretive link to the vision of the 144,000. Robert Gundry sees a clear connection between the 144,000 and the measurements of the new Jerusalem.[73] He writes,

> Twelve thousand stadia long, wide, and high (21.16), the city is reminiscent of the twelve thousand from each of the twelve tribes of Israel, especially since the cubical shape of the city makes twelve edges of twelve thousand stadia each, coming to a total of 144,000, just as in the case of the Israelites (7.1-8; 14.1-5).[74]

---

[69] It is not clear what this latter measurement represents with respect to the wall perhaps it represents width.
[70] See the parallel analysis in Aune, *Revelation 17–22*, 1202–3.
[71] Beale, *Revelation,* 1081; Murphy, *Fallen is Babylon*, 419; Geyser, "Twelve Tribes," 397.
[72] This view along with the vision of the new Jerusalem is discussed in more detail in chapter 5.
[73] Robert H. Gundry, "The New Jerusalem People as Place, Not Place for People," *NovT* 29 (1987) 254–64; cf. Beale, *Revelation*, 416-17; Murphy, *Fallen is Babylon*, 222.
[74] Gundry, "New Jerusalem," 260.

This symbolic link between the new Jerusalem, the bride of the Lamb, and the 144,000 sealed proposes conclusively an interpretation of the 144,000 as the universal church composed of both Jews and Gentiles.

It should be observed that through the vision of the new Jerusalem John has once again employed Jewish imagery for the church. The visions of the 144,000 and the new Jerusalem form metaphorical book ends to the Apocalypse to hold erect the eschatological hope of the beleaguered Asian believers. Though John is likely writing to primarily Gentile believers, he is unabashed in his belief that they represent the new spiritual Israel of God. This belief is first suggested in his messages to the churches of Smyrna and Philadelphia, where he insinuates that ethnicity is no guarantee of membership in the people of God (2.9; 3.9). The Philadelphian message is of notable interest because it is a message with a particularly Jewish tone. The one who holds the "key of David" commends this spiritually pure church and promises to keep them from "the hour of trial that is coming on the whole world to test the inhabitants of the earth" (3.10). To the one who overcomes he promises, "I will write on you the name of my God, and the name of the city of my God, the new Jerusalem that comes down from my God out of heaven, and my own new name" (3.12). These promises made to this primarily Gentile church are symbolically fulfilled and affirmed in the vision of the 144,000 sealed and in the vision of the descent of the new Jerusalem where the sealed enjoy the presence of God eternally (22.4). Each one of these passages affirms a consistent view throughout the Apocalypse that John views the church, both Jews and Gentiles, as God's new spiritual Israel.

The Innumerable Multitude

If one understands the 144,000 as representing the church universal, what then can be said of the relationship between this group and the innumerable multitude of the subsequent vision of chapter 7? A response to this question has already been hinted at in the preceding discussion, but some detailed analysis is presently in order. There are those who have objected to drawing any kind of relationship between the 144,000 and the innumerable multitude based on John's very different description of these two groups. The 144,000 are a numbered group located on earth and the multitude is innumerable and located in the presence of God. In addition, the 144,000 are sealed out of the tribes of Israel while the innumerable multitude is "from every nation, from all tribes and peoples and languages"

(7.9). It has equally been argued that this innumerable multitude should be limited to Christian martyrs, since they are described as having "come out of the great ordeal" (7.14).[75]

While the two visions are admittedly quite different, these differences are not insurmountable obstacles to understanding their unity. Many scholars see a relationship between the two visions even if they disagree as to whom these two groups represent.[76] Although the innumerable multitude is described as having "come out of the great ordeal" (7.14), it is not likely that they are solely Christian martyrs. The language here is vague and the passage lacks the usual descriptors associated with other martyr passages.[77] They are, for example, not described as having been "slain" (6.9) or "beheaded" (20.4) for their testimony. They are rather described as an innumerable multitude "from every nation, from all tribes and peoples and languages" (7.9), which is a nearly identical descriptive phrase used of all saints in the preceding vision of chapter 5 (5.9). In addition, if one postulates a link between this group and the 144,000, who represent all believers, then such an interpretation precludes the innumerable multitude being Christian martyrs.

In fact, there is another literary parallel between the visions of chapter 7 and chapter 5 that may serve to support a unity between the two visions of chapter 7. Bauckham discusses extensively a parallel pattern he observes in both 5.5-6 and 7.4 and 9 where John first hears a description but then sees an image that serves to interpret what he has heard. Just as in 5.5-6 John *hears* about the Lion of the tribe of Judah but *sees* a lamb standing in the midst of the throne, so in chapter 7 he *hears* the 144,000 numbered but *sees* the innumerable multitude.[78] Bauckham believes that this pattern suggests a unity between the visions of chapter 7 that argues for these two visions being representative of the same group. The strength of this argument lies in the fact that this pattern is not unique to these two passages, but can be observed throughout the Apocalypse. What John *sees* is immediately interpreted by what he *hears* (5.6 and 5.7-14; 7.1-2 and

---

[75] So Charles, *Revelation*, 1:199–203; Lohmeyer, *Offenbarung*, 70.

[76] So Beckwith, *Apocalypse*, 540; Beasley-Murray, *Revelation*, 141; Lohmeyer, *Offenbarung*, 70; Caird, *Revelation*, 94–96; Mounce, *Revelation*, 164; Beale, *Revelation*, 424–26; Stevenson, *Power and Place*, 253–55; Prigent, *L'Apocalypse*, 221–22; Osborne, *Revelation*, 302–3.

[77] So Beckwith, *Apocalypse*, 530; cf. Mounce, *Revelation*, 173.

[78] Bauckham, *Climax*, 214–16; cf. Stevenson, *Power and Place*, 254–55.

7.4; 14.1 and 14.2-5; 15.2 and 15.3-4; 17.1-6 and 17.7-18) or vice versa (5.5 and 5.6; 9.13-16 and 9.17-21).[79]

While this literary pattern offers one more link between the visions of chapter 7, the strongest argument for their unity lies in the overall literary purpose of the interlude. It seems undoubtedly clear that this vision of 7.9-17 is shared for the purpose of reassuring the saints of their certain eschatological victory before the opening of the seventh seal and the unleashing of the judgments to come. The two visions of chapter 7 speak of the same group of people and have in common their attempt to reassure the saints in the face of assured tribulation.[80] In the first vision, the faithful of God on earth are sealed against the coming wrath and in the second vision they are assured of their eventual reward.[81] This twofold assurance serves to fortify John's hearers against the horrific events to come. Through the interlude of chapter 7, John is offering assurance to the saints that as God's spiritual Israel on earth, they will be preserved by God from "the hour of trial" (3.10), and as "pillars" in the temple of God (3.12), they will enjoy ultimate victory with God and the Lamb in his presence forever (7.9-17; cf. 21.1–22.5). Just as the 144,000 on Mount Zion "follow the Lamb wherever he goes" (14.4), so John writes of the innumerable multitude, "The Lamb at the center of the throne will be their shepherd, and he will guide them to springs of the water of life, and God will wipe away every tear from their eyes" (7.17). John here finishes his visions of chapter 7 with a description of the salvation that will be enjoyed by all who remain faithful to the Lamb, a description that he will repeat again in greater detail at the end of the Apocalypse (21.4).[82] This salvation will be enjoyed by all without exclusion, which John assuredly promises to the suffering saints of Asia through the two visionary images of chapter 7.

Conclusion

The vision of the seven seals is the beginning of the revelation of the apocalyptic events surrounding the end of time and God's judgment. John is writing to churches that are under a great deal of stress from within and without. They are threatened by internal corruption that tugs at the very fiber of their faith and by external pressures that may have resulted in economic hardship and even physical danger (2.9-10; 13). Even if one argues

---

[79] Beale, *Revelation*, 424–25.
[80] So Osborne, *Revelation*, 302–3.
[81] So also Lee, *New Jerusalem*, 258.
[82] So Stevenson, *Power and Place*, 240.

that physical persecution has not as of yet become a major factor for the churches, the Apocalypse vividly anticipates that it will be (e.g., 2.10, 13; 6.9-11; 11.7; 12.17; 13.7, 15; 15.2; 17.6; cf. 1.9).

In each of the messages to the seven churches of Asia, John has communicated not only words of correction and encouragement but also promises of reward to "the one who overcomes" (2.7, 11, 17, 26, 28; 3.5, 12, 21). The overall message to the churches throughout the Apocalypse is a call to persevere (e.g., 2.2-3, 19; 3.10; 13.10; 14.12; 15.2; 21.7). As an encouragement to perseverance, the churches are shown immediately in chapters 4 and 5 the sovereign power of both God and the Lamb. John's artful use of the phrase, "the one who sits on the throne," (4.2; 5.1) paints a picture of God's sovereign authority that vividly colors the entire Apocalypse. As further reassurance, the churches are made aware that in the midst of this heavenly throne stands the Lamb in whom they have put their faith. It is he who has conquered and who is worthy to bring to final conclusion God's salvific plan. In chapter 6, the Lamb begins to lay open the revelation of God's design.

One by one the seals of chapter 6 reveal that war, sickness, death, famine, and even persecution of the saints are all part of what must be before the eschatological Day of the Lord. When the wrath of God and the Lamb is finally revealed, it will be a day before which the wicked will be unable to stand. The sealing of the 144,000 provides a visionary and literary interlude that allows John to reassure his readers that, in the midst of what are clearly difficult times for the church, God will keep those who belong to him to the end. The two visions of chapter 7 perform this function by showing the protection of God's people on earth (7.1-8) and their ultimate triumph in heaven (7.9-17).

The sealing of the 12,000 from each of the twelve tribes of Israel should not be seen as a call for the protection of a remnant from Israel; rather John draws imagery from his Jewish heritage that expresses to the recipients of the Apocalypse a guarantee of their spiritual security as God's new spiritual Israel. The symbolic nature of this imagery is confirmed by John's restructuring of his tribal list and through numeric symbolism to reflect messianic reality. The 144,000 represent the church, not just martyrs, in symbolic completion, as John affirms in his final vision of the new Jerusalem. They follow "the Lamb wherever he goes" (14.4) and join him in eschatological reward at the end of the age (7.9-17). Thus the two-vision interlude provides a response to the final question of chapter 6, Who can stand? It is the faithful who answer the call to persevere and who overcome that will stand before God and the Lamb.

The chapter 7 interlude, and more specifically John's vision of the 144,000 out of the tribes of Israel, serves to reinforce the present thesis that John views the church as God's new spiritual Israel. In Rev 2.9 and 3.9, John confronts the churches' Jewish opponents and begins to hint at his theological redefinition of a "true Jew." Since John sees no discontinuity between the redemptive plan of God worked out through Israel and fulfilled in the messianic Lamb, he draws no artificial lines between Jews and Christians. He does, however, make a clear distinction between those who belong to God and those who do not. This distinction is begun in 2.9 and 3.9 and is continued in the sealing of the 144,000. The fact that John views the church as new spiritual Israel is underlined in his vision of the 144,000 sealed, juxtaposed to his vision of the innumerable multitude. These two visions side-by-side, in combination with 14.1-5 and 15.1-5, reveal a consistent pattern of John's use of symbols from his Jewish heritage in tandem with his broader understanding of a people of God from every nation (5.9; 7.9; cf. 21.24-25; 22.2). This pattern is further highlighted in the second major interlude of the Apocalypse, the trumpet interlude.

4

The Temple, the Two Witnesses, and the Heavenly Woman:
The Church as Spiritual Israel

IN the previous chapter, the identity of the 144,000 was discussed and the conclusion drawn that this group is symbolic of the people of God, both Jews and Gentiles, as represented in the church. In the two visions of chapter 7, the spiritual protection of God's people is symbolized in the sealing of 12,000 from the twelve tribes of Israel (7.3-8). In the subsequent vision (7.9-7), the victory of the saints who have come out of the great ordeal is portrayed by means of an eschatological scene before the throne of God and the Lamb. This two-fold interlude offers a "before and after" picture of assurance to the beleaguered believers of Asia and forms a pause before the opening of the seventh seal and the sounding of the seven trumpets.

This twofold message of spiritual protection and eschatological reward reverberates throughout the Apocalypse. This conclusion is demonstrated through the reappearance of the 144,000 on Mount Zion (14.1-5; cf. 15.1-5), set in contrast to the marked of the beast (13.16-18), and through the final vision of the new Jerusalem (21.1–22.5). The visions of the 144,000 and the new Jerusalem appear at key moments in the Apocalypse to provide an assurance and an incentive to the Asian saints of the reward for those who persevere. The continuity between the visions of the 144,000 and the new Jerusalem is revealed through a common numeric symbolism in their affinity for multiples of twelve and, more important, in that their central visionary images symbolize a universal people of God, which John now identifies with the church. Like the 144,000 who are redeemed from humankind and who follow the Lamb (14.4-5), the innumerable multitude is from every nation, tribe, people and language (7.9; cf. 5.9) and also follows the Lamb (7.17). These two groups seen from different visionary perspectives are really the same group, representative of all believers who remain faithful to the end.

This unified interpretation is reinforced through the vision of the new Jerusalem. It is the new Jerusalem, the bride of the Lamb (21.9; cf. 21.2), which is the reward of the faithful (21.7). This reward is not a city but the city symbolizes the true reward—the saints in unadulterated communion with God. The symbolic nature of the vision is revealed distinctly but not exclusively in John's use of numeric symbolism, particularly multiples of twelve. In this composite vision, John sees the Holy City built to enormous proportions, also in multiples of twelve (12,000 stadia cubed), founded on the twelve apostles and to which entrance is gained through gates named after the twelve tribes of Israel (21.12-14; cf. 7.3-8). Into this city enter saints from every nation who bear the name of God on their forehead to enjoy fellowship in his presence forever (21.6; 22.3-4; cf. 3.12; 7.3; 14.1). The vision of the new Jerusalem brings together elements from the visions of the 144,000 and the innumerable multitude, and reinforces the conclusion that John sees the church as subsumed in, and the clear extension of, God's covenant people, Israel. For John, the church is God's new spiritual Israel.

Although the visions of the 144,000 and the new Jerusalem, which stand at either end of the Apocalypse, begin to suggest that this view of the church is held consistently throughout, it is not, however, on these visions alone that this conclusion rests. Further support is found in the heart of the Apocalypse among John's vision of the seven trumpets. Revelation 10.1—11.13 forms the second interlude of the Apocalypse, and like the first interlude, which creates a pause between the sixth and seventh seals, the second interlude is inserted between the sixth and seventh trumpets. The fact that these interludes occur at precisely the same juncture in both the sevenfold visions of the seals and the trumpets is no literary accident. In the trumpet interlude, John pauses to relate visionary experiences quite distinct from, but not unrelated to, the surrounding sevenfold vision.

As has been noted under the previous discussion of the first interlude, John's insertion of these interludes has purpose both at the literary and visionary levels. The first interlude forms a prelude to the opening of the seventh seal, which provides a visionary link to the subsequent sevenfold vision of the trumpets. This interlude offers an assurance of protection and victory before the unfolding of the trumpet judgments. This offer of assurance is not a guarantee that the saints will not suffer persecution, but it is an offer of hope that God will bring them to an eventual place of eschatological rest. This first interlude is indicative of the overall tenor of the

Apocalypse as it maintains a dynamic tension between the eschatological vindication of the saints and their present and future suffering.

The second interlude of 10.1—11.13 further elucidates this tension. As Prigent observes in his comparison of the two interludes, John reveals "le caractère double de leur [the saints] existence: préservée et levrée aux nations."[1] This second interlude offers a pause between the sixth and seventh trumpets whose judgments follow the opening of the seventh seal (8.1). The first six trumpets initiate eschatological judgments reminiscent of the exodus plagues that are directed against the land, the sea, the celestial bodies, and humankind. The judgments appear to be limited in that they affect only a third of these created realms. The second trilogy of the first six trumpets contains judgments that are particularly directed against the human inhabitants of the earth (8.13) and hence are comprised of three woes.

The six trumpets are an expansion of the judgments of God, first introduced with the opening of the sixth seal. In fact, the liaison between the seven seals and the seven trumpets seems to begin with the fifth seal (6.9-11). It is the cries for vindication from the martyred saints under the altar that call forth God's wrath in 8.6—9.21 (cf. 8.3-5).[2] This judgment, which is briefly addressed in the sixth seal, is expanded in great detail by means of the first six trumpets.[3] These judgments, however, fail to elicit a penitent response from the earth-dwellers, as John notes in 9.20-21.

The connection of the seven trumpets to the opening of the seventh seal reveals a progressive and uninterrupted (excepting the two major interludes already mentioned) visionary flow from 4.1 through 11.19. It is the Lamb's taking of the sealed scroll and the subsequent opening of the seven seals that initiates the fulfillment of the eschatological plan of God. This plan, which is set in motion by the redemptive work of the Lamb (5.9-10), is fulfilled with the sounding of the seventh trumpet as heavenly voices cry out, "The kingdom of the world has become the kingdom of our Lord and of his Christ" (11.15). The sounding of the seventh trumpet, however, does not conclude John's apocalypse, but simply serves as a literary precursor to the expanded account of the eschatological victory in chapter 19. The intervening chapters (12–18) elaborate on the continued suffering of the saints as well as on the eventual judgment of their enemies.

---

[1] Prigent, *L'Apocalypse*, 263.
[2] Beale, *Revelation*, 521.
[3] Compare the similar response of the judged in 6.16 and 9.6.

Structurally, there seems to be a natural break in the Apocalypse with the conclusion of the seventh trumpet and the opening of chapter 12. Adela Yarbro Collins argues that this is the structural midpoint of the Apocalypse and thus divides the Apocalypse into "two great halves" (1.9—11.19; 12.1—22.5).[4] While this may be true structurally, thematically John continues in 12.1—22.5 to elaborate on themes introduced in 4.1—11.19. The visionary content of the second interlude (10.1—11.13) prepares the hearer for the revelations of 12.1 and following. Not only is there a proleptic introduction of the beast in 11.7, but the visions of chapters 11, 12, and 13 all share in common the cryptic symbolic number borrowed from Daniel of three and one half years expressed in various manners as forty-two months (11.3; 13.5), 1,260 days (11.4; 12.14), and "a time, times and a half a time" (12.6).[5]

Chapters 11 and 12 particularly share visionary content rich in Jewish imagery that must be interpreted in light of the overall purpose and literary context of the Apocalypse. In Rev 11.1-2, John is given a rod to measure the temple and its worshipers, and in Rev 11.3-13, God's two witnesses, who are reminiscent of Moses and Elijah, exercise a powerful ministry in "the great city, which is spiritually called Sodom and Egypt, where their Lord was crucified" (11.8 translation mine). Revelation 12.1 opens with a heavenly vision of a woman clothed in the sun, with the moon at her feet and a crown of twelve stars, who gives birth to a male child "who is destined to rule the nations with an iron rod" (12.5; cf. 2.27; 19.15; Ps 2.9; *Pss. Sol.* 17.23-24). While the original source of some of this imagery is debated, most agree that it has likely passed to John through Jewish tradition.

These three images of chapters 11 and 12 will be the focus of the present discussion. The identity of these symbols will provide further insight into John's perception of the relationship between the church and Israel in the kingdom of God. Each of these images of chapters 11 and 12 shares a common symbolic referent; all three symbolize the collective people of God as represented in the church. Thus they support the present thesis that John understands the church as subsumed in, and the full expression of, God's salvific plan through Israel and fulfilled in the church—the new spiritual Israel. It is this common symbolic referent to the church that unites the first and second interludes of John's apocalypse

---

[4] Collins, *Combat Myth*, 20.

[5] So Joseph S. Considine, "The Two Witnesses: Apoc. 11.3-13," *CBQ* 8 (1946) 386; Aune, *Revelation 6–16*, 594.

and in turn unites these two interludes to the vision of 12.1-14. It is this common thread that delineates the scope of the present discussion: What is the meaning of the visionary content of Revelation 11–12 and what insight does it provide into John's perception of the relationship between the church and Israel in the kingdom of God?

The Trumpet Interlude (10.1—11.14)

Understanding the symbolic meaning of John's measuring of the temple, the two witnesses, and the woman clothed in the sun is fraught with difficulty as is evident from the plethora of scholarly literature available on the subject. The view has already been offered above that each of these visions shares the church as their common symbolic referent, but such an interpretation is not without its difficulties. In treating the visionary content of these two chapters, it is best first to address chapter 11, since it forms with chapter 10 John's second interlude, while chapter 12 will be taken up in a subsequent related discussion.

Like the first interlude, John's second interlude also follows the revelation of divine judgment on humankind. A question naturally follows: like the first, does John's second interlude also address the welfare of the people of God? A preliminary response to this question would be in the affirmative, although this second interlude should not be confined to this limited purpose. The second interlude is located between the sixth and seventh trumpets and can be divided into three related units: 10.1-11; 11.1-2; 11.3-14.[6]

John's Prophetic Recommissioning and the "Little Scroll" (10.1-11)

In the first section, 10.1-11, John signals a visionary shift with his frequent introductory formula, καὶ εἶδον. He is no longer observing the trumpet angels but sees instead "another mighty angel" (10.1) descending from heaven whom he describes with language reminiscent of his first

---

[6] These three divisions are based on content rather than formulaic language, as might be done with John's other visions. All three units form part of the same interlude and the same visionary experience introduced in 10.1 with καὶ εἶδον. Aune, *Revelation 6–16*, 585, observes that the literary material of 11.1-13 is not in the usual form of a "vision report" and appears to be more characteristic of narrative material. He notes, however, that John has couched the narrative in language similar to his other vision material. While the material of 11.1-2 and 11.3-13 may simply be extensions of John's vision experience begun in 10.1, it seems reasonable and for ease of discussion to refer to these units as separate but related visions or vision narratives in the following discussion.

encounter with "one like *the* Son of Man"[7] (1.12-16 italics mine). It is from this angel that he receives an open scroll which he is instructed to eat. The scroll is sweet to the taste but bitter in his stomach. Upon eating the scroll, John is told that he "must prophesy again about[8] many peoples and nations and languages and kings" (10.11). The meaning and purpose of John's experience in 10.1-11 is difficult to ascertain but appears to rest partly on the identity of the open scroll. An in-depth analysis of chapter 10 will not be undertaken at this juncture since the present focus is the imagery of chapters 11 and 12 in relationship to the quest of discerning John's view of the church as new spiritual Israel. Some summary remarks are in order, however, since chapter 10 forms the first section of John's second interlude and, in the opinion of some scholars, may also be linked to chapter 11 by content.[9]

There are only two scrolls mentioned in the Apocalypse, the sealed scroll of chapter 5 and the open scroll of chapter 10. A central question surrounding the identity of the chapter 10 scroll is its relationship to the sealed scroll of chapter 5. A number of extensive comparisons have been drawn between the two scrolls and their respective visions, suggesting that the two scrolls are identical.[10] Both of John's scrolls appear to trace their imagery back to Ezek 2.8-3.4 where Ezekiel is told to take a scroll with

---

[7] This translation proposed by the NRSV, while acceptable, reflects an interpretation on the part of the translators not necessarily inherent in the text, since υἱὸν ἀνθρώπου is anarthrous.

[8] Some modern English translations (e.g., RSV, NRSV, NIV) translate ἐπί as "about," and this is in keeping with the suggested meaning found in BDAG. See "ἐπί," 366, *BDAG on CD-ROM*. Version 1.0d. 2000, 2001. Beale, *Revelation*, 554, however, argues for "against" as a more precise translation, citing precedent from the LXX, in particular Ezek. Beale also observes that John's use of the fourfold formula, "peoples and nations and languages and kings," in 10.11 now takes a negative tone from this point in the Apocalypse (cf. 11.9; 13.7), in contrast to his positive use of the phrase in 5.9 and 7.9. This latter observation seems to be the most persuasive argument for the use of "against;" however, since 10.1-11 appears to be a recommissioning of John's prophetic ministry ("you must prophesy again"), "about" seems more appropriate given the fact that his ministry has and will continue to encompass both saints and nonbelievers. Cf. Ladd, *Revelation*, 148; Osborne, *Revelation*, 404–5 in favor of "about."

[9] Some scholars see the visionary material of 11.1-13 as the content of the open scroll John ingests in chapter 10 (e.g., Charles, *Revelation*, 1:260; Lohmeyer, *Offenbarung*, 89–90; Mounce, *Revelation*, 218). Considine, "Two Witnesses," 378, says that 10.1-11 forms the introduction for 11.1-13 and also announces the fulfillment of the "mystery of God" that is revealed in 12.1 through the rest of the Apocalypse. Bauckham, *Climax*, 257–66, argues that the open scroll of chapter 10 is identical to the sealed scroll of chapter 5, the contents of which begin to be revealed in chapter 11.

[10] See Beale, *Revelation*, 530–32, 548; Bauckham, *Climax*, 243–57.

writing on both sides (cf. Rev 5.1) and to eat the scroll, which is sweet to the taste (cf. Rev 10.8-9). Upon ingesting the scroll, he is told to go and prophesy to Israel (cf. Rev 10.11) and, similar to John, his message is a message of judgment (Ezek 2.10).

A major objection to equating the two apocalyptic scrolls stems from a morphological debate. The primary Greek term used for the scroll of chapter 10 is βιβλαρίδιον (10.2, 9, 10), which is usually considered a diminutive of βιβλίον and is normally translated "little scroll."[11] It is often observed, however, that John does not use βιβλαρίδιον exclusively for the chapter 10 scroll since βιβλίον is used in 10.8 for the same scroll. Bauckham downplays this lexical disagreement in his quest to equate the two scrolls.[12] He observes that the confusion in this matter first begins at the level of the textual evidence, noting the disagreement among manuscripts as to the precise terminology John uses, and he further argues that diminutives in the first century often no longer carried a diminutive meaning. He cites the use of other diminutives in the Apocalypse as evidence in favor of this latter assertion as well as in the *Shepherd of Hermas*, which is the only other known Greek text that uses both βιβλίον and βιβλαρίδιον and does so interchangeably.

Beale acknowledges that Bauckham's overall argument for equating the two scrolls is persuasive, but he raises some important cautionary points.[13] One observation he makes is that John uses βιβλαρίδιον only here in the Apocalypse (as opposed to βιβλίον, used twenty times throughout), which suggests that he uses it purposefully as Beale argues John does diminutives elsewhere.[14] This shift in terminology, as well as the anarthrous βιβλαρίδιον (10.2), may indicate that John wishes to draw a distinction between the two scrolls.[15] While Beale believes that it is "plau-

---

[11] "βιβλαρίδιον," 176, *BDAG on CD-ROM*. Version 1.0d. 2000, 2001; G. Schrenk, "βιβλίον," 1:617, *TDNT on CD-ROM*. Version 1.0d. 2000, 2001; "βιβλαρίδιον," 1:6.65, *L&N on CD-ROM*. Version 1.0d. 2000, 2001.

[12] Bauckham, *Climax*, 243–45.

[13] See the discussion Beale, *Revelation*, 530–32.

[14] Cf. Osborne, *Revelation*, 395, who takes an unsatisfactory middle position in this discussion in that he sees the open scroll of chapter 10 as the previously sealed scroll of chapter 5, yet he believes that βιβλαρίδιον is being used as a diminutive, indicating some distinction. Osborne solves this apparent contradiction by suggesting that the little scroll is only a "small" part of the whole scroll that reveals the eschatological plan of God.

[15] For those who see a distinction between the two scrolls see Charles, *Revelation*, 1:260; Beckwith, *Apocalypse*, 578–79; Kiddle, *Revelation*, 168; Lohmeyer, *Offenbarung*, 89–90; Prigent, *L'Apocalypse*, 253–54. Collins, *Combat Myth*, 19–32, sees the two scrolls as the "organizing principle" of the Apocalypse. She argues that the sealed scroll of chapter 5

sible" that the two scrolls are identical, he correctly observes that, in the final analysis, the identity of the chapter 10 scroll has little effect on the interpretation of this passage.

It is impossible to ascertain with any certainty the identity or content of the chapter 10 scroll, but some interpretive remarks can be offered as to the nature of the visionary event. Bauckham believes that there is indicated here a shift in John's prophetic focus because the judgment meted out in 6.1—9.19 has been ineffectual in bringing about repentance among the nations, which is confirmed by the unresponsiveness of the judged in 9.20-21. Thus the unique revelation of the opened scroll in chapter 10 is that the effective tool for the conversion of the nations is not judgment, but is the church's testimony as they follow their Lord in suffering, death, and resurrection, so potently illustrated in 11.3-13.[16]

Collins sees 10.1-11 as playing a structural role. Within her theory of an interlocking structure of the Apocalypse, she sees this passage as transitional, pointing back to John's previous revelations (namely chapters 1 and 5) and looking ahead (10.11) to the prophetic call that he must now fulfill in Rev 12.1—22.5.[17] In this latter section, John does just what he is instructed to do in 10.11; he prophesies "about" many nations and kings.

Collins seems correct in her observation that there is a transition at 12.1 in John's apocalyptic material, and the trumpet interlude helps in this transition. Not only is John recommissioned in this section, but there is a proleptic introduction of the beast in 11.7, who becomes a dominant figure in subsequent visions. John is now coming to the end of the series of seven trumpets that were initiated with the opening of the seven seals. Thus there is a continual literary and structural flow from 4.1—11.19 with two interludes at 7.1-17 and 10.1—11.14. John's recommissioning forms the first part of this second interlude and sets the stage for the renewed prophetic experience to follow.

Bauckham's alternative explanation for John's prophetic recommissioning is more difficult to defend. His view that there is a move away from judgment toward an emphasis on the church's witness does not seem

---

represents the contents of 1.9–11.19 and that the open scroll of chapter 10 contains the remainder of John's revelation.

[16] Bauckham, *Climax*, 283.

[17] Collins, *Combat Myth*, 16–21, 27–28; cf. Elisabeth Schüssler Fiorenza, *The Book of Revelation Justice and Judgment*, 2d ed. (Minneapolis: Fortress, 1998) 53–54, who notes a similar structural role for chapter 11. See especially Mark Seaborn Hall, "The Hook Interlocking Structure of Revelation: The Most Important Verses in the Book and How They May Unify Its Structure," *NovT* 44 (2002) 278–96.

so clear-cut. As Beale observes, judgment continues to be a dominant theme of the chapters that follow Revelation 10. In 11.3-13, the focus is not the testimony of the two witnesses, but the world's rejection of the witnesses, which lays the groundwork for coming judgment.[18] Bauckham is, however, at least partially correct in his observation that there is a shift in the focus of the apocalyptic material following 10.1-11. The shift in John's use of the fourfold formula, "peoples and nations and languages and kings," for the people of the earth as opposed to the people of God may be a small indicator of this; but there is also a more detailed focus on the fate of both the nations and the saints and their relationship to one another. This shift in focus, however, is not a clean break with the preceding material since both the preceding and subsequent chapters of the Apocalypse share common themes.

John's Prophetic Recommissioning and the Vision Narratives of 11.1-13

The next two sections of the trumpet interlude are found in 11.1-2 and 3-14. In 11.1, John is given a measuring rod and told to "arise and measure the temple of God and the altar and those who are worshiping in it" (translation mine). In 11.2, however, he is told not to measure the outer court[19] "for it is given over to the nations, and they will trample over the Holy City for forty-two months." The vision of 11.3-13 follows immediately and is John's vision of God's two witnesses who bear testimony for this same period of forty-two months, although expressed now as 1,260 days (11.3). When their testimony is complete, John writes that they are slain by the beast, which arises from the abyss, and their dead bodies remain on open display for three and one half days in "the great city, which is spiritually called Sodom and Egypt, where their Lord was crucified" (11.8; translation mine).

The link, if any, between John's subsequent visions of chapter 11 and the preceding prophetic commission of chapter 10 has been difficult to ascertain. As mentioned above, some scholars see in 11.1-13 the revelation of the contents of the scroll of chapter 10. Aune further suggests that in 11.1-2 John begins to exercise the prophetic call of chapter 10 through the symbolic measuring of the temple.[20] Revelation 11.1-2 has at least some affiliation with the visionary experience of chapter 10 because of their

---

[18] Beale, *Revelation*, 531; cf. Osborne, *Revelation*, 395, n.5.
[19] John is literally told to "throw or cast out" (ἔκβαλε) this outer court.
[20] Aune, *Revelation 6–16*, 594.

similarities to Ezekiel's prophetic experience.[21] The similarities between John's and Ezekiel's prophetic calls have already been outlined above, but Ezekiel also has a visionary experience in which he observes the measuring of the Jerusalem temple (Ezek 40.3—42.20). There are, however, some key differences between John's and Ezekiel's temple visions. In Ezekiel's vision, the temple is measured by a divine or angelic figure, and no part of the temple compound is excluded. John's subsequent vision of the measuring of the new Jerusalem, however, adopts these characteristics of Ezekiel's vision (21.15-17).

The vision of the two witnesses (11.3-13) does not evoke Ezekiel-like images but does allude to other OT images, such as the two olive trees of Zech 4.3 (cf. Rev 11.4) and the ministries of Moses and Elijah (cf. Rev 11.5-6). Prigent suggests the possibility that John's recommissioning in chapter 10 finds expression in the prophetic ministry of the two witnesses.[22] If one interprets the two witnesses as the church, then such an association is in a general way possible, but it is not at all clear that the vision of the two witnesses has this intended purpose.

The relationship between John's recommissioning and the two visions of chapter 11 is not critical to establish in order to accomplish the present task of interpreting the symbols of the chapter 11 visions. What can be said with some certainty concerning the visions is that they are at a minimum united because they makeup the totality of the trumpet interlude, which itself has a unified literary purpose in the plan of the Apocalypse. Each of the visions within the interlude flows one into the other with no major structural break as in 10.1 (καὶ εἶδον) and 12.1 (καὶ σημεῖον μέγα ὤφθη).

More important for the present discussion are the significant thematic links shared among the two vision narratives of 11.1-13 that extend even into the visions of chapters 12 and 13. These common themes will be discussed in more detail below but are evident in three major areas. First, these visions all deal with the symbolic time period of three and one half years expressed in various denominations as forty-two months (11.2; 13.5), 1,260 days (11.3; 12.6), and "a time, times and half a time" (12.14). Second, it will be argued that the major figures of these visions share a common symbolic referent—the church. Third, it will be further argued that there is a common message among the visions regarding the spiritual protection of God's people in the face of certain opposition.

---

[21] See Bauckham, *Climax*, 266–67.

[22] Prigent, *L'Apocalypse*, 260.

A Hermeneutic of Sources

Interpreting the vision of 11.1-2 is one of the more challenging tasks in the study of John's apocalyptic imagery. The purpose and meaning of the vision are not clearly discernable. In order to elucidate the meaning of this vision narrative, many scholars have turned to a study of source material for both this vision and the subsequent vision of 11.3-13. The geographical setting of both visions appears to be Palestine, indicated by references to the temple, the Holy City, and the location of Christ's crucifixion.[23] The Palestinian venue, as well as the allusions to an Ezekiel-like measuring of the temple and the power-driven prophetic ministries of Moses and Elijah, gives both visions a Jewish tone. It is, therefore, tempting to see behind these two visions a Jewish source or sources that have been adopted and adapted by John for his apocalyptic purposes.

R. H. Charles, who views chapter 11 as a digression from the current theme of the Apocalypse, argues that there are two pre-70 CE independent Jewish sources behind 11.1-13 borrowed by John and adapted for his own purposes.[24] He offers five reasons for this conclusion that are largely based on a stylistic analysis of this passage.[25] Charles believes that 11.3-13 particularly reflects a version of a Jewish antichrist myth circulating at some date prior to 70 CE.[26] Beasley-Murray essentially follows Charles, arguing that 11.1-2 could conceivably be a short apocalyptic narrative that survived the First Jewish Revolt. He adds that 11.3-13 is conspicuously Jewish in tone with a curious omission of any Christian reference to Christ's parousia (11.11-12).[27]

While interesting, such source analysis must end in speculation since no extant witnesses exist to verify these hypotheses.[28] Even after Charles' elaborate analysis, he acknowledges, as do most scholars, that 11.1-13 in its

---

[23] Aune, *Revelation 6–16*, 588, adds the threat of drought (11.6), a particular concern in Palestine.

[24] Charles, *Revelation*, 1:269–73; cf. Beckwith, *Apocalypse*, 586–87. See Considine, "Two Witnesses," 377–92, for a counter analysis particularly of 11.3-13. Considine argues against Charles' conclusions and finds no reason not to see 11.1-13 as a unified whole from the hand of John.

[25] Charles, *Revelation*, 1:270.

[26] Ibid., 1:274, 285–86; cf. Aune, *Revelation 6–16*, 588–93, who also believes that 11.1-13 reflects two originally Jewish sources but disagrees with Charles' comparison of 11.3-13 to a Jewish antichrist myth.

[27] Beasley-Murray, *Revelation*, 176–78.

[28] So Beale, *Revelation*, 556; Kiddle, *Revelation*, 174–75; cf. David Flusser, *Judaism and the Origins of Christianity* (Jerusalem: Magnes, 1988) 391–92.

present context cannot be interpreted historically, but must be interpreted eschatologically and figuratively.[29] This latter observation is an important one in the discussion of both source material and interpretive methodology and brings to the fore an important point of agreement among most exegetes of the Apocalypse. Regardless of one's source critical view, in the final analysis, one must recognize that John has adapted all of his sources for his own use within the Apocalypse. Thus the material has become "his" and must be interpreted primarily within its literary context.

This is the hermeneutical approach de Villiers argues should be given priority when analyzing John's use of symbols. He eschews any eclectic approach that attempts to find meaning in Jewish or pagan sources and calls for a "syntagmatic" and "paradigmatic reading" of the symbolic language.[30] A syntagmatic reading is one that recognizes the relationship of symbols within the textual unit being studied, and a paradigmatic reading analyzes how these symbols are developed throughout the entire text. The social world of the author becomes a secondary "grid" against which symbols are to be understood, but this social setting may at times be difficult if not impossible to discern.[31] When considering the relationship of symbols, de Villiers cautions that the approach should not be overly simplistic, but must recognize that some symbols have a closer relationship to one another than others. Their interrelationship is hierarchical.

De Villiers's hermeneutical approach is not unique, but is an important reminder that the socio-cultural background of particular symbols or narratives should not be given undue influence in any interpretive approach. While John's apocalyptic material, indeed, the genre of literature which he uses, is largely the product of his own social location, these symbols have taken on their own meaning through his use of them within the context of the Apocalypse. John is a Jew for whom Jesus is the Messiah, and it is this messianic understanding through which he reinterprets the Jewish scriptures and that significantly influences his use of Jewish imagery, much of which is borrowed from these same scriptures.[32] The OT background to John's images should, therefore, be given priority in any source analysis, while recognizing the overarching importance of John's

---

[29] Charles, *Revelation*, 1:274; cf. Beasley-Murray, *Revelation*, 178.

[30] P. G. R. de Villiers, "The Lord was Crucified in Sodom and Egypt: Symbols in the Apocalypse of John," *Neot* 22 (1988) 125–38.

[31] Ibid., 132–33.

[32] G. K. Beale, *John's Use of the Old Testament in Revelation*, JSNTSup 166 (Sheffield: Sheffield Academic, 1998) 127.

own use of these images.³³ It is this lens through which one must peer in order to understand John's use of apocalyptic symbols.

Source Material (11.1-13)

With this interpretive perspective in mind, some attempt can be made to explain the vision narratives of 11.1-13. As has been observed earlier, the vision of 11.1-2 comprises the measuring of the temple and the altar and a strict command not to measure the outer court, which has been given over to the nations who will trample the Holy City for forty-two months. It has already been suggested that this vision narrative may be an allusion to Ezekiel's measuring of the temple (Ezekiel 40–42) and that this connection to Ezekiel may form a link with the preceding passage of 10.1-11.

Bauckham proposes another OT background to this passage, which he says has not yet been fully recognized. He views Dan 8.11-13 as a common source for all of chapter 11 observing, that both visionary sequences, the measuring of the temple, and the two witnesses speak of the trampling of the Holy City and the persecution of the saints for the danielic period of three and one half years (Rev 11.2-3).³⁴ In addition, Bauckham argues that Zech 12.3 also plays an interpretive role since John has extended Daniel's trampling of the "host" and the sanctuary to the entire city. Bauckham's discussion bypasses Ezekiel 40–42, rather seeing this latter passage as background for the measuring of the new Jerusalem (21.15).³⁵

The connection between Rev 11.1-2 and Dan 8.11-13 is an important possibility since both vision narratives of chapter 11 and even chapters 12 and 13 allude to Daniel's symbolic three and one half year time period (Rev 11.2-3; 12.6, 14; 13.5). In addition, the beast of Rev 13.1-3, first introduced in 11.7, is clearly a conglomeration of the beasts of Dan 7.1-8. This beast has many of the same characteristics as Daniel's "little horn," which, for a similar period of time overcomes the "host" (i.e., God's people), and, like the dragon of Rev 12.4, sweeps a portion of the stars from heaven (Dan 7.8, 11; 8.9-14; cf. Rev 12.4; 13.6-7).

It may best be said that John has both Ezekiel and Daniel in mind when he pens this vision narrative of 11.1-2. There are clear allusions to

---

³³ See Ian Paul, "The Use of the Old Testament in Revelation 12," in *The Old Testament in the New Testament: Essays in Honor of J. L. North*, ed. Steve Moyise, JSNTSup 189 (Sheffield: Sheffield Academic, 2000) 273–74; cf. Hirschberg, *Das eschatologische Israel*, 217, who also proposes that the OT and early Jewish traditions should be given priority.

³⁴ Bauckham, *Climax*, 269–73.

³⁵ Ibid., 269, n.46.

Ezekiel's prophetic commission in Rev 10.1-11, and the subsequent command to "rise up and measure the temple" (11.1) carries similar though less exacting allusions to Ezekiel 40–42. Although John, rather than an angel, does the measuring, the connection between Rev 11.1-2 and Ezekiel 40–42 seems closer in some ways than that of Rev 21.15. As in Ezekiel, the focus of the measuring in Rev 11.1-2 is the temple rather than the Holy City, and the measuring serves to delineate between what is clean and unclean.[36] This is not to suggest, however, that Rev 21.15 and its accompanying vision of the new Jerusalem do not carry allusions to the same Ezekiel passage.

Bauckham seems to overemphasize the connection between 11.1-2, Dan 8.11-14, and Zech 12.3 to the neglect of the Ezekiel allusion. This overemphasis is likely a result of his own hermeneutical agenda, since his goal is to prove that John's new emphasis is now on the role of the church's witness in the conversion of the nations. He believes that the vision narratives of chapter 11 reveal what remained mysterious to Daniel (Dan 12.8-10) and that is the salvation of the nations through the witness of the church.[37] While it is difficult to prove Bauckham's ultimate conclusion, it is at least possible to see a connection to Daniel through John's description of the trampling of the Holy City for forty-two months. The measuring of the temple and the altar, however, show clearer allusions to Ezekiel 40–42 (cf. 43.14-17). Thus it could be said that the vision narrative of 11.1-2 provides a transition between John's recommissioning in 10.1-11 and the subsequent vision of 11.3-13, as well as the visions of chapters 12 and 13, through its allusions to both Ezekiel and Daniel.

The discussion of background material leads naturally to the next point of analysis and that is John's adaptation of this material within the Apocalypse. Some scholars see in John's vision of the measuring of the temple and the subsequent vision of the two witnesses a prophecy concerning the fate of ethnic Israel.[38] Walvoord interprets this passage literally as a prophecy of a rebuilt temple in earthly Jerusalem during a future time of tribulation.[39] Beckwith and Ladd, who take a different hermeneutical approach, do see here a prophecy concerning the salvation of Israel.[40] This

---

[36] So Jeffrey Marshall Vogelgesang, "The Interpretation of Ezekiel in the Book of Revelation" (Ph.D. diss., Harvard University, 1985) 79.

[37] See particularly the concluding remarks Bauckham, *Climax*, 273.

[38] So Beckwith, *Apocalypse*, 588–89; André Feuillet, *The Apocalypse*, trans. Thomas E. Crane (Staten Island: Alba, 1964) 61; Ladd, *Revelation*, 151.

[39] Walvoord, *Revelation*, 175–83.

[40] Beckwith, *Apocalypse*, 588–89; Ladd, *Revelation*, 152–53.

approach to the passage, however, is fraught with difficulties, not the least of which is that John never seems to set up such a dichotomy between Israel and the church. His concern throughout is for the people of God, both Jews and Gentiles, as represented in the corporate church. Considine poses a valid question when he wonders what role such an interpretation would play in the Apocalypse. John is not writing to a Jewish audience and 2.9 and 3.9 have already shown John's attitude toward some of those in Judaism.[41]

Beckwith argues that chapter 11 reflects a recurring Christian concern (as in Romans 9–11) for the fate of Israel. He contrasts the two interludes of the seals and trumpets by suggesting that the sealing of the 144,000 from the twelve tribes of Israel shows a concern for the "final safety of the whole church," while the trumpet interlude demonstrates a concern for the "final safety of Israel."[42] Such a distinction, however, is inconsistent not only with the message of the Apocalypse but also in its treatment of the symbols. How can 144,000 from the twelve tribes of Israel represent the church when the temple of 11.1-2 cannot?

It is more reasonable to see in John's use of Jewish imagery in these two interludes, as well as elsewhere, a consistent message concerning the church communicated in symbolic fashion. These often very Jewish symbols are a product of John's own social location, but they also reveal an inherent perspective of how John views the church as the new Israel. In 11.1-13, his allusions to Ezekiel and Daniel reinforce this idea that John intends the images within his vision to be understood symbolically. Indeed, this conclusion seems to be confirmed by the close association within the Apocalypse between 11.1-2 and 21.9-27. In order to understand the message of 11.1-2, then, attention must be turned to understanding the nature and interpretation of these symbols and the purpose of this text within the narrative as a whole. The three symbols of particular importance in this passage are the temple, the Holy City, and the act of measuring.

The Meaning of the Measuring of the Temple (11.1-2)

In the vision of 11.1-2, John is specifically told to "rise up and measure the temple of God" (τὸν ναὸν τοῦ θεοῦ) and the altar and the ones who worship in it" (11.1). The outer court of the temple, however, is to be strictly left out of the measurement (ἔκβαλε ἔξωθεν), for it has, along with the Holy City, been given over to the nations (11.2). Many scholars, in an at-

---

[41] Considine, "Two Witnesses," 381–84.
[42] Beckwith, *Apocalypse*, 588–89; cf. Ladd, *Revelation*, 151, who follows Beckwith.

tempt to interpret this vision, have tried to associate the specific areas of the temple mentioned in the vision with the historic temple. John's reference to the "temple of God and the altar and the ones who worship in it," for example, is argued by some to be a reference to the temple area serviced by the priests: the holy place and the most holy place. The altar, therefore, would be the altar of incense located within the temple building itself as opposed to the altar of burnt offering.[43]

There is considerable debate, however, as to what John means by the "outer court" of the temple. Many scholars understand this area as a reference to what has become known as the "court of the Gentiles," which is one of several outer courts of the first-century Herodian temple.[44] The reference in 11.2 to the giving over of this court to the "nations" (ἔθνεσιν) or the "Gentiles" seems to reinforce this historical connection. Bauckham, however, takes exception to this identification, noting that the designation, court of the Gentiles, is not original to the first-century temple, but is modern nomenclature. He rather argues that this outer court is a reference to the court of the priests just outside of the temple building where the altar of burnt offering was located in the first century. He believes that this interpretation would be more consistent with the interpretation of Dan 8.11-12.[45]

The principle difficulty in the identification of the outer court in 11.2 is determining which temple (Solomonic, Ezekielian, or Herodian) John might have in mind as he communicates his vision narrative. If John envisions Ezekiel's temple, which is possible because of the apparent allusions already observed to Ezekiel's measuring of the temple, then the identity of the outer court must be related to this earlier temple complex and not the first-century Herodian temple, which had a much more complex court system. This latter observation would also be true of the less complex Solomonic temple.

A final possibility is that John does not have in mind a historical temple but a heavenly one. Throughout the Apocalypse, John uses ναός to refer consistently to God's heavenly temple. Revelation 11.19 is an excellent example of this usage as John here refers to ὁ ναὸς τοῦ θεοῦ (cf. 11.1) being opened in heaven after the sounding of the seventh trumpet. It is quite possible, then, that John's reference in 11.1-2 is not to any

---

[43] So Bauckham, *Climax,* 268–69; Mounce, *Revelation,* 220.

[44] So Kraft, *Offenbarung,* 152; Mounce, *Revelation,* 220; Beale, *Revelation,* 560; Osborne, *Revelation,* 412–13.

[45] Bauckham, *Climax,* 268–69, however, does acknowledge that the textual difficulties surrounding Dan 8.11-12 do make any such conclusion provisional.

historical temple but to the heavenly one.[46] One objection that could be raised to this point is that the chapter 11 visions seem historically located in Palestine (cf. 11.8); however, John is not above moving between heaven and earth in his visionary material, as can be seen, for example, in the vision of the heavenly woman of 12.1-17, who is at one moment in heaven and at another on earth. This being acknowledged, however, it does seem that the visions of 11.1-13 are purposely tied to an earthly venue, which is an important element in their overall meaning.

The focus of the vision material following chapter 10 centers significantly on the fate of the saints and the judgment of their enemies. Revelation 11.1-13 begins to develop a tension between the saints and the nations that is expanded more fully in chapters 13 through 20. This focus naturally results in much of the visionary material dealing with earthly entities (e.g., the beast, false prophet and the saints [13.1-14.5], the fate of Babylon [17-18] and the millennium [20.1-10]), although heavenly scenes are still common. Chapter 12 is perhaps indicative of this focal shift as John moves the cosmic battle from heaven to earth. In this manner, the second half of the Apocalypse begins to give the Asian saints some explanation for their suffering and some hope of their eventual vindication.

Although the identity of the historical or visionary temple John refers to in 11.1-2 is not possible to determine precisely, it seems more likely that John has in mind, at least to some degree, the earthly temple, which is reinforced by the apparent location of the subsequent vision (11.3-13). The identity of the temple, however, is not a prerequisite to understanding the overall message of this vision. Like much of John's apocalypse, this vision is meant to be understood symbolically. This symbolism can be seen in the clear distinction drawn between that which is measured and that which is not. It is the temple, the altar, and the worshipers who are measured, while the outer court and the Holy City are cast out. The concern here, as in the chapter 7 interlude (cf. 9.4), is for the preservation of the saints. The church is described elsewhere in the NT as God's spiritual temple (1 Cor 3.16-17; 6.19; 2 Cor 6.16; Eph 2.21), and this is frequently taken as the intended meaning here. The measuring of the temple, therefore, is a symbolic representation of the preservation of the saints.

Stevenson postulates a more precise identification of these symbols, preferring rather to see the worshipers as symbolic of the church fulfilling their role as priests (cf. Rev 5.10) and the temple as symbolic of the place

---

[46] See Beale, *Revelation*, 562; Considine, "Two Witnesses," 380–82.

of protection for God's people.[47] The measuring of the temple, the altar, and the worshipers signifies the purity as well as the protection of God's people and heightens the contrast between what is measured and what is not.[48] Stevenson's desire for more precision at this point serves his thesis that the temple is a place of identity for the people of God and a place where God's presence is found. Hence it is through the temple language of 11.1-2 that John not only symbolizes the care and preservation of God's people (as in chapter 7) but also envelopes the church in temple language, suggesting its identity as the new Israel of God.[49]

Stevenson's interpretation is advantageous in that it solves a perceived problem with interpreting the temple as the church. If the temple symbolizes the church, then who do the worshipers represent? Osborne makes an awkward attempt at resolving this issue by postulating that the temple represents the corporate church while the worshipers represent the individual believers.[50] Most scholars, however, gloss over the issue by simply seeing all of the cultic imagery combined as indicative of God's people. Aune cautions against an over-allegorization of the imagery and suggests that a focus on the theological message of the vision is of greater importance. The message, he says, "centers on the salvation and protection that lie at the center (the temple of God), while danger and destruction lie at the periphery (the outer court and the Holy City)."[51]

Aune pushes the debate in the right direction and his theological interpretation would be supported by Stevenson.[52] Stevenson's precise interpretation of the symbols is not ultimately necessary. While his argument is appealing, it does seem plausible that the temple itself can also symbolize the church. In addition to previously cited NT precedent, further support might be found in a comparative analysis of John's description of the Holy City in chapter 21. Here is a city that is at once the bride of the Lamb and the new Jerusalem (21.9-10); and, like the temple in 11.1-2, it is measured. Its cubic measurements recall those of the holy of holies in the Jerusalem temple and suggest that in this culminating apocalyptic vision,

---

[47] Stevenson, *Power and Place*, 259–60.

[48] Cf. Beale, *The Book of Revelation*, 560–61, who points out that the express purpose for the measuring of the temple in Ezekiel was to exclude idolaters.

[49] Stevenson, *Power and Place*, 263; cf. 224.

[50] Osborne, *Revelation*, 411–12.

[51] Aune, *Revelation 6–16*, 598.

[52] Stevenson, *Power and Place*, 259, 263.

John is merging images of both the temple and the Holy City into one symbol that represents the people of God.[53]

This discussion leads nicely into the next symbol to consider in John's vision of 11.1-2, and that is John's reference to the Holy City (11.2). Beale groups this reference to the Holy City with those to the new Jerusalem of 21.2, 10 and 22.19, suggesting that John consistently intends for the Holy City to represent the people of God. Thus he argues that there is in 11.2 an "already-and-not-yet" reference to the heavenly city. This identification of the Holy City as the people of God is not intended to conflict with the similar symbolic meaning of the temple.[54] Rather the Holy City in 11.2 represents the believers who are being persecuted on earth and who are also part and representative of the heavenly Jerusalem.[55] Osborne furthers this comparison between 11.1-2 and the new Jerusalem by noting that in the measuring of the new Jerusalem, no portion of the city is excluded as in 11.2, symbolizing the eventual and complete victory of the saints.[56] Thus the message being conveyed in 11.1-2 is similar to that of the seal interlude: while God promises the spiritual protection of his people, the nations, for a period of time, will be allowed to oppose and at some point to overcome the people of God. John's reference to the trampling of the Holy City emphasizes the pervasiveness of both the opposition and profanity of the world until the time of the nations is fulfilled (cf. Luke 21.22). This same message is conveyed in the subsequent vision of 11.3-13.

The act of measuring the temple has been reserved for a final analysis because it embodies the focus of John's message. As has already been observed, what is central to this vision is the dichotomy between what is measured and what is not. The act of measuring, like the other images in this vision, is intended to be symbolic, particularly in light of the fact that the measuring actually never takes place in the narrative. Measuring in the OT is often used figuratively to symbolize judgment (e.g., 2 Sam 8.2a; 2 Kgs 21.13; Lam 2.8; Amos 7.7-9), restoration (Jer 31.38-40; Zech 1.16; 2.1-2),[57] sanctification or protection (e.g., 2 Sam 8.2b; Isa 28.16-17; Jer

---

[53] This analysis is similar to that of Stevenson, *Power and Place*, 267–72 (particularly 269–70); however, Stevenson sees no conflict in separating the identity of the temple from God's people in 11.2, while merging this identity in Revelation 21. Cf. Beale, *Revelation*, 1070. For a more detailed discussion see the following chapter.

[54] Beale, *Revelation*, 562.

[55] Ibid., 568; cf. Osborne, *Revelation*, 413.

[56] Osborne, *Revelation*, 411–12; cf. Beale, *Revelation*, 1072–73.

[57] Osborne, *Revelation*, 752–53.

31.38-40; Ezek 42.20; Zech 1.16; 2.5; cf. *1 En.* 61.1-5),[58] and the latter meaning is best understood in the context of Rev 11.1-2. The measuring of the temple is a symbolic visionary act that represents the preservation of the people of God,[59] while those who are outside the temple are the objects of God's wrath.

Typical of the Johannine apocalypse is this dichotomy between the people who belong to God and those who stand outside of God's kingdom in opposition to him and his people.[60] John has already recounted for his hearers a vision of the 144,000 and the great multitude in the chapter 7 interlude, who enjoy the protection and victory of God while the inhabitants of the earth are judged by God (6.12-17; 8.13; 9.4, 20-21). This dualism continues throughout the rest of the Apocalypse and comes to a crescendo with the destruction of Babylon (Rev 18), juxtaposed to the vindication of the saints and the triumph of the rider on the white horse (19.1-16). The fate of the nations is the "great supper of God" (19.17) and that of the beast and false prophet is the "lake of fire" (19.20), but the people of God enjoy the marriage supper of the Lamb (19.9) and find their reward in a renewed heaven and earth filled with the presence of God (Rev 21.1–22.5).

The first and second interludes of John's apocalypse, therefore, have in common that they pause to promise the people of God a certain protection in difficult times. What is made clear for the Asian Christians is that their suffering will continue but is only temporary. For a specified period of time, designated with danielic symbolism as three and one half years (11.2-3; 12.6; 12.14; 13.5), the nations or earth-dwellers will temporarily have the upper-hand, they will trample the Holy City (11.2), and will even be allowed to overcome the saints (11.7; cf. 13.7). What the saints

---

[58] Aune, *Revelation 6–16*, 604; Beale, *Revelation*, 559–61; Stevenson, *Power and Place*, 259–60.

[59] This is the view held by a majority of scholars. Charles, *Revelation*, 1:275; Lohmeyer, *Offenbarung*, 89; Kraft, *Offenbarung*, 152; Kiddle, *Revelation*, 179; Considine, "Two Witnesses," 384; Mounce, *Revelation*, 219; Bauckham, *Climax*, 269; Aune, *Revelation 6–16*, 598; Beale, *Revelation*, 558–60; Prigent, *L'Apocalypse*, 263; Stevenson, *Power and Place*, 260; Osborne, *Revelation*, 411–12.

[60] The division between these two groups is noticeable in the language of the Apocalypse. The participles κατοικοῦντες (those who inhabit; 11.10; 13.8, 12) and σκηνοῦντες (those who tabernacle; 12.12; 13.6) are used to describe these two groups. The first is used to describe "those who inhabit the earth," while the latter is used for those who "tabernacle" in heaven. This division becomes particularly pronounced in chapters 12 and 13, which will be observed in more detail later. The verb σκηνόω is also used in 7.15 to speak of the saints before the throne of God. See Osborne, *Revelation*, 478; Bauckham, *Climax*, 240.

must do is hold to the testimony of Jesus and keep the commandments of God; in other words, they must persevere in their faith. It is their spiritual fortitude even unto death that guarantees their ultimate victory.

"My Two Witnesses" (11.3-13)

The measuring of the temple is followed immediately by the vision of the two witnesses in 11.3-13. The heavenly voice that had summoned John to measure the temple continues to speak, introducing the vision of the two witnesses.[61] The two visions are not strictly linked by common images, but are certainly linked by the narrative voice, by venue, by the reference to the similar time period of three and one half years, and, more importantly, by a common theological message. John is told that the Holy City will be trampled by the nations for forty-two months (11.2), and during this same time period, although now expressed as 1,260 days, the two witnesses will be given authority to prophesy (11.3). The linking of these two visions implies that John intends for them to be interpreted in relationship to one another.

Something should be said at this point about the time period of three and one half years that is first introduced in 11.2 as forty-two months and becomes a common feature of the subsequent visions of chapters 11, 12, and 13. The predominance of this time period suggests that it plays an important interpretive role in understanding the message that John wishes to communicate. The number finds its source in Daniel, and it is likely John's intention to allude to and carry forth in a similar apocalyptic direction the symbolic use of this number. John expresses the three and one half years as forty-two months (11.2; 13.5), 1,260 days (11.3; 12.6), and "time, and times, and half a time" (12.14). The latter expression is used only once and is a virtual quote of the similar expression in Daniel (Dan 7.25; 12.7). The 1,260 days recalls Daniel's 1,290 days (Dan 12.11), the difference resulting from John's use of perfect thirty day months. Daniel, however, does not use the figure of forty-two months, and John's peculiar use of this denomination may perhaps be explained by his attempt to draw an allusion to Elijah's ministry or Israel's wilderness wanderings.[62] The drought under Elijah's ministry came to be designated in later tradition as three and one half years (e.g., Luke 4.25; Jas 5.17) and Israel's forty-two encampments during its wilderness wandering have been generally understood to have

---

[61] It is difficult to determine when the direct speech ends and John's recounting of what he sees begins (possibly 11.4).
[62] Beale, *Revelation*, 565–66; Osborne, *Revelation*, 414.

occurred over forty-two years (Num 33.5-49). Both of these periods in Israel's history were periods of judgment.[63]

Whether John's use of forty-two months is intended to recall these periods of Israel's history is uncertain, but what is certain is that he wishes his readers to recognize the apocalyptic significance of the three and one half year period. He removes any doubt of his intention by his use of the danielic phrase "time, and times, and half a time" in 12.14. This period of time first found its fulfillment in Daniel's "abomination of desolation," which occurred under the reign of Antiochus Epiphanes (167–163 BCE), when the temple was desecrated and Jerusalem was trampled by the Gentiles. Josephus summarizes this period of time in his *Jewish War* first as three years and three months (1.19) and later as "three years and six months" (5.394). This danielic threat of the "abomination of desolation" in the temple is renewed in the gospel tradition (Mark 13.14; Matt 24.15) and is later, at least partially, fulfilled in the period between the beginning of the First Jewish Revolt (fall of 66 CE) and the fall of Jerusalem (70 CE),[64] which lasted about three and one half years. This period of conflict with the Romans is described in Luke 21.24 as the trampling of Jerusalem by the Gentiles (or nations; ἐθνῶν), "until the times of the Gentiles are fulfilled"—a description seemingly echoed by John in Rev 11.2.[65] John's intention in his apocalypse is to renew once again the apocalyptic symbolism behind this number by suggesting that the previous fulfillments have only been partial and that a similar suffering of the people of God at the hands of the world powers has yet to be completed.

This renewed significance given to the three and one half year period naturally leads to a discussion of what historical era corresponds to this symbolic number. There is some difference of opinion on this matter as some scholars see John's three and one half year period as representative of the church age inaugurated by the Messiah and completed at his Parousia,[66] while others interpret this time frame as a final eschatological period when the antichrist will arise and persecute the church, but will finally be defeated at the Parousia.[67] Of course, the assumption is often

---

[63] Beale, *Revelation*, 565.
[64] See Aune, *Revelation 6–16*, 609; Beale, *Revelation*, 566.
[65] Beale, *Revelation*, 565–66.
[66] So Considine, "Two Witnesses," 387; Beale, *Revelation*, 567–68; Prigent, *L'Apocalypse*, 261.
[67] So Ladd, *Revelation*, 153; Bauckham, *Climax*, 273; Osborne, *Revelation*, 420.

made that each instance of John's use of this three and one half year period designates the same historical era.

Beale, however, does allow for the possibility that John is referring to the church age in 11.2-3 and 12.6, 14, but to an intense period of eschatological tribulation in 13.5.[68] This latter interpretation of 13.5 is the most logical and preferred interpretation since it coincides with the rise of the beast that marks the beginning of such a period of persecution (cf. Rev 11.7; 17.8; 2 Thess 2.1-12). Revelation 11.7 seems to support such an interpretation for it indicates that the saints will face an intense period of persecution just before the end. This is what John may term as the "great ordeal" (7.14; τῆς θλίψεως τῆς μεγάλης). Daniel's three and one half year time period is a similarly limited but intense time of oppression for the people of God that is brought to completion through the establishment of the eschatological reign of God (Dan 7.25-27). Although Daniel's prophecy was fulfilled during the reign of Antiochus Epiphanes, John's allusion to it plays on its dual status as both a historical and eschatological reality. It is interesting to note that the poetic discourse of Dan 7.25-27 declares, as does the hymn of Rev 11.14-18, the establishment of the kingdom of God and the triumph of the saints following this period of oppression.

If Rev 13.5 refers to an intense eschatological period of persecution for the people of God, then how might one interpret the other sometimes identical references for this same time period in 11.2-3 and 12.6, 14? It has already been mentioned above that John designates this three and one half year time period through three different expressions, forty-two months, 1,260 days, and "time, and times, and half a time." One may ask why John varies his reporting of this time period, in such a manner, and what if any significance it might have. It is interesting to observe that both the designations forty-two months and 1,260 days are each used twice throughout Rev 11-13. The variations in John's accounting are not without rhyme or reason, but are purposeful and meaningful.[69]

Each time John uses the designation of forty-two months, he uses it to speak of the period of domination by either the nations or the beast (11.2; 13.5). These two periods of domination are not mutually exclusive, but are related in that the full and ultimate expression of the trampling of the Holy City by the nations is found in the eventual rise and reign of

---

[68] Beale, *Revelation*, 567.

[69] The following observations concerning John's use of 42 months and 1,260 days, although developed independently, are affirmed to some degree by Bauckham, *Climax*, 402.

the beast. It is during the time of trampling that the nations rage against God (Ps 2.1-3) and resist the testimony of his people. The church struggles against its archenemy, Satan, which John dramatically illustrates in 12.1-17, but the struggle will end with the triumph of God and his people through the one who will rule the nations with an iron rod (Rev 19.15; cf. 2.27; 12.8; Ps 2.9; *Pss. Sol.* 17.23-24).[70] This period of domination by the nations and conflict for the church corresponds, not to a final eschatological tribulation period, but to the church age. Both Luke 21.24 and Rom 11.25 indicate that this period of the Gentiles is that period of the church age inaugurated by the coming of the Messiah and completed at his return (cf. Rev 12.5-12 in this light as well). It is reasonable to propose, however, that this period may see an intensification of persecution just before the end as indicated in 11.7 and 13.5.

The vision of the two witnesses (11.3-13) bears out this interpretation. John has just reassured the Asian believers through his vision of the measuring of the temple that, although they are presently suffering, they have hope and security in their fellowship with God. This is the same message they received through the sealing of the 144,000 and the innumerable multitude. His message, however, remains a mixed one. Their spiritual protection is assured as they follow the Lamb, but there is also a call to perseverance, for Satan has been cast down and his fury will be felt (12.12) through the oppression from the ungodly and the rise of the beast (13.1-10).

This period of domination by the nations introduced in 11.2 becomes the springboard for John's next vision of the two witnesses. The heavenly voice tells John that the Holy City will be trampled for forty-two months, but "I will give my two witnesses authority to prophesy for 1,260 days wearing sackcloth" (11.3). This period of time during which the two witnesses are given prophetic authority corresponds to the forty-two months expressed in the previous sentence; it is the period of the church age and the domination of the nations. This period, however, will end with an intense time of persecution that is marked by the rise of the beast and the apparent defeat of the church (11.7-10; cf. 13.1-7). Why does John change his numeric designation of this very same three and one half year period? John's switch signals his change of subject matter. When he speaks of three and one half years from the perspective of God's people (i.e., the

---

[70] It should be noted that this idea of a conflict between the nations and God and his Messiah finds clear expression in Psalm 2, to which John makes reference. Psalm 2 is understood to be a messianic Psalm throughout the NT (Acts 13.33; Heb 1.5; 5.5; cf. Mark 1.11; Luke 3.22).

two witnesses), he uses the designation 1,260 days. This observation is confirmed by his use of 1,260 days once again in 12.6 for the period during which the woman is protected by God in the wilderness. This similar numeric designation for the period of the two witnesses and the woman suggests that these two symbols should be interpreted by a common referent, a subject that will be developed more below.

What, then, is the significance of using 1,260 days for the two witnesses and the woman of chapter 12? It is because John is recording the visions of 11.3-13 and 12.1-17 from the perspective of the community of God with which he closely identifies. This is the similar perspective of Daniel and a second reason for the use of 1,260 days (cf. Dan 12.11). Rather than repeating the designation of 1,260 days for a third time in 12.14, John uses for the first and only time in the Apocalypse the danielic expression "times, a time and a half time" (cf. Dan 7.25; 12.7). Since 12.14 is mainly a literary recapitulation of 12.6, the story having been interrupted by the battle and hymn of 12.7-12, John varies the formulaic expression, eliminating any doubt about his allusion to Daniel. Like Daniel, John is a prophet among and on behalf of his people (Rev 1.1, 9) who wishes to encourage God's suffering people of their eventual deliverance.

In 11.3-13 and 12.1-17, John is writing from the perspective of the believing community, and the main characters of these two visions have some connection to this community. At a minimum, they have a connection because they stand in opposition to the forces that oppose God, whether those forces are physical or metaphysical. These visionary characters also enjoy the protection of God, at least for a period of time, and ultimate victory with him. This latter statement is particularly true of the two witnesses of 11.3-13, but is also reflected to some degree in 12.1-17. The woman is "nourished" by God in the wilderness for 1,260 days and is protected from the onslaught of her enemy the dragon. What is not revealed in the vision of 12.1-17 is her ultimate deliverance, but this is certainly purposeful since this vision establishes the parameters of the eschatological struggle in the following chapters and lays the basis for the final judgment and victory to come.[71]

These two visions continue to portray John's dualistic worldview. It is the forces of good, allied with God and opposed by the forces of evil, allied with Satan who are exposed through the vision of 12.1-17. It is this latter vision that is often seen as the center of the Apocalypse because it encapsulates the theme of John's message throughout. The struggle between these

---

[71] Collins, *Combat Myth*, 29–31.

two forces is reflected not just in the heavenly sphere but also in the earthly one. This patterning of earthly existence upon heavenly reality is a commonly accepted ancient perspective[72] that helps John's hearers gain some understanding of their own struggle in their present reality. This is perhaps one of the reasons the visions of 11.3-13 and 12.1-17 so easily move between heaven and earth. The believing community on earth to whom John writes is an extension of God's heavenly community ([οἱ] οὐρανοὶ καὶ οἱ ἐν αὐτοῖς σκηνοῦντες, 12.12; τοὺς ἐν τῷ οὐρανῷ σκηνοῦντας, 13.6) and thus suffers the disdain that he also suffers (e.g., 11.10; 13.6). The nations of the world or the earth-dwellers (τοὶς κατοικοῦντας ἐπὶ τῆς γῆς, 8.13; 13.8) are under the judgment of God and follow the beast, who is the earthly personification of God's archenemy, Satan (6.12-17; 8.13; 9.20-21; 12.18—13.10; 16.9, 11, 21).

With this overarching perspective in mind, the task of identifying the key figures in these two visions becomes less cumbersome. The identity of the two witnesses in 11.3-13 has been a matter of considerable debate and there is no shortage of speculation as to whom these figures represent. Their identity hinges on one's interpretive approach. A literal interpretation anchors their identity in some historical personages, either past or future,[73] while a symbolical interpretation allows for an allegorical or thematic identity.[74]

The hermeneutical approach taken to understand the measuring of the temple was to interpret the imagery of that vision narrative as symbolic, and this approach seems best in the subsequent vision of the two witnesses. There are some clues within the vision narrative itself that may help to clarify the identity of these two witnesses. The voice speaking with

---

[72] Collins observes that the Jewish tabernacle and temple were both considered to be patterned after heavenly prototypes (cf. Heb 8.5), an idea that seems to be reflected in the Apocalypse (6.9; 7.15; 8.3; 9.13; 11.19; 15.5-8; 16.1); ibid., 135.

[73] So Walvoord, *Revelation*, 175. Ladd, *Revelation*, 154 and Osborne, *Revelation*, 418, take a middle position in that they interpret the possibility that two prophetic figures will appear during a final eschatological period, but they also see them as symbolic of the church's witness through the ages.

[74] A number of scholars interpret these two prophetic figures as the church that exercises its prophetic witness to the world either during the church age or during a final eschatological period. See Kiddle, *Revelation*, 180–83; Considine, "Two Witnesses," 386; Mounce, *Revelation*, 222–23; Bauckham, *Climax*, 273–74; Aune, *Revelation 6–16*, 598–603; Beale, *Revelation*, 572–73. These two witnesses have also been identified idealistically as the Law and the Prophets or the "word of God" and "the testimony of Jesus." See Kenneth Strand, "The Two Witnesses of Rev 11:3-12," *AUSS* 19 (1981) 134, who identifies them as the latter set with a possible secondary identity as the church.

John tells him that the two witnesses will be given authority to prophesy for 1,260 days (11.3). They are clad in sackcloth, which is a sign of humility before God and grieving over sin and the judgment to come.[75] In 11.4, the two witnesses are further identified as "the two olive trees and the two lampstands that stand before the Lord of all the earth." This is a clear allusion to the visionary experience of Zechariah in 4.1-14. In Zechariah's vision, the two olive trees are identified as "the two anointed ones who stand by the Lord of the whole earth" (4.14). They are Zerubbabel and Joshua who have political and religious authority in Israel. The golden lampstand, which has seven bowls that represent the seven all-seeing eyes of God (4.10), is the community of God that Zerubbabel and Joshua are responsible to rebuild, the focus of which is the temple of God.

John has borrowed this imagery and combined it in the symbol of the two witnesses. They are not only the two olive trees, but they are also the lampstand that stands before the Lord. John represents them not as a single lampstand, as in Zechariah, but as two lampstands in his vision. This maintains consistency in his representation of a dual witness.[76] What is significant is that these two prophets are represented as both the olive trees and the lampstand of Zechariah. This lends credence to their identification as a corporate symbol representing the entire community of God rather than two historical figures. As has been noted above, Zechariah's golden lampstand is described as having seven bowls that represent the all-seeing eyes of God. John similarly represents the churches of Asia as seven golden lampstands in the midst of which "one like the Son of Man" (1.13) stands. Although these seven lampstands represent seven historical churches in the Roman province of Asia, they also symbolize the corporate church to which the message of the Apocalypse is ultimately written. John's use of the number seven throughout the Apocalypse to denote completeness allows for this broader secondary interpretation.[77] The representation of the two witnesses as two lampstands provides symbolic consistency with the seven lampstands of chapter 1 and suggests that these two witnesses should be identified as another symbol of the corporate church.[78]

---

[75] Beale, *Revelation*, 576.

[76] This emphasis on a dual witness may be inspired by the Mosaic Law, which requires all truth to be validated by the testimony of two witnesses (Deut 17.6; 19.15).

[77] Bauckham, *Climax*, 273–74.

[78] Ibid.; Beale, *Revelation*, 574.

Additional observations can be made from the text that argue for the corporate identity of these two witnesses.[79] The language of 11.7 is revealing. Here John writes that when the two witnesses have finished their prophesying, they are overcome by the beast which "will make war on them and conquer them and kill them" (ποιήσει μετ' αὐτῶν πόλεμον καὶ νικήσει αὐτοὺς καὶ ἀποκτενεῖ αὐτούς). This is nearly identical language to 13.7a (cf. 12.17b) in which the beast is given authority "to make war on the saints and to conquer them" (ποιῆσαι πόλεμον μετὰ τῶν ἁγίων καὶ νικῆσαι αὐτούς). It would seem, then, that the language of 11.7 anticipates the visionary scene of 13.7a and reinforces the idea that these two witnesses represent the corporate people of God. In addition, the further descriptive phrase of 13.7b concerning the beast warrants observation. The beast is not only given power to make war on and overcome the saints, but he is also given authority over "every tribe and people and language and nation." These are the earth-dwellers (οἱ κατοικοῦντες ἐπὶ τῆς γῆς) who worship the beast (13.8). This is again the same language used to describe those who rejoice over the death of the two witnesses in 11.8-9. They are first described as "peoples and tribes and languages and nations," and second as earth-dwellers (οἱ κατοικοῦντες ἐπὶ τῆς γῆς). The same inclusive phrase that designated the redeemed of God, who are "from every tribe and language and people and nation" (5.9; cf. 7.9) has, since 10.11, become John's descriptor for the unredeemed, those "whose name has not been written in the book of life of the Lamb that has been slain from the foundation of the world" (13.8 translation mine; cf. 11.9; 13.7; 14.6; 17.15). It would seem, therefore, that the description of the beast in 13.1-10 is an expansion of the scene in 11.7-10 and that the images in the two visions may be interpreted in light of each other.

The movement of the vision from a local to an international venue also argues for the corporate identity of the two witnesses as the church. While it seems at first that John has localized their witness in 11.8, he remarks in 11.9 that it is "the peoples and tribes and languages and nations" who will view the dead bodies of the two witnesses that lie in the street of the city. In 11.10, these onlookers are further described as the "inhabitants of the earth" who rejoice over the demise of these two prophets because their witness had been "a torment to the inhabitants of the earth." The enlargement of the scene from a specific locality to an international setting argues that John wishes the scope of their witness and their downfall to be

---

[79] The following is an adaptation of a similar list in Beale, *Revelation*, 574–75.

understood globally, which would be logical if these witnesses represent a larger entity, such as the universal people of God.

The nature of their testimony and the unified attribution of power to both witnesses indicate that the symbolic focus of these two witnesses is on their corporate identity. Although the message that the two witnesses bear to the world is never actually delineated in the vision narrative, they are nevertheless called "my two witnesses" (τοῖς δυσὶν μάρτυσίν μου) and their ministry is termed prophetic. Beale correctly points out that the use of the term μάρτυς in the Apocalypse usually refers to those who bear testimony to Jesus (cf. 1.9; 2.13; 12.11, 17; 17.6).[80] These prophets, dressed in sackcloth, are intended to elicit an image of OT prophets who bear a message from God of both repentance and judgment. This is a calling and message in which the entire church participates throughout its tenure on earth.

The testimony that these two prophets bear is reinforced through a display of prophetic power. This power, however, is not to confirm their message but is specifically given to them in defense of the opposition from the world. The nature of their power is parsed out in some detail in the vision, with great acts of judgment being attributed to both witnesses. Fire comes from their mouths to consume any who might want to kill them; they have power to stop the rain, turn water into blood, or to bring plagues on the earth (11.5-6). All of these prophetic acts are judgments on those who refuse to receive their message. Each of these attributes can easily be traced back to the OT prophets, particularly Moses and Elijah. This detailing of the witnesses' prophetic powers has caused many to identify these prophets as Moses and Elijah *redivivus* or as other historical figures endued with similar powers.[81] This detailing of their prophetic power is not, however, for the purpose of limiting their identity to certain historical figures. These powers are never attributed to either of the witnesses individually but corporately, lending further strength to their common identity.[82] The description of their powers is, again, intended to invoke in John's hearers the idea that these witnesses stand in the tradition of God's

---

[80] Beale, *Revelation*, 572.

[81] Another popular alternative to Moses and Elijah is the identification of these two witnesses with Enoch and Elijah, since both of these figures appear to have never experienced death. On the expectation of the return of Enoch and Elijah, see e.g., *4 Ezra* 6.26; *Apoc. El.* (H) 4.7; 5.32; *Apoc. Pet.* (Eth.) 2. For an extensive listing of the historical personages suggested for the two witnesses of Rev 11.3-13 see Beale, *Revelation*, 572–73, n.293; cf. Considine, "Two Witnesses," 390–92; Prigent, *L'Apocalypse*, 270, n.31.

[82] So Strand, "Two Witnesses," 130–31.

OT prophets. Just as those prophets faced opposition from an idolatrous audience—whether it be Egypt, as in the case of Moses, or Israel, as in the case of Elijah—so those who bear the testimony of Jesus face similar opposition.

The emphasis in 11.3-13 is not on the content of the message that these two witnesses bear. It is understood that, as prophets of God, they bear God's message which, as observed above, can be assumed to be the testimony of Jesus. What receives greater emphasis is the fact that there is opposition to their message and that they are given divine protection in the face of that opposition. Their safety and the success of their witness are guaranteed for the symbolic period of 1,260 days, at the end of which their mission will be deemed complete (11.7a). At the end of this allotted time, they will appear to be defeated by the beast, but their ultimate victory is assured, as evidenced in their resurrection from the dead (11.7b-10). The vision of the two witnesses, therefore, is a symbolic presentation of the church's experience consistently portrayed throughout the Apocalypse. The saints bear the testimony of Jesus (1.2, 9; 12.17; 19.10) despite withering opposition, but their protection in the face of seeming defeat is guaranteed, as is ultimately expressed in their resurrection from the dead (11.11-12; cf. 20.1-6).

It is this scene of resurrection and vindication that provides a final argument for the corporate identity of the two witnesses as the church. John writes that the two witnesses lay in the street of the city for three and one half days, after which time the "breath of life from God entered them" (11.11) and they ascended "up to heaven in a cloud" in full view of their enemies (11.12). Although John opened the vision of the two witnesses with numerous allusions to the OT prophetic tradition, the vision concludes with allusions befitting the Christian tradition. Their resurrection and ascension "in a cloud" recalls Jesus' similar experience, as portrayed in the Acts account (1.9), and no doubt is a proleptic introduction to the vindication and resurrection of the saints more fully portrayed in 19.1—20.6. The two witnesses, therefore, are figures that unite two traditions, the Jewish prophetic tradition and the gospel tradition. John sees the union of these two traditions not only fulfilled in the church but also fulfilled in his own apocalyptic ministry, for John sees himself as a Christian prophet standing within the tradition of the Hebrew prophets.[83] This union of Jewish and Christian tradition displays the essence of John's perception of

---

[83] This is clear in a number of instances throughout the Apocalypse the most recent of which is scene in John's Ezekiel-like call of chapter 10 already discussed.

the church. It is subsumed in, and the full extension of, God's covenant people Israel; it is God's new spiritual Israel.

Thus the vision of the two witnesses is not a story concerning the fate of ethnic Israel or of literal eschatological prophets, but it is a microcosm of the church age from beginning to end. The church, like the two witnesses, has been given God's prophetic commission and power to witness to the nations who oppose this testimony. A time is coming when this opposition will reach its climax with the metaphorical rise of the beast (11.7), at which time the church will seem defeated (11.7-10). The church's vindication is assured, however, through the resurrection of the righteous and the judgment of the wicked (11.11-12). This vision, like 11.1-2, serves to assure the Asian saints of their certain victory in the face of present opposition. This was the message of John's first interlude, and it is equally the message of his second.

"The Great City": Jerusalem or Rome? (11.8)

With the corporate identity of the two witnesses established, the discussion must turn to one of the more difficult interpretive aspects of the vision narrative, and that is the identity of the city described in 11.8. When the testimony of the two witnesses is finished, John states that the beast arises out of the abyss and conquers and kills the two prophets (11.7). Upon their death, their bodies lie unburied for three and one half days in the "street of the great city which is spiritually (πνευματικῶς) called Sodom and Egypt, where also their Lord was crucified" (11.8 translation mine). The difficulty with this latter passage is determining what city, if any specific one, John has in mind. The opening description of this locale as "the great city" immediately evokes images of Babylon, metaphorical Rome, since this is consistently the description of Babylon throughout the Apocalypse (16.19; 17.18; 18.2, 10, 16, 18-19, 21). However, John's final description of this same locale as the place of the Lord's crucifixion indicates not Rome but Jerusalem.[84]

---

[84] Some scholars (Feuillet, *Apocalypse*, 61; Beagley, 'Sitz im Leben', 68; Osborne, *Revelation*, 426–27; cf. Beale, *Revelation*, 603–4) have also posited that 11.13 tilts the evidence in favor of identifying the city with earthly Jerusalem. John writes that a tenth of the city was destroyed by an earthquake at the time of the ascension of the two witnesses, and as a result of this disaster, 7,000 inhabitants lose their lives. If this is 10% of the population, then it has been observed that a population of 70,000 best fits first-century Jerusalem rather than Rome. While intriguing, this argument provides little support for identifying the city as Jerusalem. First, one would have to make the assumption that the destruction of a tenth of the city means that an equal percentage of the population died as well. This is an

Most scholars try to solve the issue by positing a compromise between these two alternatives. Many see here a primary reference either to Rome or to Jerusalem with a broader and more important metaphorical meaning as a city that encompasses all the evil and rebellion of the world against God.[85] Beale, who resists any definitive reference either to Rome or to earthly Jerusalem, postulates that the key to this problem is found in John's use of πνευματικῶς, which signals a figurative rather than a literal interpretation of the city. This adverb applies equally to Sodom and Egypt as well as the phrase "where also their Lord was crucified." Sodom and Egypt suggest persecution (Wis 19.14-17) and the seduction of God's people (Ezek 16.26, 44-57). Israel became like them (Amos 4.10-11) and was punished; so the world is like them and will be equally punished. The "world-city" is, therefore, spiritually like Jerusalem, which became ungodly and rejected the Messiah.[86]

Beale is correct to point out the significance of πνευματικῶς, and it would seem that this passage does lend itself ultimately to a figurative understanding of the city. This interpretation seems particularly warranted in light of the above argument for the corporate identity of the two witnesses as well as the fact that the subsequent verses (11.9-10) indicate that the venue is international rather than local.[87] This interpretation, however, must not undermine the significance of John's obtrusive reference to this city as the place "where also their Lord was crucified." Revelation 12.9 may lend support here by demonstrating that when John so chooses, he identifies important symbols through multiple descriptive phrases that are

---

inference not clear from the text. Second, numbers in the Apocalypse are usually symbolic rather than literal; therefore it seems possible that the number here is symbolic since 7,000 is a multiple of seven.

[85] Mounce, *Revelation*, 226–27, sees the city as Rome, with the reference to the crucifixion as indicative of the typical pagan response to righteousness. The martyrs, therefore, lie dead in the streets of a city that represents the world under the "oppressive sway of Antichrist." Marshall, *Parables of War*, 163–65, 172, who sees the context as the First Jewish Revolt, proposes that the city is Rome and that John condemns Rome for its rebellion against God and "surprisingly" for its crucifixion of Jesus "*in Rome*" (emphasis his). Hirschberg, *Das eschatologische Israel*, 218–19, believes that 11.8 is primarily a reference to Rome with a secondary allusion to Jerusalem. He similarly sees in 11.8 an inference to the Roman responsibility for the crucifixion of Jesus. Considine, "Two Witnesses," 388; Michaels, *Revelation*, 141–42; Bauckham, *Climax*, 172; Osborne, *Revelation*, 426–27, see the city as Jerusalem with a broader figurative reference to all the profane cities of the world.

[86] Beale, *Revelation*, 591–93. Cf. Kiddle, *Revelation*, 185–87; de Villiers, "The Lord was Crucified," 133–35, who eschew any historical reference to Rome or Jerusalem but opt, like Beale, for a broad metaphorical interpretation.

[87] So Kiddle, *Revelation*, 184; Beale, *Revelation*, 593–94.

intended to leave no doubt in his hearers' minds as to the identity of that image.

In 12.9, John describes the dragon as "that ancient serpent, who is called the Devil and Satan, the deceiver of the whole world." The dragon here is renamed with descriptors that leave no doubt as to its identity ending in an action phrase that describes its role on the cosmic stage. A similar pattern can be seen in 11.8 as the great city is first identified as Sodom, then Egypt, and finally as the place "where also their Lord was crucified"—a descriptive action phrase that describes its role on the cosmic stage. If John had simply referred to the city as "the great city," then his hearers may have likely identified this metropolis, so described later in the Apocalypse, as Babylon (i.e., Rome). However, John adds the additional relative clause in order to clarify the identity of this symbol, with the final descriptive phrase being the most definitive.

This analysis, then, argues that John had in mind earthly Jerusalem. This interpretation is further validated by the fact that the previous vision also takes place in or around the temple complex and finishes with a reference to the trampling of the Holy City for forty-two months by the nations. This last phrase of 11.2 sets the stage for the vision of 11.3-13 and helps to locate both visions at least figuratively in Palestine and more specifically in Jerusalem.[88] This is not to imply, however, that John wishes his readers to understand simply a reference here to earthly Jerusalem. This is preempted by the use of πνευματικῶς, and thus allows a broader interpretation in which the city also represents all that is ungodly in the world. There should be no interpretive struggle, therefore, over whether John intends to refer here to Babylon (Rome) or to Jerusalem. He intends to allude to both. What is significant is that he has allied earthly Jerusalem with the enemies of God. What was once holy is now profaned as is signified by the "casting out" of the outer court of the temple, the trampling of the Holy City (11.2), and the negative tripartite description of the "great city" in 11.8. While earthly Jerusalem may be profaned, heavenly Jerusalem, like the inner court of the temple, is secure in God's care and represents the redeemed people of God (Rev 21.9-10; cf. Gal 4.21-31).

The distinction between the portrayal of earthly Jerusalem and heavenly Jerusalem is an important one. Throughout the Apocalypse, with the exception of 11.1-13, John consistently describes the temple/tabernacle, the Holy City, and Jerusalem positively in association with God's throne and his dwelling (3.12; 6.9; 7.15; 11.19; 14.15, 17; 15.5-6, 8;

---

[88] So Aune, *Revelation 6–16*, 588.

16.1, 17; 21.1—22.5, 19). In 11.1-2 and 8 the temple, the Holy City, and Jerusalem are portrayed in a negative context and appear to be located on earth. While the temple is less negatively portrayed, being measured and thus protected, its outer court and the Holy City are cast out and trampled by the nations. This profaning of what was once godly begins to establish the context of the visions of 11.1-13. The disregard for godliness is a characteristic of God's enemies and comes to its climax in the blasphemies of the beast (13.1, 6-7). The contextualization of the opposition as being on earth serves to give to the Asian saints some explanation of their own suffering and furthers the apocalyptic dichotomy between the earthly as profane and the heavenly as holy.

What is of particular interest for the present study is the association in this context of Jerusalem with the enemies of God and his people. John's description of Jerusalem as "Sodom and Egypt, where their Lord was crucified," evokes the worst images of Israel's history from the Jewish prophets, as well as the gospel tradition, and arguably carries anti-Jewish overtones. The responsibility for the death of the Messiah becomes a major weapon in the anti-Jewish and anti-Semitic arsenal of later church tradition (e.g., Melito, *Peri Pascha* 55). Is it John's intention, however, to be anti-Jewish (i.e., to reject the Jews as the people of God)? Although later church tradition may have interpreted John in this manner, this is not likely John's intention. John never demonstrates in the Apocalypse overt hostility to or rejection of the Jewish traditions or scriptures. On the contrary, he makes extensive use of them. Indeed, it has been observed that even in his virulent condemnation of Jewish opposition in Smyrna and Philadelphia, he maintains the integrity of the appellation "Jew." Although John gives no clear indication of his stance on the fate of ethnic Israel, it would be difficult to envision him as anti-Jewish.[89]

This being acknowledged, one cannot overlook the overtly negative description of earthly Jerusalem in 11.8, which is no doubt intended to evoke a negative response in his recipients. John, who sees himself as an extension of the Jewish prophetic tradition (10.1—11.2), draws from this tradition images associated with rebellious Israel, Sodom and Egypt (e.g., Isa 1.9-10; Jer 9.26; 23.14; Ezek 16.26, 44-57; Amos 4.10-11). However, he does not stop here but, as a Christian prophet, extends the condemnation of Jerusalem as the place of the Lord's crucifixion, thus identifying himself with a deeply rooted gospel tradition. The identity of the city with

---

[89] Revelation 11.13 has been offered as a possible indication of Jewish repentance, but such a conclusion is unwarranted and would require the Jews to be the focal group of the vision—a conclusion that is not supported by the context (cf. 11.9-10).

the crucifixion of Christ leaves no doubt that he intends earthly Jerusalem and is a description catered to his Christian audience. In addition, the descriptor, "where *their* Lord was crucified" (emphasis mine), also serves to identify the two witnesses with the followers of Jesus, thus bolstering their identity as representatives of the church. Like their Lord, these two witnesses suffer the same fate in the same city and similarly enjoy a bodily resurrection and ascension into heaven. This association of the church's fate with that of their Lord's legitimizes the present suffering of the saints and reminds them that their future hope is also guaranteed through him (e.g., Matt 24.9; Mark 13.9; Luke 21.12; 2 Cor 1.5; 2 Tim 2.3, 12).

John's negative description of the city could easily be likened to his condemnation of the Jewish opposition in Smyrna and Philadelphia as a "synagogue of Satan" (2.9; 3.9).[90] In both instances, the Jewish opposition to God's people is characterized as being allied with God's enemies. They are cohorts of Satan, who is the ruler of the earthly realm (Revelation 12–13). John is not, however, rejecting outright all Jews or even Judaism as a religion. He is redrawing the parameters that designate the people of God. Faithfulness, not ethnicity, is the distinguishing mark of the people of God. Faithfulness implies keeping God's commandments and holding to the testimony of Jesus (1.2; 1.9; 12.17; 19.10). These are the "true Jews" who are the heirs of God's covenant promises and who will be part of God's new Jerusalem.

An Overview of the Vision of the Two Witnesses

John writes that the death of the witnesses is cause for rejoicing throughout the world, to the extent that the occasion is marked with the exchange of gifts (11.9-10), because these two prophets have been "a torment to the inhabitants of the earth" (11.10). The bodies of the two witnesses lie in the streets of the city for a period of three and one half days. The importance of this latter figure should not be overlooked since it likely has some symbolic correspondence to the three and one half years previously mentioned in 11.2-3. The difficulty lies in determining what exactly this symbolic correspondence is.

The answer can be found by considering the overall picture presented by the vision of 11.3-13. Taken as a whole, this vision is a microcosm of the church age from an apocalyptic perspective. It has been observed above

---

[90] This is not to suggest with Beagley, '*Sitz im Leben*', 28, however, that these passages (2.9; 3.9; 11.8) provide incontrovertible evidence that the Jews, as the enemy of the church, are the primary focus of the Apocalypse.

that when John speaks of the danielic three and one half years as the period of domination of the nations or of the beast, he uses the designation forty-two months (11.2; 13.5); however, he uses the figure 1,260 (11.3; 12.6; cf. 12.14) days to speak of the same period from the perspective of God's people. Therefore, the 1,260 days during which the witnesses prophesy corresponds to the forty-two months during which time the Gentiles trample the Holy City. These 1,260 days figuratively correspond to the church age that began with the completion of Jesus' messianic ministry (cf. 12.5-6). With the understanding that the two witnesses symbolize the believing community, then their prophetic ministry during this period corresponds to the church's call to bear the testimony of Jesus to the nations. This is a call similar to the commission John has already received in 10.11. The church is guaranteed, like the two witnesses, that it will be protected during this time and that its testimony will be completed (11.5-7a).

When the testimony of the church is finished, the beast will arise from the abyss to overcome and to destroy it (11.7; cf. 13.6). This eschatological period of time near the end of the church age is symbolized by the three and one half days in which the corpses of the two witnesses lie in the street of the "great city." John remains consistent in his use of the number three and one half because of its symbolic importance; however, he relates this figure in days rather than months to create a distinction between the forty-two months (or the 1,260) days previously referenced. This eschatological ordeal, during which the church appears to be defeated, is a limited time of tribulation that John proleptically introduces in 11.7-10 and develops in more detail beginning in 13.1. At the end of the three and one half days, however, the two witnesses rise from the dead and ascend into heaven in similar fashion as their Lord (11.11-12). They suffered the same fate as their Lord and will in turn share his victory. This part of the vision corresponds to material John will develop later in the Apocalypse and that is the victorious resurrection attained by believers as part of their vindication over Satan and his cohorts (19.1–22.7).[91]

In 11.13, the ultimate victory of the witnesses is marked by another extension of God's judgment through an earthquake in which a tenth of the city is destroyed. Seven thousand lose their lives while the rest of the earth-dwellers give glory to God. This reaction from the inhabitants of the earth is unprecedented in the Apocalypse and has been seen by some as indicative of a conversion experience. Bauckham believes that this verse speaks of the conversion of the nations in response to the prophetic wit-

---

[91] See Prigent, *L'Apocalypse*, 273, 276; cf. Considine, "Two Witnesses," 389.

ness of the church.[92] Even though the preaching of the witnesses seems to be accompanied by acts of judgment, he believes this is not primarily their message, but it is rather a call to repentance. So far in the Apocalypse, judgment has failed to elicit a positive response from the earth-dwellers (9.20-21), but the result of the church's witness and its vindication will yield a positive result (11.13).

There is, however, some debate as to whether this passage actually describes a conversion experience. John simply says that those who survive the earthquake "become terrified" (ἔμφοβοι ἐγένοντο) and "give glory to the God of heaven." Whether this is a conversion experience or simply a fear-induced acknowledgment of the sovereignty of God is difficult to say. The fact that this response is unique in the Apocalypse gives it significance but does not provide an answer to this overarching question. Beale suggests that this is a similar response and may even be an allusion to Nebuchadnezzar's acknowledgment of the God of Daniel as sovereign over the "inhabitants of the earth" (οἱ κατοικοῦντες τὴν γῆν; Dan 4.35 LXX Theod; cf. 2.46-47; 4.34). If so, then Beale argues that 11.13 may not be a reference to a true conversion. Even after Nebuchadnezzar's acknowledgment of God, he is still portrayed in chapter 3 as forcing others to worship idols and in chapter 5 his son is equally still an idolater.[93]

The allusion to Daniel is uncertain and the debate highlights the difficulty inherent in the interpretation of this passage. Bauckham's argument that this represents a conversion of the nations is somewhat persuasive, but not completely convincing. It is not clear whether the terror experienced by those who have witnessed not only the vindication of the witnesses but also the earthquake judgment should be interpreted as godly fear. While it is true that their secondary response is to give glory to God, this may simply imply that the ultimate victory of the church will finally result in the recognition of the sovereignty of God and the Lamb (cf. Phil 2.6-11) hitherto denied by the inhabitants of the earth (9.20-21; cf., 16.9, 11, 21).

The Purpose of the Trumpet Interlude

With the close of the vision narrative of 11.3-13 comes the close of the trumpet interlude and the announcement that "the second woe has passed" and that "the third woe is coming very soon" (11.14). John, therefore, has paused near the end of the sevenfold trumpet cycle to relate three distinct but not unrelated visions. In the first act of the interlude, John receives

---

[92] Bauckham, *Climax*, 278; cf. Considine, "Two Witnesses," 392.
[93] Beale, *Revelation*, 603–4.

a recommissioning to prophesy to the nations. This Ezekiel-like commissioning is a prelude to the next vision in which John is told again in Ezekiel-like fashion to rise up and measure the temple. The vision of 11.1-2 is linked to the commissioning vision by the same heavenly voice(s)[94] that instructs John throughout. This voice continues to speak in 11.3, and thus links the final vision of the interlude to the previous one. The visions of 11.1-2 and 3-14 are not only linked by the same divine messenger but also through common purpose. Both visions address issues related to the apocalyptic three and one half year period during which time the people of God must exercise their prophetic call in the face of international opposition. Second, they both promise protection to the people of God through the symbolic act of measuring and the prophetic power of the two witnesses. This promise of protection is a message that John reiterates from the chapter 7 interlude and reveals a shared purpose behind these two interludes.

Both interludes communicate an important message to the church just before the end. It is a message of protection and promised victory, but not a promise of exemption from persecution. The church will be protected spiritually, though it will suffer physically, but in the end it will be vindicated. This is the threefold message of both chapters 7 and 11. In addition, the trumpet interlude focuses particularly on the church's role during the time of domination by the nations. This focus on the church's ministry to the world has led some scholars to posit that the second interlude complements the first by completing its message.[95] The vision of the two witnesses of 11.3-13 provides this ministry focus, but the tone of the entire interlude is set by John's recommissioning in the opening half of the interlude. John's call to prophetic witness to the nations seems to be played out in the ministry of the two witnesses. John's call is also the call of the church, and the two are linked as members of the community of faith. The purpose of the second interlude, therefore, is to communicate an end-time message to the church. The message is not only a promise of protection and ultimate triumph but it is also indirectly a call to faithful perseverance through bearing the testimony of Jesus before the nations.

---

[94] The heavenly voice that first speaks to John in 10.4 becomes plural in 10.11 and once again singular in 11.3.

[95] Kiddle, *Revelation*, 167; Considine, "Two Witnesses," 379.

The Woman Clothed in the Sun (12.1-17)

In 11.15-19, the seventh angel sounds the seventh trumpet and the victory of God and his people is announced. In this manner, the sevenfold cycle of trumpet visions is concluded and John's visionary material moves to a new vision sequence in 12.1. The shift in vision sequence is signaled by John's introductory formula, καὶ σημεῖον μέγα ὤφθη ἐν τῷ οὐρανῷ. Collins sees in the introduction of the vision of 12.1-17 a major shift in the apocalyptic material. This division fits neatly into her structural analysis of the Apocalypse, which she divides into a sevenfold series of visions.[96] Hence the vision of chapter 12 begins a new cycle of what she calls seven unnumbered visions.

There is, however, some debate as to whether a major structural division in the text should be acknowledged here at 12.1. Prigent does not see a structural break because of what he observes as a continuous thematic flow between chapters 11 and 12. He argues that the themes of chapter 12 build upon those of chapter 11. The vision of the two witnesses symbolizes, for example, the ministry of the church and the proclamation of the kingdom of God against which the beast inspired by Satan fights. This beast, which is introduced in 11.7, is expounded upon in chapter 13 while chapter 12 elucidates the cosmic power behind the beast.[97]

Prigent's thematic analysis is valid but does not necessarily preclude a structural division at 12.1. As has already been observed, the visions of chapters 12 and 13 are clearly connected to the preceding material of chapter 11 in that all of this vision material deals in some way with the apocalyptic time period of three and one half years.[98] In addition, the measuring of the temple, the two witnesses, and, as will be argued below, the heavenly woman of chapter 12 all share a common symbolic referent—the church. Collins does not deny this continuity, but incorporates it into her structural outline, calling it "the technique of interlocking" by which John overlaps material in the Apocalypse.[99] Thus in the case of the trumpet interlude, the open scroll of chapter 10 looks back to the sealed scroll of chapter 5 while the recommissioning of 10.11 and the proleptic

---

[96] Collins, *Combat Myth*, 19. See Bauckham, *Climax*, 15–16, 21–22, who also sees here a "fresh start" in the literary structure of the Apocalypse.

[97] Prigent, *L'Apocalypse*, 283–84.

[98] So also Prigent, *L'Apocalypse*, 283.

[99] Collins, *Combat Myth*, 16. See Beale, *Revelation*, 112–14, and his review of this theory of interlocking. Cf. Bauckham, *Climax*, 2–29, who also sees an interlocking of John's visionary material.

introduction of the beast in 11.7 anticipates the material of chapters 12 and 13.[100]

Collins, following Farrer, observes that the usual indication for a visionary shift in the Apocalypse is the use of either εἶδον or ὤφθη.[101] This terminology, along with the often recognized division of the book into series of sevens, is used to form the structural plan of the book.[102] Of course, opinion varies as much on the structure of the book as the literary markers that delineate that structure. For example, the appearance of ὤφθη in 11.19 might suggest a structural division here instead of at 12.1.[103] Bauckham makes similar observations about the use of καὶ εἶδον as a structural marker, concluding that this introductory phrase alone fails to lead to a legitimate structural analysis.[104]

As can be observed from this brief survey, a consensus on the structural division of the Apocalypse has not yet been found. This disagreement, however, does not prevent a successful attempt at interpreting the text. While there does appear to be an important structural shift at 12.1, it is far more important to observe that the material that precedes and follows this structural break maintains thematic unity throughout. It is this thematic unity that will be the focus of the following discussion and that will provide a basis for interpreting John's vision of Revelation 12.

Source Material (12.1-17)

The source critical analysis of Revelation 12 can be divided essentially into two camps, with some scholars arguing for significant parallels to pagan mythology and others arguing for closer allusions to the OT. Most scholars, who argue for a mythological background, do not believe that John is borrowing directly from pagan sources, but that the material he uses has passed to him through Jewish tradition.[105] The more conservative ap-

---

[100] Collins, *Combat Myth*, 27–28.

[101] Collins also uses these introductory formulae in her division of 12.1—15.1 (ibid., 14). Cf. Beale, *Revelation*, 621, who uses both καὶ εἶδον and καὶ ἰδού as structural markers to divide 12.1—15.4, like Collins, into seven visions.

[102] Collins, *Combat Myth*, 13.

[103] As Prigent, *L'Apocalypse*, 283, notes in citing André and Allo. Stevenson, *Power and Place*, 263, suggests that 11.19 is a transition verse that concludes chapter 11 but also introduces chapter 12.

[104] Bauckham, *Climax*, 5–6, 17–18.

[105] So Beckwith, *Apocalypse*, 613–15; Charles, *Revelation*, 1:300–14; Kraft, *Offenbarung*, 164; Collins, *Combat Myth*, 101, 104–7; Aune, *Revelation 6–16*, 680–81, 712–13; Paul, "Use of the Old Testament," 269–73.

proach, as Le Frois terms it,[106] argues that the primary source of Revelation 12 is Jewish literature, in particular the OT.[107] These scholars do not completely deny parallels to pagan combat mythology, but view John's own Judeo-Christian perspective as overwhelming more influential.

The study of the Greco-Roman parallels to the vision of Revelation 12 is fascinating and should not be overlooked. Collins's influential work in this area investigates the relationship between Revelation 12 and the combat myths of other cultures (e.g., Greek, Egyptian, Ugaritic, and Hittite) and concludes that the story expressed through the vision of chapter 12 finds its closest parallel in the myth of the birth of Apollo or the Python–Leto–Apollo myth.[108] In the Python–Leto–Apollo myth, Leto has been impregnated by Zeus and is about to give birth to their child, Apollo. Python, the dragon, tries to destroy Apollo, but Zeus, through the use of the north wind, and Poseidon come to her aid. Apollo is born, defeats Python, and establishes the Pythian Games.

The parallels with the story line of Revelation 12 are readily apparent. A woman, who is portrayed in goddess like fashion, is about to give birth while a dragon waits to destroy her child. The child, who appears to be of divine progeny (12.5), is rescued from the dragon through his immediate ascension into heaven. The woman is pursued by the dragon, but she is protected by God with the aid of the earth (12.16). The dragon, unlike that of the Python–Leto–Apollo myth, is not defeated by the divine child himself, but rather by the angelic warrior, Michael (12.7-9). One might argue, however, that Michael's victory is directly the result of the influence of the child himself as is stipulated in the subsequent celebratory hymn (12.10-11).[109]

---

[106] Bernard J. Le Frois, *The Woman Clothed with the Sun (Ap 12): Individual or Collective: An Exegetical Study* (Rome: Orbis Catholicus, 1954) 1–3.

[107] So J. Edgar Bruns, "The Contrasted Women of Apocalypse 12 and 17," *CBQ* 26 (1964) 459–63; Beale, *Revelation*, 634–35; Prigent, *L'Apocalypse*, 285, 287–88; Osborne, *Revelation*, 456–60.

[108] See her comparative analysis; Collins, *Combat Myth*, 66–67.

[109] It is unnecessary to see any difficulty in Michael defeating the dragon rather than God or his Messiah. Michael is portrayed throughout Jewish literature as the protector of God's people (*1 En.* 20.5; *As. Mos.* 10.1-2; *T. Levi* 5.7; cf. 1QM 9.14-15; 13.10-13; 17.6-8) and is particularly featured in Daniel (10.13, 21; 12.1), a book well represented not only in this vision sequence but throughout the Apocalypse. See the discussion in Beale, *Revelation*, 651–54. Osborne, *Revelation*, 469, suggests that Michael, rather than a divine figure, is seen fighting not only because of Jewish precedent but also because of the lack of equality between Satan and God throughout the Apocalypse.

In addition to these storyline parallels, Collins equally observes similarities between the description of the heavenly woman and contemporary pagan goddesses. The woman of Revelation 12 is clothed in the sun with the moon at her feet and crowned with twelve stars. Contemporary coinage has been discovered with Artemis of the Ephesians depicted in similar fashion with the crescent moon and stars. In addition, Collins has suggested that the crown of twelve stars in Rev 12.1 may be a reference to the twelve signs of the zodiac.[110] She acknowledges, however, that the association of the entire zodiac with a god or goddess was fairly rare in the Greco-Roman world. Usually the zodiac was associated with a male "high-God such as Zeus, Zeus-Jupiter, Helios, or Sarapis-Zeus." She does, however, note that "the zodiac was a standard part of the iconography of the Ephesian Artemis."[111] She also finds similarities with the goddesses Atargatis and Isis, the latter of which becomes Collins choice for the closest parallel to the woman of Revelation 12. Thus she sees a combined parallel to Isis and the Python–Leto–Apollo myth.

Collins's analysis does not end here, but she continues to hypothesize that the combat myth has likely passed into Jewish tradition and from there to the redactor of the Apocalypse.[112] Charles argues in some detail from his own unique perspective for a similar conclusion.[113] He too believes that the original source of the vision is neither Jewish nor Christian but is found in pagan mythology. The storyline, however, has not come to John directly from pagan sources but has been shaped by Jewish tradition. Charles is quite specific in his analysis, suggesting that there are two Semitic sources (oral or written) behind Revelation 12. Revelation 12.1-5 and 13-17ab are likely of pagan mythic origin but were adapted by a Pharisaic Jew about 67–69 CE. Revelation 12.14-16 are now meaningless in the present context but originally referred to the flight of the Pharisees into the wilderness, while the elite stayed in the temple and suffered the consequences of the Roman siege.[114] He further surmises that Rev 12.7-10, 12 are probably borrowed from an original Jewish source and that

---

[110] Collins, *Combat Myth*, 71–72; cf. Aune, *Revelation 6–16*, 681; Malina and Pilch, *Revelation*, 155–56. Charles, *Revelation*, 1:315–16, and Beckwith, *Apocalypse*, 622–23, believe that the stars represent the signs of the zodiac but do allow in the context of the Apocalypse that the stars may represent the twelve tribes of Israel (Gen 37.9).

[111] Collins, *Combat Myth*, 71–72.

[112] Ibid., 101, 104–7.

[113] Charles, *Revelation*, 1:299–300.

[114] Ibid., 1:310.

John's adaptation of the entire material for his purposes is evident in 12.3, 5, 9-10, and 17c.[115]

Charles' rather fragmentary analysis of Revelation 12 is based largely on conjecture, especially since there are no extant oral or written sources to verify his hypothesis. Beale, who acknowledges that Revelation 12 has a certain affinity with pagan myth, argues for a stronger dependence on OT imagery.[116] He believes that at most the OT, especially Daniel, may be a filter through which pagan mythology has passed, but he writes, "John stands in the tradition of Christ and of the OT and interprets everything through those two lenses."[117] He sees John doing what he typically does, using OT imagery to express NT ideas.[118] The purpose of this "combat myth" is to show that the church's ultimate struggle is not with flesh and blood but with Satan himself. Beale sees Revelation 12 as a replay of the exodus motif in which Rome is now the one who pursues God's new Israel (cf. *Sib. Or.* 8.88).[119]

A number of noticeable parallels can be observed between Revelation 12 and several OT passages including Israel's exodus (Gen 3.15, 16a; 37.9; Exod 19.4; Deut 32.11; Ps 2.9; Isa 14.12-15; 26.18 LXX; 27.1; 7.14; 51.2-3, 9-11; 66.7 LXX; Mic 4-5). The imagery of the sun, moon, and twelve stars is frequently associated with Gen 37.9 (cf. Cant 6.10; *T. Naph.* 5.1-5; *Midr. Rab.* Num 2.13), in connection with the woman's role as representative of the people of Israel. In Isa 66.7-8 (cf. Gal 4.26; *4 Ezra* 10), Zion, like the heavenly woman of Revelation 12, is in travail and gives birth to a son, who represents the eschatological people of God.[120] The enmity between the dragon and the woman's offspring is often traced to Gen 3.15,[121] and the description of her son as one "who will rule the nations with an iron rod" is a certain reference to Ps 2.9 (cf. *Pss. Sol.* 17.23-24). The casting down of the dragon or Satan from heaven finds Jewish precedent in Isa 14.12-15 as well as in Jewish apocalyptic works (*1 En.* 6–11,

---

[115] Ibid., 1:307, 309.

[116] Beale, *Revelation*, 624, 634–35.

[117] Ibid., 635.

[118] Ibid., 623–24.

[119] Ibid., 633.

[120] Ibid., 629.

[121] Raymond E. Brown, et al., eds., *Mary in the New Testament: A Collaborative Assessment by Protestant and Roman Catholic Scholars* (Philadelphia: Fortress, 1978) 230, n.501, observe that the same description of the dragon is given in both Rev 12.9 and 20.2, suggesting that this description is a deliberate creation of the author to assure the connection with Gen 3.15 (cf. 2 Cor 11.3; Rom 16.20) as opposed to pagan mythology.

86; *2 En.* 29.4-5 [the longer version may be a Christian interpolation]; *Sib. Or.* 5.528-29; cf. Luke 10.18).[122]

The parallels between Revelation 12 and Israel's exodus or wilderness wanderings are numerous. Prigent observes similarities between OT descriptions of Pharaoh and that of the dragon in Revelation 12 (Isa 5.9; Ezek 29.3; 32.2). In addition, the flood water that the dragon spews forth against the woman (Rev 12.15) mimics the pursuit of the Israelites by the Egyptians (Exod 14.5-9), who themselves were swallowed up by the earth (Exod 15.12).[123] The nourishment of the woman for 1,260 days, and her flight into the wilderness on eagle's wings (Rev 12.14), invokes images of God's care for Israel in the wilderness as he "bore [her] on eagle's wings and brought [her] to himself" (Exod 19.4; cf. Deut 32.11).[124] Beale also finds "striking" the similarities between Revelation 12 and Isa 51.2-3 and 9-11 in which Israel's history is retold in poetic format. The passage speaks of Sarah, as the matriarch of Israel, giving birth "in pain" (ὠδίνουσιν; Isa 51.2 LXX; cf. Isa 66.7 LXX; Rev 12.2) and of God's promise to comfort Zion in "her waste (desert) places" (51.3). The passage also recalls the exodus when God "cut Rahab in pieces" and "pierced the dragon" (Isa 51.9; cf. Ps 74.13-14).[125] Beale believes that the parallels here are so convincing that John must have had this passage somewhere in mind when writing Revelation 12.[126]

One other Jewish parallel, often cited as a possible background source for John's heavenly vision, comes from the Dead Sea Scrolls. 1QH 3.6-18 tells a somewhat similar story as Revelation 12 of a woman who, "amid the pains of Hell," gives birth to a male child called "a Marvellous Mighty Counsellor" (Vermes). The similarities with Revelation 12 are noticeable but limited. Both accounts speak of a woman in child-birth who, through great pain, gives birth to a male child of messianic significance. The similarities, however, end with these general parallels. Finding further correspondence is complicated by a lack of consensus on the interpretation of the text and support for its relevance to the study of Revelation 12.[127]

---

[122] Osborne, *Revelation*, 468–69.

[123] Prigent, *L'Apocalypse*, 287–88.

[124] Beale, *Revelation*, 669–70; Brown, et al., *Mary in the New Testament*, 231; Collins, *Combat Myth*, 120–22. Osborne, *Revelation*, 482, cites these passages as well and further suggests that this kind of rescue may have become a standard motif in Judaism (*1 En.* 96.2; *As. Mos.* 10.8; cf. Isa 40.31).

[125] So also Osborne, *Revelation*, 482.

[126] Beale, *Revelation*, 631.

[127] See Collins, *Combat Myth*, 67–70, for an analysis of this text, against its use as back-

Regardless of one's perspective on the background material for Revelation 12, there seems to be at least one point of agreement among scholars and that is that John has adapted this material for his own Christian purpose. This observation brings the discussion full circle to the comments made earlier concerning the use of sources in interpreting the Apocalypse.[128] In that discussion, the hermeneutical approach suggested was to give interpretive primacy to John's use of symbols within the Apocalypse, with his socio-cultural background providing a secondary resource. Of course, in considering the influence of John's socio-cultural background, it seems proper to give emphasis to his Jewish tradition, particularly the literary allusions to extant Jewish literature. This was the approach taken to the interpretation of the visionary material of the trumpet interlude, and this seems to be a right approach to the visionary material of Revelation 12.

John's cultural background does play a certain role in his choice of images and story line for his material in the Apocalypse. While there may be some similarities to pagan mythology, John's handling of the material is likely not influenced by this association. As Beale and Prigent question, why would John use pagan mythology in a work that has a clear polemic against idolatry?[129] The vision of Revelation 12 clearly portrays the classic struggle between good and evil that is a part of John's Jewish heritage and need not find its origin in pagan mythology. *The War Scroll* found at Qumran is an example of this dualistic apocalyptic thinking that also found a home among the early believers in Jesus.[130] John is a Christian Jew who draws upon his Jewish heritage to understand his present world.[131] The primary source for his imagery and thought can be solidly located in Jewish literature and in particular the OT.[132]

While it is true that John is also located within a Greco-Roman world and is writing to churches that are probably predominantly Gentile,

---

ground material for Revelation 12. She also analyzes another text, *Apoc. Adam* 78.6-26, which has also been suggested as a Jewish source text. Cf. Prigent, *L'Apocalypse*, 285, who notes the similarities between 1QH 3.6-18 and Revelation 12, but does not believe this text is a background source for John.

[128] See above "A Hermeneutic of Sources," 117–19.

[129] Beale, *Revelation*, 634; Prigent, *L'Apocalypse*, 285.

[130] This contrast between light and darkness can be found in the Gospel of John, 1 John, and the Pauline epistles (e.g., Rom 2.19; 13.12; 1 Cor 4.5; 2 Cor 4.6; 6.14; Eph 5.8; 1 Thess 5.5).

[131] Paul, "Use of the Old Testament," 273–74.

[132] So Bruns, "Contrasted Women," 460; Beale, *Revelation*, 635; Prigent, *L'Apocalypse*, 285; Osborne, *Revelation*, 456.

one need not argue that this aspect of his culture plays a dominant role throughout the Apocalypse or more specifically in Revelation 12. Collins offers John's apparent use of the Nero *redivivus* myth in chapter 13 and its seeming dominance in the "eschatological schema" of the Apocalypse as justification for his use of pagan mythology in the vision of chapter 12.[133] The weakness of this argument, however, seems to lie in the difference between the Nero *redivivus* myth and pagan religious mythology. The Nero *redivivus* myth did not develop out of the deeply rooted religious traditions of the ancient world, but it was a late first-century legend that likely erupted out of a fear of the return of one of the more diabolical Roman emperors.

In addition, there seems to be a difference between the literary purposes of chapters 12 and 13. Chapter 12 begins in heaven but ends on earth, which helps to elucidate John's desire to reveal the cosmic forces behind present earthly realities. At the end of chapter 12, the dragon is standing on the shore of the sea from which arises the seven-headed beast who will become his earthly emissary. Chapter 12 unveils the cosmic battle between good and evil that is the impetus behind the earthly struggles of God's people. It is God who has won this battle through his Messiah, and this victory is the determining factor in the outcome to be portrayed in the rest of the Apocalypse. This victory, which is already a reality in heaven, will now become an earthly reality. God's people figure prominently in this battle, and it would seem unlikely that John would rely on pagan mythology rather than his own Jewish heritage to communicate this message.

Chapter 13 develops the earthly counterpart to this battle by symbolic allusions to the imperial cult and possibly the Nero *redivivus* myth. The predominance of the imperial cult in Asia made the use of these images particularly poignant to communicate the reality the churches of Asia were facing. Yet, even after acknowledging these allusions, a close inspection of the images of chapter 13, particularly the seven-headed beast, returns the interpreter to OT sources, in particular the book of Daniel. The Jewish imagery and OT allusions found throughout the Apocalypse clearly predominate and this is no less true of the vision in Revelation 12.

The Identity of the Woman of Revelation 12

With the establishment of some hermeneutical parameters, the discussion can now focus on the major interpretive question of chapter 12 for this study: Who or what does the woman of Revelation 12 symbolize? A his-

---

[133] Collins, *Combat Myth*, 187.

torical overview of the exegesis of Revelation 12 reveals no consensus on the woman's identity and this lack of consensus continues among modern commentators.[134] Le Frois identifies three lines of interpretation that seem to emerge as early as the third century: the woman is identified as the church, as the people of God of both the Old and New Testaments, or as Mary the mother of Jesus.[135] He further states that a combination of the first and third interpretations is known as early as the fifth century but may be earlier.[136] These three historical views are still the predominant interpretations among modern scholars, but to these three might be added a fourth view, the woman as representative of Israel.[137]

The view that has gained the majority of support is what is sometimes called the "collective view," which interprets the woman as the people of God of both the Old and New Testaments.[138] This view combines the interpretations of the woman as the church and Israel into a single view. The collective view offers the most advantageous interpretation not only because it provides a cogent explanation of the seemingly contradictory description of the woman, but more important it is the view most consistent with John's own perception of unbroken continuity between the old and new covenant people of God. Before discussing this majority view, however, it would be helpful to work through the other major interpretations to gain some sense of their value as well as the intrinsic difficulties inherent in attempting to find a solution to the identity of the woman of Revelation 12.

The identification of the woman as Mary the mother of Jesus is a predominantly Roman Catholic interpretation. This view suits best the opening section of chapter 12 (12.1-6), since the woman is portrayed as pregnant and giving birth to a male child "who is to rule all the nations with a rod of iron" (12.5). This latter description is almost unanimously interpreted as a messianic reference (Ps 2.9; cf. *Pss. Sol.* 17.23-24), and

---

[134] For a historical overview of the first eight centuries of exegesis see Le Frois, *Woman Clothed*, 11–61; cf. Pierre Prigent, *Apocalypse 12: Histoire de l'exégèse,* BGBE 2 (Tübingen: Mohr/Siebeck, 1959).

[135] Le Frois, *Woman Clothed*, 11.

[136] Le Frois adopts this combined interpretation based on his exegesis of the passage (ibid., 255).

[137] So Collins, *Combat Myth*, 134; Walvoord, *Revelation*, 188.

[138] So Beckwith, *Apocalypse*, 616; Charles, *Revelation*, 1:315; Feuillet, *Apocalypse*, 115; Bruns, "Contrasted Women," 459; Kraft, *Offenbarung*, 163, 171; Mounce, *Revelation*, 236; Beale, *Revelation*, 628–31; Prigent, *L'Apocalypse*, 292–93; Craig R. Koester, *Revelation and the End of All Things* (Grand Rapids: Eerdmans, 2001) 118, 123–24; Osborne, *Revelation*, 456.

thus the child is identified in this Christian document with Jesus.[139] The difficulty with this Marian interpretation, however, is that it seems too focused to fit well with the entire context of the vision.[140]

In 12.13-17, the story of the woman is briefly summarized and resumed after a brief interlude in 12.7-12. The woman, who flees to the desert for "a time, and times and half time" (12.14), is pursued by the dragon who attempts to destroy her; however, she is rescued by miraculous intervention. Frustrated, the dragon turns "to make war on the rest of her children, those who keep the commandments of God and hold the testimony of Jesus" (12.17). The obvious problem that arises at this juncture is explaining why the dragon continues to persecute the woman even after the birth of her male child.[141] It does not seem historically or even metaphorically accurate to postulate such a considerable interest on the part of Satan in the persecution or death of Mary. In addition, "the rest of her children" are clearly identified with the Jesus community, which further complicates the Marian identity of the woman. The symbolism and message of the vision seem to demand that the woman be interpreted more broadly as a group rather than an individual. Some Catholic scholars have recognized this inherent difficulty and have proposed a solution.

Le Frois says that many Roman Catholic scholars have recognized that John is speaking here in some way of the church but that he chooses to represent the church through a symbol with Marian features. Therefore, Mary is seen as integral to the symbolism of the vision, even if this interpretation is secondary. This view of Mary as symbolically embodying the church, Le Frois says, has historical roots in the Western church (e.g., Augustine),[142] and it is the interpretation for which he argues when he writes, "Mary is the Ideal Realization of the People of God, the perfect Church."[143] Therefore, Revelation 12 is a "vision of Mary as the Church, in whom is embodied all that is truly Israelitic, in whom the role of Mother of Christ coincides."[144]

Many scholars, who hold other interpretive positions, recognize to varying degrees the possibility that the woman could be identified with

---

[139] So Beckwith, *Apocalypse*, 615–16; Charles, *Revelation*, 1:320; Walvoord, *Revelation*, 189–90; Aune, *Revelation 6–16*, 688; Beale, *Revelation*, 639; Prigent, *L'Apocalypse*, 284; Osborne, *Revelation*, 462.

[140] So also Osborne, *Revelation*, 457.

[141] So Collins, *Combat Myth*, 105–6.

[142] Le Frois, *Woman Clothed*, 58–61.

[143] Ibid., 255.

[144] Ibid., 269.

Mary. However, they usually relegate such an interpretation to a secondary position, indeed often to a position of little importance.[145] It should be observed that the features in common between the woman of Revelation 12 and Mary are quite limited. Outside of the fact that the two are women who give birth to a messianic child, they have little in common. The woman of Revelation 12 is clothed in the sun with the moon at her feet and wears a crown of twelve stars. While some scholars have suggested that these stars represent the signs of the zodiac,[146] they are in this context likely indicative of the collective people of God, particularly in view of John's use of twelve and its multiples throughout the Apocalypse to symbolize the people of God (e.g., 144,000; new Jerusalem).[147] In addition, the fact that she continues to be the object of Satan's pursuit after the birth of her child and her close identity with those "who hold the testimony of Jesus" (12.14) implies a wider interpretation than that of Mary. As John describes, she is a heavenly portent, and she should be interpreted within the context of the vision as a symbol with broad meaning.

The portrayal of the woman as the mother of the Messiah might suggest her identity as Israel. Indeed, her flight into the wilderness and her nourishment and protection there recall Israel's exodus from Egypt. Walvoord argues that the woman is earthly Israel who is experiencing an eschatological persecution from which the church has already been delivered.[148] Collins also sees the woman as Israel, but from a clearly different perspective.[149] She believes that the woman is heavenly Israel, the background of which comes from the OT where Israel is often portrayed as the wife of God (Hos 1.2; 2.4-5; Isa 50.1; 54.5-8). John has borrowed this imagery and "intensified this metaphor," portraying the woman as the "Queen of Heaven." She finds support for this view in "the ancient idea that all earthly entities have heavenly prototypes" (e.g., the tabernacle),

---

[145] So Bruns, "Contrasted Women," 459–60; Brown, et al., *Mary in the New Testament*, 239; Aune, *Revelation 6–16*, 712; Koester, *Revelation*, 118, 123–24; Beale, *Revelation*, 628–29; Osborne, *Revelation*, 457.

[146] See above, 148, n. 110.

[147] So Beale, *Revelation*, 625–27; Roloff, *Revelation*, 145; Kraft, *Offenbarung*, 164. Beale cites a number of OT and Rabbinic texts that associate the symbols of the sun, moon, and stars with Abraham, Isaac, Jacob, and their seed. Josephus (*Ant.* 3.164-72, 179-87) and Philo (*Mos.* 2.111-12, 12-24; *Spec.* 1.84-95) also make the correlation between the heavenly bodies and the twelve tribes of Israel. Thus it is possible to suggest that John uses this imagery to symbolize the people of God of both the OT and the NT, which is consistent with his pattern of using Jewish imagery for the church.

[148] Walvoord, *Revelation*, 188, 194–96.

[149] Collins, *Combat Myth*, 134.

an idea which she finds common in Jewish apocalyptic literature.[150] Thus the woman represents heavenly Israel and the birth of the male child is a heavenly prototype of the earthly event. The birth pangs of the woman are the eschatological woes leading up to the messianic coming and the reference to the "rest of her children" is the "redactor's" attempt to portray the "establishment of the Christian community as an eschatological event parallel to the coming of the messiah."[151]

This latter explanation attempts to resolve a weakness with the interpretation of the woman as Israel in that the woman gives birth to both the Messiah and the believing community. This is not, however, a serious weakness since it might be argued that the church sprang from Jewish roots. Of course, the fact that the woman is subject to the same pursuit and persecution as the "rest of her children" (Rev 12.14-17) might be more difficult to explain in this light. On the other hand, this objection might not even present an insurmountable difficulty, since Israel had been an object of persecution long before the first century. The real difficulty, however, is that this interpretive approach draws a distinction between the church and Israel that does not seem consistent with the rest of the Apocalypse.[152] This is a common objection to her identity as either earthly Israel or a heavenly prototype. A further difficulty with Collins's argument is that the vision of Revelation 12 moves between heaven and earth in such a way that the woman is seen not only as a heavenly figure but also an earthly entity.

For Collins, the justification for seeing the woman as Israel arises out of a belief that the portions of the passage that describe the woman (12.1-6, 14-17) come originally from Jewish sources.[153] This is also the justification given for the terse presentation of the birth of the Messiah rather than a more Christian portrayal, which may have included some reference to Jesus' ministry and death.[154] The objection to this rationale is that whether

---

[150] Ibid., 135; also, see above, 132, n. 72.

[151] Ibid., 135. Cf. Marshall, *Parables of War*, 137–38, who similarly interprets the woman as heavenly Israel. She struggles to bring forth the Messiah whose birth inaugurates a final conflict between good and evil. Marshall, however, interprets the vision of chapter 12 strictly within the context of the First Jewish Revolt against the Romans.

[152] So Roloff, *Revelation*, 145; cf. Prigent, *L'Apocalypse*, 292–93, who writes, "L'Apocalypse ne semble jamais distinguer entre le peuple de Dieu de l'ancienne et de la nouvelle alliance."

[153] Collins, *Combat Myth*, 106–7.

[154] Ibid., 105; cf. Aune, *Revelation 6–16*, 688, for remarks contrary to this conclusion. Both Beale, *Revelation*, 639, and Osborne, *Revelation*, 463, explain the brief reference to the Messiah as a "telescoping" of events in this passage, especially with regard to the life of

these passages originate from some possible Jewish source, either written or oral, does not alter the fact that they have been used and admittedly redacted by the Christian author.[155] Thus the question remains as to what John intended the woman to symbolize.

The interpretations that come the closest to answering this question are the ecclesiastical view and the collective view. The ecclesiastical view interprets the woman as the church, while the collective view fine tunes her identity as the corporate people of God of both the old and new covenants. The difficulty with the ecclesiastical view is the problem of explaining how the church gives birth to the Messiah.[156] The collective view has the advantage of rectifying this inherent weakness by interpreting the woman first as ideal Israel (12.1-6), who gives birth to the Messiah, and then as the church, who is the mother of those who hold to the testimony of Jesus (12.17).

This view, however, is not without its critics. Collins, for example, objects to it on the grounds that it is artificial and fragmentary because it divides the woman's identity within the vision narrative.[157] While this may appear to be the case, such a fluid interpretation of this symbol does not seem unwarranted in light of the fact that John consistently blurs the line of distinction between Israel and the church, seeing an unbroken continuity between them. The previous analysis of the visions of the 144,000 (7.1-8) and the two witnesses (11.3-13) has already demonstrated John's affinity for the metaphorical use of Jewish symbols for the church.

The vision of the two witnesses particularly offers a helpful interpretive parallel to the heavenly woman. The description of the two witnesses, like that of the woman, relies heavily on imagery from Israel's tradition. They are the lampstands of Zechariah, they wield the power of Moses and Elijah, and, yet, they are clearly symbols of the church proclaiming God's message to the nations and suffering the fate of "their Lord" (11.8). This mélange of Jewish and Christian traditions is typical of John and is no less so in the vision of the heavenly woman. She represents the faithful people

---

Christ. Beale comments that the telescoping of events has precedent in both the NT (John 3.13; 8.14; 13.3; 16.5, 28; Rom 1.3-4; 1 Tim 3.16) and in the Apocalypse (1.5; 2.8; 17.8). This observation is reasonable in view of the fact that John's focus here is not to portray a detailed messianic ministry, but the defeat of Satan and the result of that defeat for the people of God. The birth and immediate ascension of the Messiah encapsulates the important fact of the success of the messianic ministry and the resulting defeat of Satan through the exaltation of the one "who rules the nations with an iron rod" (12.5).

[155] So Collins, *Combat Myth*, 101–45.
[156] So ibid., 105–6.
[157] Ibid., 106.

of God of both ideal Israel and the church who have become heirs together of God's covenant promises. This union of the best of the old with the new, however, does not imply a tacit acceptance of all who claim participation in these covenants. Not all Jews are allied with God as is implied in Rev 2.9; 3.9; and 11.8. Likewise, as is so evident in the warnings of the seven messages to the Asian churches, only those saints who remain faithful until the end will escape the judgment of God.

The collective view, therefore, best explains the imagery of the heavenly woman. She is at once Israel and the church. She portrays an unbroken continuity between the people of God of both the old and new covenants consistent with John's own perspective. In this manner, she can be at once represent the mother of the Messiah as well as the church. As the object of Satan's pursuits, she represents the faithful of God on earth who suffer persecution. For John's contemporaries, this imagery is painfully real and begins the unveiling of the root cause of their present suffering.

Conclusion

The parallel references to 1,260 days in both visions of 11.3-13 and chapter 12 propose a common interpretation of the major figures in these visions, and to this discussion should be added the vision of 11.1-2. All three visions have in common the symbolic time period of three and one half years, and all three visions recount the protection of the major figures in the face of external opposition. These commonalities imply that these visions, though differing in imagery, share a similar thematic point and that the major figures of each vision share a common symbolic referent.

It has already been argued that the vision of the two witnesses is a vision in microcosmic format of the church age in which the church exercises its call to speak prophetically to the nations. During this period, the church enjoys a level of protection in the face of anticipated opposition until it has completed its prophetic task. At the end of the age, the beast will arise and "make war" on the church and seemingly overcome it. God, however, has the final word through both the vindication of the saints and his judgment on those who refuse to acknowledge him.

If one understands the 1,260 days of 11.3 as symbolic of the church age, then it would be naturally coherent to interpret this same figure in 12.6 as indicative of the same time period. This time period begins with the completion of the messianic ministry (12.5) and will end with the defeat of the dragon and his cohorts.[158] In the vision of Revelation 12,

---

[158] Beale, *Revelation*, 646–47. Kiddle, *Revelation*, 211, sees the references to this time

John signals his hearers that this period has begun, but does not bring it to a conclusion as he seems to in 11.7-13. This open-ended approach, however, is purposeful because John intends to use this vision as a springboard from which he will expand the discussion of this final period of tribulation and the ultimate victory of the saints (Rev 13.1—20.15).

The vision of Revelation 12, then, is very much an opening vision for the last half of the Apocalypse. What it has in common with the preceding visions of the two witnesses and the measuring of the temple is its overall message. John conveys a threefold message in these visions that not only echoes the message of his first interlude but also prepares his hearers for the events that will unfold in the rest of the Apocalypse. This message is that the saints will be spiritually protected by God, they will experience certain opposition among the nations—who have temporarily been given an upper-hand in the world—but their vindication is assured. This message is communicated through increasingly lengthier and more detailed presentations by a variety of images and perspectives as the visions unfold.

The vision of the measuring of the temple tells the story in very brief form of the protection of God's spiritual temple, the church, while the Holy City is trampled by the nations for forty-two months. This latter numeric designation for the 1,260 days is John's reference for the church age from the perspective of the nations. The vision of the two witnesses expands on this period of time from the perspective of the church and offers a more detailed view of the church's responsibility as well as the eschatological outcome of this period (11.7-13). Then, the final trumpet is sounded in 11.15-18 as a proleptic announcement of the victory of God that will be portrayed repeatedly in increasing detail later in the Apocalypse (14.6–19.21).

The vision of Revelation 12 retakes the themes presented in 11.1-13 with the intent to offer some explanation for the present opposition experienced by the saints, as well as to set the scene for a final intense period of opposition (begun in 13.1) that will end in the eschatological defeat of all who oppose God and his people (19.17—20.3). The particular message that Revelation 12 communicates is the central message of the Apocalypse. The opposition that the saints are presently experiencing has its roots in a cosmic struggle between God and Satan. Thus the vision purposely moves from heaven to earth, as does the cosmic battle. Both the woman and the dragon first appear in their adversarial positions in heaven (12.1-6) and later on earth (12.12-17). This movement between heaven and earth

---

period in Revelation 12 and 13 as the church age, while the references in Revelation 11 would refer to an intense eschatological period before the end.

should not be a source of interpretive difficulty, but must be understood as an integral part of the vision's message, for it is John's intention to give the historical opposition to the Asian saints a cosmic significance. Therefore, it is not necessary to propose that the woman represents a heavenly prototype of Israel or of the church on earth. She represents the collective people of God of both covenants who are presently represented in the followers of Jesus (12.17). The woman can, therefore, represent both Israel and the church in a single symbol. This is entirely consistent with John's view throughout the Apocalypse that the church is God's new spiritual Israel. Indeed, John's use of Jewish imagery in 11.1-13 expresses this same idea. The church is representative of God's collective people that finds its roots in the Jewish faith.

The woman, who is portrayed in 12.1-6 as the mother of the Messiah, is Israel as the people of God in the OT who give rise to the Messiah. Their opposition has been the dragon or Satan (12.9), who has attempted to thwart God's planned redemption of his people since the beginning (12.4). The dragon's failure to destroy the child results in his eschatological defeat at the hands of Michael and his angels (12.7). This defeat, however, is clearly attributed to the success of God's Messiah (12.10-11) and results in the loss of Satan's "place" in heaven (12.8).

This battle between Michael and Satan has primordial significance in that it alludes to Satan's fall before creation, at which time he swept a third of the "stars" from heaven (12.4).[159] These stars symbolize Satan's angels who join him in battle against Michael and his angels.[160] Although this vision carries primordial significance, John has transferred the full and final import of this battle to a time after the birth and ascension of the messianic child. Satan, though fallen, appears to have a "place" in heaven (cf. Job 1.6) that he does not lose until after the messianic child is caught up to God (cf. Luke 10.17). This exaltation of the Messiah gives Michael and his angels the authority to complete the dragon's defeat. All of God's saints share this victory; however, it is a victory with an already-and-not-yet quality. Satan has been cast to the earth, which brings joy to those who dwell in heaven but "woe" to the earth, for Satan "knows his time is short"

---

[159] Osborne, *Revelation*, 468–69; cf. Charles, *Revelation*, 1:320; Brown, et al., *Mary in the New Testament*, 233–34.

[160] This interpretation seems the most likely since the casting down of these stars forms part of the opening description of the dragon and since these stars share the dragon's fate of being cast from heaven to earth. See Osborne, *Revelation*, 461. Contra Beale, *Revelation*, 635–37, who does not believe they are satanic angels, but proposes that they are saints (cf. Dan 8.10; 12.3) or possibly "deceived" Israel.

(12.12). The saints will not be exempt from this woe, but will in fact be the object of Satan's wrath (12.17). In this manner, the vision provides cosmic significance to the eschatological suffering of the saints. Satan goes "to make war" on the offspring of the woman, who are clearly identified as those who "hold the testimony of Jesus" (12.17; cf. 1.2, 9; 19.10). John uses the same expression in 12.17, "to make war" (ποιῆσαι πόλεμον), as he used in 11.7[161] and will use again in 13.7 to express Satan's intent. This language serves as a further literary link to tie together the visions of 11.3-13; 12.1-18 (as well as 11.1-2 by association) with the vision of 13.1-10 and the remainder of the Apocalypse. John is about to expand on the final period of time to which he briefly alludes in 11.7-10, which is the rise and reign of the beast. Rev 12.1-17 provides the cosmic background to this earthly reality and sets the stage for the final eschatological showdown (12.18).

Collins seems correct, therefore, in her structural conclusions that the trumpet interlude provides a link to the next major section of the Apocalypse begun in 12.1. John's recommissioning in chapter 10 provides the basis for his prophetic direction taken up in chapter 11 and continued in chapter 12. Chapters 11 and 12 continue some of the earlier themes of the Apocalypse, particularly God's protection of the saints so clearly illustrated in the seal interlude (7.1-8), but with particular focus on the earthly plight of the saints both at the level of their call and their eschatological fate (cf. 7.9-17).[162]

Of particular interest for the present discussion is John's continued use of Jewish imagery in each of the three visions of chapters 11 and 12 and even in his Ezekiel-like recommissioning of chapter 10. The visions of the measuring of the temple, the two witnesses, and the heavenly woman all draw heavily on Jewish imagery with significant allusions to OT texts. This affinity for Jewish imagery is indicative of John's socio-religious heritage and certainly his familiarity with Jewish sources, particularly the Hebrew Scriptures; but it is also indicative of his perspective on the relationship between Judaism and the emerging Christian movement.

Once again, what is clear from the analysis of these visions, as well as from previous discussion, is that John sees continuity between the traditions of the old and new covenants. The privileges and hopes of God's covenant people Israel have been realized in the sacrificial actions of the Lamb

---

[161] In this passage, John uses the finite verb form of ποιέω rather than the infinitive as he does in the other two passages. The sense, however, is the same.

[162] As has been particularly drawn out by Bauckham, *Climax*, 238–337.

(5.9-10), and the heirs of these promises are the Lamb's followers. For this reason, John is able to draw from the best of Israel's prophetic tradition to express this reality, and his visions flow freely between Jewish tradition and Christian hopes. Thus the 144,000 are sealed out of the twelve tribes of Israel, but they are also an innumerable multitude; the two witnesses are like Moses and Elijah *redivivus*, yet also members of the Jesus community (11.8), and the heavenly woman is at once faithful Israel and the church.

It must not be overlooked, however, that as in Rev 2.9 and 3.9, John seems to impugn once again the reputation of Judaism through his description of earthly Jerusalem in 11.8. Historic Jerusalem is called Sodom, Egypt, and the place where the Lord was crucified (11.8). This latter designation is nearly as vicious as the synagogue of Satan accusation. What differentiates 11.8 from 2.9 and 3.9 is that while the latter passages may be explained as condemnation of local Jewish opposition, 11.8 is a condemnation of the symbol for Jewish religious and political identity. Jerusalem is placed in league with the "great city" and thus is in league with the dragon and all those who oppose God and his people. Furthermore, the purposeful and decidedly Christian denunciation of Jerusalem as the place of Jesus' crucifixion implies Jewish culpability in the death of the Messiah, which the church eventually saw as a product of Jewish unfaithfulness to God.

This condemnation of Jerusalem as the place of Jesus' death once again appears to orient John conspicuously close to later Christian writers who similarly denounced the Jews for their rejection of the Messiah.[163] However, such a close affinity is more an illusion than a reality. John's denunciation of earthly Jerusalem should more accurately be placed in the same category as the synagogue of Satan accusations. Although the condemnation may be broader than in 2.9 and 3.9, John is still maintaining here a consistent apocalyptic line of demarcation between those who belong to God and those who belong to Satan. Any who have placed themselves in opposition to Christ and his church, represented by the two witnesses, are condemned along with the pagan culture of the day, as represented in the great city. The dragon, who represents Satan, is himself portrayed as waiting to devour the messianic child in the next vision of Revelation 12, and he is the ultimate force behind all opposition to God metaphorically embodied in the beast, the great city Babylon, and all the earth-dwellers who follow the beast.

---

[163] E.g., Melito, *Peri Pascha* 55 calls the Jews "God-killers."

John no doubt recognizes, perhaps as Paul (Romans 9–11), that a majority of Jews have rejected the gospel message. Their rejection of the Lamb began with his crucifixion and continues in their opposition to God's people, as in Smyrna and Philadelphia. This rejection of God's Messiah places them in league, wittingly or unwittingly, with Satan, as does their opposition to the churches in Smyrna and Philadelphia. It must be reiterated, however, that John's denunciation does not imply a blanket rejection of all Jews or Judaism as a religion. Insiders and outsiders are measured, not by ethnicity, but by faithfulness to God and the Lamb. Just as the faithful are comprised of both Jews and Gentiles, so the unfaithful have a similar mix.

While John's reinterpretation of Jewish scripture and tradition from a christological perspective as well as his denunciation of certain Jewish elements appears to have some affinity with a similar anti-Jewish offensive undertaken by later elements within the church, a careful contextual analysis of the Apocalypse reveals some important distinctions. For John, the church is never portrayed as Israel's replacement. It is subsumed in, and the clear extension of, God's covenant people Israel. John does not emit the anti-Jewish or anti-Semitic tone characteristic of later Christian writers. John has, however, redrawn his definition of a "Jew" (i.e., the covenant people of God) along theological lines. This new people of God, not limited by ethnicity, are drawn from every nation (5.9; 7.9), faithfully follow the Lamb, and bear the seal of God—a mark of their faithfulness as God's new spiritual Israel.

5

The New Jerusalem as the Eschatological People of God

> Just as the Gospels were composed with a view to the Passion and Resurrection and progress carefully toward that goal, so also the Revelation of John was constructed with the heavenly Jerusalem in mind and unfolds inexorably toward this culmination.[1]

WILLIAM Reader's statement succinctly captures the importance of the vision of the new Jerusalem to the Apocalypse of John. As the final climactic vision of the Apocalypse, it brings together in one magnificent menagerie of images the themes upon which John builds throughout the Apocalypse. It provides the beleaguered believers of Asia with a glimpse of the reward for which they long but can barely imagine in the midst of their present struggles. It is the goal of their pilgrimage, as Hebrews so eloquently states it (Heb 12.22), and the prize of their high calling toward which Paul encouraged the Philippians (3.14) to press. It is the city whose builder and maker is God (Heb 11.10); it is the end to which John calls them to persevere.

The vision of the new Jerusalem (NJ) is the final vision to consider in the present study of John's use of Jewish imagery for the church. In this vision, as has been argued in the previous chapters, John once again reveals his own perception of the relationship between the church and Israel. It is perhaps this vision that outlines most clearly this perception of John's that the church is God's new spiritual Israel, for this vision centers on one of the most powerful symbols in Jewish tradition—the Holy City (21.2). In this vision is expressed the Jewish eschatological hope of the restoration of Jerusalem and the people of God. Although John's Jerusalem has no temple, the dimensions of the city powerfully suggest that it is in itself a holy

---

[1] William W. Reader, "The Twelve Jewels of Revelation 21.19-20: Tradition History and Modern Interpretations," *JBL* 100 (1981) 433.

of holies. This restored Jerusalem is, however, founded on the apostles of the Lamb (21.14) and is a gathering place for the nations (21.26). Indeed, the city itself is called the bride of the Lamb (21.9). Although John has adopted significant images from Jewish prophetic tradition, he has redefined them and reapplied them within a Christian context. The NJ is a symbol for the eschatological people of God redeemed by the Lamb from every nation (5.9; 7.9; cf. 21.26), who are heirs of God's new creation (21.7; 22.3).

The vision of the NJ skillfully combines many of the images from the previous visions discussed, reinforcing the current thesis that John envisions the church as a new spiritual Israel. As in the vision of the 144,000 sealed, the twelve tribes of Israel are once again present as the names on the gates of the NJ. In addition, the measurements of the city in 12,000 stadia, like the 12,000 from each of the tribes of Israel (7.4-8), continue John's affinity for multiples of twelve as symbolic of the people of God. As in the vision of the innumerable multitude, John emphasizes the universal nature of the people of God, a countless multitude from every nation comprising the NJ (7.9; 21.3, 24, 26), and the woman of chapter 12, who represents the universal church, is now "the bride, the wife of the Lamb" (21.9).[2] It is the details of this final vision of the Apocalypse that make these parallels clear and the interpretation of the NJ as the people of God—new spiritual Israel—so inescapable.

The Vision's Structure and Purpose (21.1—22.5)

Revelation 21.9—22.5 encompasses the section of the Apocalypse known as the vision of the NJ. One would be remiss, however, not to study 21.1-8 in conjunction with this vision since it acts as a transitional passage, both concluding 19.11—22.15[3] (being introduced as the last in a series of καὶ εἶδον)[4] and introducing the very detailed vision of the NJ that follows. In 21.1-2, John sees a new heaven and a new earth, as well as "the Holy City, the new Jerusalem, coming down out of heaven from God, prepared as a

---

[2] For the latter comparison see Jonathan A. Draper, "The Twelve Apostles as Foundation Stones of the Heavenly Jerusalem and the Foundation of the Qumran Community," *Neot* 22 (1988) 42.

[3] So Collins, *Combat Myth*, 19; Celia Deutsch, "Transformation of Symbols: The New Jerusalem in Rv 21:1—22:5," *ZNW* 78 (1987) 109–10; Bauckham, *Climax*, 21–22; Lee, *New Jerusalem*, 267; Osborne, *Revelation*, 728.

[4] As observed by Osborne, *Revelation*, 728.

bride adorned for her husband." Then John hears a "loud voice from the throne," which in hymnic fashion provides an explication of what John is about to see.[5] This is a common pattern in the Apocalypse in which hymnic or auditory sections are used to introduce subsequent detailed visions.[6] Therefore, Rev 21.9–22.5 provides a detailed account or recapitulation of the themes introduced in 21.1-8.[7]

Revelation 19.11—20.15 recounts the final defeat of the enemies of God at the hands of the rider on the white horse whose name is "Faithful and True" (19.11). He defeats them with the sword of his mouth[8] and sets up his millennial kingdom. Satan, who only experiences temporary imprisonment during this millennial reign, is finally released only to face his ultimate defeat, which sets the stage for the final judgment of both "great and small" (20.12). All who are not found written in the "Book of Life" are cast into the lake of fire with Satan, the false prophet, and the beast (20.10, 15). Revelation 21.1 provides a transition from this final moment of judgment from which even the old heaven and earth flee (21.11) and the old evil order is done away. Now John sees a new heaven and earth in which God's rule is made complete; the state of affairs anticipated in 19.1-9 (note particularly 19.7-8; cf. 19.10; 22.6-10) has now become a reality.

There are three main themes that John introduces in 21.1-8 that are detailed in 21.9—22.5: a new creation, the NJ, and the tabernacle of God among humanity (21.3). As will be demonstrated, each of these themes is united in John's following description of the NJ in 21.9—22.5. This pericope can be further subdivided into two separate but related sections: 21.9-27 and 22.1-5.[9] The unifying factor for the three sections—21.1-8 and 21.9-27; 22.1-5—is the NJ, which John sees as synonymous with the new heaven and earth. Thus the unity of 21.1—22.5 is apparent and easy

---

[5] Elisabeth Schüssler Fiorenza, *Revelation: Vision of a Just World*, Proclamation Commentaries (Minneapolis: Fortress, 1991) 109.

[6] See the discussion in chapter 3, 103. What John *sees* is immediately interpreted by what he *hears* in 5.6 and 5.7-14; 7.1-2 and 7.4; 14.1 and 14.2-5; 15.2 and 15.3-4; 17.1-6 and 17.7-18, or vice versa in 5.5 and 5.6; 9.13-16 and 9.17-21. See also Vogelgesang, "Interpretation of Ezekiel," 82; Bauckham, *Climax*, 214–16; Beale, *Revelation*, 424–25.

[7] Vogelgesang, "Interpretation of Ezekiel," 82; Beale, *Revelation*, 1039.

[8] John's description of this rider in 19.11-16 (he wears a robe dipped in blood, his name is the "Word of God," and he leads the army of heaven) leaves no doubt that he wishes his hearers to understand not only that he is describing the giver of this apocalypse (1.16) but that this victor is none other than Jesus Christ himself (1.1).

[9] So Prigent, *L'Apocalypse*, 448–50, 452.

to maintain in contrast to those who argue that this section is a convoluted patchwork of textual units.[10]

The purpose of 21.9—22.5 is to provide the conclusion the entire Apocalypse has been anticipating. It is a multifaceted conclusion that supports John's consistent call to persevere while maintaining the dualistic message of reward for the faithful and judgment for the unfaithful. John brings the message of the Apocalypse full circle by assuring the churches addressed in chapters 2 and 3 that the benefits of the new order are the reward of those who remain faithful in this present life (21.7), while those who compromise will suffer the ultimate fate of Satan and the beast in the lake of fire and will be excluded from God's eternal Holy City (21.8, 27).[11]

This dualism extends even into the structure of the Apocalypse itself, as this passage forms a dual conclusion with 17.1—19.10 in which the judgment of Babylon is recounted.[12] The first part of this section, 17.1-18, is John's vision of the whore of Babylon, which contains a number of similarities to John's vision of the NJ.[13] The first striking comparison is the nearly identical literary repetition between the introductions to the two visions (17.1; cf. 21.9). Both visions are revealed by one of the angels that holds one of the seven bowls of the last plagues,[14] and in both visions John is carried in the spirit to a visionary locale (desert, 17.3; high mountain, 21.10) where he is shown in one the "judgment of the great whore" (17.1) and in the other the "bride, the wife of the Lamb" (21.9). Both figures are bedecked with jewels but the contrasts are more arresting than the comparisons, as one is sullied and drunk with the blood of the saints (17.3-6) while the other is pure and reflects the glory of God (21.11). John's message is clear: who one chooses to serve determines one's eschatological

---

[10] Contra Charles, *Revelation*, 2:144–47, who finds that 20.4 through chapter 22 exhibits "mental confusion" and has been "disarranged in an astonishing degree and does not at present stand in the orderly sequence originally designed by our author." Charles is forced to hypothesize that John was martyred before the completion of the Apocalypse, after which a faithful disciple arranged the final pieces left by the author. Cf. Aune, *Revelation 17–22*, 1115.

[11] So Osborne, *Revelation*, 747, who suggests that the eschaton has two foci—judgment and reward.

[12] Lee, *New Jerusalem*, 275.

[13] See Aune, *Revelation 17–22*, 1144–45, for a detailed literary comparison of 17.1—19.10 and 21.9—22.9; cf. Deutsch, "Transformation," 123, who has a comparative table of the description of the whore and the NJ.

[14] Whether it is the same angel or two different angels from among the seven is not clear.

destiny. An alliance with the corrupted contemporary culture means separation from God and certain judgment, but faithfulness to the testimony of Jesus brings certain reward and eternal intimacy with "the Lord God the Almighty and the Lamb" (21.22).[15]

"The Tabernacle of God Is with Humanity" (21.1-8)[16]

As was noted above, John introduces three themes in this transitional section that anticipate the detailed vision of the NJ in 21.9—22.5. John opens this transitional section with the vision of a new heaven and earth, which serves to establish the underlying theme of the entire vision section (21.1—22.5)—is the renewal of all things, a new creation. John's audience would no doubt be reminded of the previous flight of the old heaven and earth from before the judgment of God (20.11), and they are now assured of God's plan of restoration through a new heaven and earth. The eschatological renewal of heaven and earth is not an expectation unique to the Apocalypse but can be found throughout Jewish literature (e.g., *1 En.* 72.1; 91.16; *4 Ezra* 7.30-31; *Sib. Or.* 5.212; *Jub.* 1.29; 4.26; *Apoc. El.* 5.38[17]; 1QS 4.25; 2 Pet 3.13; cf. Matt 5.18; 19.28; 24.35; Rom 8.21; 2 Cor 5.17; Gal 6.15).[18] Isaiah prophesies such a renewal as part of the expected future restoration of Israel (65.17; 66.22), which John here adopts as the eschatological hope of his contemporary hearers. This theme of renewal pervades this section (21.1-8) of the Apocalypse and provides the backdrop for the description of the NJ (21.9—22.5).

There are several ways in which this passage reflects the theme of renewal. One has already been noted through the mention of John's opening declaration that he saw a new heaven and earth. Another is John's observation that the new earth contains no more sea, which is a metaphorical

---

[15] Cf. Beale, *Revelation*, 1064–65; 1117–21.

[16] Interwoven throughout the discussion in the following sections is some analysis of John's use of the OT in the formulation of his vision of the NJ. The present project was already near completion when the recent work by David Mathewson, *A New Heaven and a New Earth: The Meaning and Function of the Old Testament in Revelation 21.1—22.5*, JSNTSup 238 (London: Sheffield Academic, 2003) was published. This writer was, therefore, not able to incorporate Mathewson's research into the present discussion but recommends it as a reference for further study.

[17] Aune, *Revelation 17–22*, 116, believes this passage to be dependent on Rev 21.1. While this is possible, the *Apocalypse of Elijah* exhibits both Jewish and Christian traditions that are difficult to distinguish within the text. See the comments O. S. Wintermute, "Apocalypse of Elijah," in *OTP* (Garden City, N.Y.: Doubleday, 1983) 1:726.

[18] For these and additional references see Aune, *Revelation 17–22*, 116.

way of indicating the thoroughness of God's judgment and the absolute distinction between the old and new order. In the Apocalypse, the sea is characterized as the place of chaos, the origin of evil (12.15, 18; 17.1-6; 13.1) and the abode of the dead (20.13).[19] It is from the sea that the beast arises to implement the dragon's demonic plan against God's people (13.1), so John assures his audience that no such evil exists in God's new world (cf. 21.8). In addition, a voice from the divine throne declares the renewal of all things, "See, I am making all things new" (21.5). In this new world there will no longer be any suffering, mourning, or pain "for the first things have passed away" (21.4), and it is this same divine declaration that reminds John and his audience that all evildoers have been judged and have no part in the new order (21.8).

Along with the theme of a new creation, the two remaining themes introduced in 21.1-8, the NJ and the dwelling of God with humanity, are detailed more fully in 21.9—22.5.[20] Immediately upon seeing the new heaven and earth John also sees "the Holy City, the new Jerusalem, coming down out of heaven from God, prepared as a bride adorned for her husband" (21.2). This vision of the NJ is set aside at this point, not to be picked up again until 21.9. John is instead distracted by a great voice which he hears coming from the throne that declares,

> Behold, the tabernacle (σκηνή) of God is with humanity. He will tabernacle with them and they will be his peoples (λαοί), and God himself will be with them and be their God." (21.3 translation mine)

This declaration by the divine being is the focus of 21.1-8 and sets the stage for the vision to follow. It clarifies for John's hearers that the renewal of all things is the responsibility of the creator of all things (4.11), and what he began at creation and sought to achieve through redemptive history has been brought to final fruition. Indeed, the new order is sustained by his very presence as will be revealed in 21.9—22.5.

John wishes to communicate in 21.1-8 a message integral to his apocalypse that he will illustrate in his subsequent vision of the NJ. This message is that God and his people are finally united in a way never before experienced, yet in a way that has been anticipated before the creation of the first world. John is going to introduce this level of fellowship in stun-

---

[19] See Beale, *Revelation*, 1042, for a list of the five identities of the sea in the Apocalypse. Cf. Osborne, *Revelation*, 73–31; Deutsch, "Transformation," 115–16.

[20] Although 21.9—22.5 primarily details the NJ, John returns to the idea of a new creation in 22.1-5.

ning and vivid detail in his description of the NJ. It is an unadulterated fellowship in which God's servants worship him day and night, look upon his face, and enjoy his presence forever (22.3). It is difficult to express such fellowship in words, so John does so through multiple images that are staggering to the human perception.

The covenant language echoed throughout the throne declaration of 21.3-8 emphasizes this primary message of unity between God and his people and is particularly rich with allusions to God's covenant promises to Israel. Throughout the OT God promises to dwell in the midst of his people, to walk among them, and to be their God (Lev 26.11-12; Jer 7.23; 11.4; 30.22; 31.33; Zech 2.10-11a; 8.3). This promise is reiterated in Ezekiel's (37.26-28; cf. 43.7) prophecy of a post-exilic restored Israel, which is the text that may lie behind Rev 21.3.[21] This idea that God dwelt in the midst of his people is even expressed in the regulations that governed everyday life during Israel's wilderness wanderings (e.g., Deut 23.12-14) and is vividly illustrated in the encampment of Israel around the tabernacle of God (Numbers 2). It is the image of God's tabernacle in the midst of his people that is adopted in the throne declaration of Rev 21.3.

The use of σκηνή and its cognate verb σκηνόω provides a link for John's audience between the images of God's dwelling among the Israelites in the wilderness and the eschatological presence of God to which he now refers. The term σκηνή is used in the LXX for the tabernacle or the Tent of the Testimony, which was the center of worship for the Israelites and the place of the shekinah presence of God.[22] The shekinah presence of God was evident to the Israelites through the pillar of cloud and fire over the tabernacle during the wilderness wanderings. The noun "shekinah" itself is derived from the Hebrew word *shakan* or *shaken*, "dwell," which may suggest an additional word play in Rev 21.3 since its LXX equivalent is σκηνόω.[23]

Moreover, Rev 21.7 echoes the Davidic promise of 2 Sam 7.14 (cf. Jer 31.9). There John writes, ὁ νικῶν κληρονομήσει ταῦτα καὶ ἔσομαι αὐτῷ θεὸς καὶ αὐτὸς ἔσται μοι υἱός. The language of the latter portion of this text is nearly identical to that of the LXX and suggests an extension of this messianic promise through Christ (note particularly the use

---

[21] This covenantal language is embraced by Paul in the NT where God's people, the church, become his spiritual temple in which he dwells (2 Cor 6.16b—7.1).

[22] It is also noteworthy that the verb σκηνόω is used in John 1.14 with regard to God's presence incarnate among his people.

[23] Osborne, *Revelation*, 726–27.

of υἱός) to God's new covenant *peoples* (21.3b).[24] This latter observation is particularly poignant when one observes how subtly but significantly John has adapted the covenant language for his present audience. In 21.3b, John changes the singular "people" (λαός; Ezek 37.27; cf. Jer 11.4; 31.33) of the OT prophetic tradition to "peoples" (λαοί),[25] reflecting his own universal perception of the people of God.[26] This inclusion of the nations in the covenant promises of Israel is not out of harmony with OT expectations, which John understands to be fulfilled in the new covenant (Rev 5.9; 7.9; 21.14, 26; cf. Gen 12.1-3; 17.2-8; Zech 2.10-11; Sir 44.21-23; Gal 3.16, 29).[27]

The throne declaration of 21.3-8 announces the major goal of God's eschatological plan: God now dwells among his people. This unadulterated presence has never before been experienced by any person or people group on earth. There are no more veils, no more holy of holies, and no more priestly intercessors. God's redeemed sanctified people now eternally serve him in his presence and look without fear upon his face (22.3-4). Encompassed in this new-found fellowship is the fulfillment of God's covenant promises throughout the ages, which becomes the secondary message within the declaration of 21.3-8. The significance of this declaration becomes clear in the details of the vision which follows in 21.9-27.

The New Jerusalem (21.9-27)

Although Rev 21.9–22.5 is set apart structurally from 21.1-8, it clearly develops the themes of this previous section. John now resumes in detail the vision of the NJ first introduced in 21.2. The description of the NJ

---

[24] See Lee, *New Jerusalem*, 272–74; Osborne, *Revelation*, 740, who suggests that it also echoes Gen 17.7.

[25] It is difficult to be certain of the original reading of the text. Some manuscripts contain the singular λαός (E, P, et al.) while others contain the plural λαοί (ℵ, A, et al.). The weight of the manuscript evidence is nearly equal with some bias in favor of λαοί. Although it is conceivable that a scribe may have changed λαός to λαοί in order to bring it in harmony with αὐτοί, it is more likely that λαοί is the original reading since it is the more difficult reading, placing the text out of harmony with OT precedent. See Bruce M. Metzger, *A Textual Commentary on the Greek New Testament*, 2d ed. (Stuttgart: United Bible Societies, 1994) 688.

[26] So Gundry, "New Jerusalem," 257; Bauckham, *Climax*, 311–12; Mounce, *Revelation*, 383; Aune, *Revelation 17–22*, 1123; Hirschberg, *Das eschatologische Israel*, 242; Beale, *Revelation*, 1047; Prigent, *L'Apocalypse*, 450; Osborne, *Revelation*, 734; contra Walvoord, *Revelation*, 314, who adopts λαός as the original reading.

[27] Gundry, "New Jerusalem," 257; Beale, *Revelation*, 1047; cf. Deutsch, "Transformation," 118–20.

will not only detail the attributes of this eternal city but will incorporate the theme of a new creation also previously introduced (21.1). It is the NJ that best describes the new order, for in John's description of the NJ he illustrates the veracity of God's promise to renew of all things (21.5). Evil has been removed (21.8, 27; cf. 22.15), nothing accursed is there (22.3), and God and his people dwell together in intimate communion (22.4).

Although 21.9—22.5 encompasses the entirety of the NJ description, 22.1-5 seems to be a natural subdivision and thus will be developed separately in the present discussion. It is in this section that John's description of the NJ turns to aspects of the new creation and the motif of a restored paradise. The particular focus of 21.9-27 is a description of the NJ, which includes the measurements of the city as well as the exquisite materials out of which it is constructed. It is to this description that the discussion will now turn.

Upon the completion of the throne declaration of 21.3-8, John is approached by "one of the seven angels who had the seven bowls full of the seven last plagues" and the angel says to him, "'Come, I will show you the bride, the wife of the Lamb.'" John is immediately taken to a "great, high mountain" where he sees "the Holy City Jerusalem coming down out of heaven from God." The opening of this vision, as has been observed earlier, is nearly identical to the opening of the vision of the whore of Babylon in 17.1-3. John obviously wants his hearers to envision the comparisons and the contrasts between that which is and that which will be, as incentive to persevere.

In contrast to 17.3, John is taken in this vision to a very high mountain where he observes the descent of the NJ. His location on a high mountain, as opposed to the wilderness (17.3), is a first contrast between his vision of the whore and the "wife of the Lamb." It is not clear whether John wishes to identify this mountain with Mount Zion, therefore, such allegorization may press the text too far.[28] John's mountain location may be simply for practical reasons, since such a high place would offer him the vantage point necessary to observe such a heavenly descent or, perhaps more likely, he may wish to invoke Ezekiel-like imagery after which his vision is patterned (Ezek 40.2). A mountain location is often the place of divine revelation in both the Old and New Testaments. Moses receives the Law on Mount Sinai (Exodus 19–20), Elijah receives his recommis-

---

[28] Bruce J. Malina, *The New Jerusalem in the Revelation of John: The City as Symbol of Life with God* (Collegeville, Minn.: Liturgical, 2000) 52–53. Malina suggests that Isa 2.2 is behind this text and also observes that the Jerusalem temple is often called God's "holy mountain" (Isa 11.9; 25.6-7, 10; 27.13; 30.29; 40.9; 56.7; 57.13; 65.11, 25; 66.20).

sioning on that same mountain (1 Kgs 19.8-18), Jesus is transfigured on a mountain, and, for Matthew, a mountain location is where Jesus delivers his first major teaching and is the location from which he gives his final commission (Matthew 5–7; 28.18-20). More significant than John's location, however, is the vision that he describes. John is shown the "bride, the wife of the Lamb." This "bride," as the NJ is first introduced in 21.2, is now about to be described in 21.11—22.5. John describes in exacting detail a city comprised of rare jewels and transparent gold and is of immense proportions. Each of the details of John's vision is significant and bears close scrutiny.

People or Place?

Before delving into the intimate details of the vision, however, it is appropriate first to deal with a major exegetical sticking point—the description of the NJ as the "bride, the wife of the Lamb." Does John intend for his hearers to understand the city as a literal place, an abode for the saints, or as symbolic of those same saints, indeed, as the wife of the Lamb? It would seem that John's intention in this passage is to describe the people of God symbolically. This impression derives chiefly from the angelic description of the NJ as the "bride, the wife of the Lamb" in 21.9 and John's similar description in 21.2. John wishes to communicate symbolically the purity, beauty and intimate union that the redeemed will experience with God at the eschaton. The chief difficulty with this interpretation, however, is that John seems to describe in earthly language a specific place that is measurable, with streets, foundations, walls, gates that never shut and a city into which the kings of the earth bring their glory.

Elisabeth Schüssler Fiorenza recognizes this difficulty and raises three primary objections to a symbolic interpretation of the city, arguing instead that John describes a literal place.[29] First, she observes that in 21.2 the city is *compared* to a bride so the city cannot be the bride. Second, 21.7 states that the saints will inherit the city which indicates that it must be a literal place. Third, in 21.24-26, the city, is described as the dwelling place of the saints, where the kings of the earth enter to bring their glory. Osborne believes that the correct view of the city lies in a synthesis of the two views, arguing that the city is both symbol and substance.[30] However, he makes an observation along the lines of Schüssler Fiorenza's first objection when he observes that it is John's literary habit first to use simile and then later

---

[29] Elisabeth Schüssler Fiorenza, *Priester für Gott* (Münster: Aschendorff, 1972) 348–50.
[30] Osborne, *Revelation*, 733.

to turn the simile into a metaphor (e.g., 15.2 "appeared to be a sea of glass . . . sea of glass"; 21.11, 18 "like jasper . . . jasper"). Thus the fact that the NJ appeared "like a bride" (21.2) and later is "the bride" (21.9) does not imply that John intends for his interpreters to envision a place symbolic of people. Osborne further observes that just as Babylon—represented by the whore in chapter 17—represents both place and people, so the NJ can be at one time both place and people.

This latter observation by Osborne bears little weight toward an argument for taking the NJ as both people and place. While one can argue that Babylon or Rome, of which Babylon is likely a symbol (17.9; cf. 1 Pet 5.13), is both place and people, one must ask if this is John's intended meaning behind the symbol of the whore. It seems not. John's intention seems rather to symbolize Rome, not as a people, but as the center of world corruption. It is the waters upon which the whore sits, not the whore, that are described as "peoples and multitudes and nations and languages" (17.15). The whore rather symbolizes Rome's corrupt power and authority as well as its idolatrous intentions. This promiscuous woman stands in contrast to the chaste and pure bride of the Lamb (19.7-8). Rome is the "mother of whores and earth's abominations" and is "drunk with the blood of the saints" (17.5-6). It is the nations of the earth that have "committed fornication and lived in luxury with her" (18.3, 9). Rome is the antithesis of God's power and has set itself up in the place of God (13.1, 6, 14-15; cf. 2 Thess 2.4). Thus it is more accurate to view the whore as a symbolic person who represents a real place, but to see the NJ as a symbolic place representing real people.

The remaining objections raised by Schüssler Fiorenza are easily surmounted if one looks closely at the text. In his article, "The New Jerusalem People as Place, Not Place for People," Gundry offers sound rebuttals to Schüssler Fiorenza's arguments. [31] To her first objection that the city is compared to a bride and therefore cannot be a bride, Gundry counters that it is more accurate to state that John compares the *preparation* of the city to the adornment of a bride rather than comparing the city itself to a bride (21.2). This observation, by implication, also negates Osborne's argument concerning John's use of simile and metaphor. To Schüssler Fiorenza's second objection concerning the city being an inheritance of the saints, Gundry notes that the text does not specifically state that the saints will inherit the city, but rather "these things" (21.7; κληρονομήσει ταῦτα). As for her third objection, Gundry believes that the entering of

---

[31] Gundry, "New Jerusalem," 263–64.

kings into the city is not communicating that they are literally entering and exiting the city, but rather entering the city is metaphorically to become a part of it (the promise of Rev 3.12 confirms this understanding). The unrepentant nations have already been judged in chapter 19, which leaves only the redeemed of the nations to enter the city. Since the city as the saints occupies all of the new earth, the nations of the new earth are the redeemed who rule it as kings (22.5).

Beale offers an additional rebuttal to this latter objection that seems more to the point. He argues that the portions of the vision that speak of the nations streaming into the city (21.24-26) are likely based on Isaiah 60, which elicits a tone of literal expectation. John, however, uses the spatial language of Isaiah, as he does the measuring of the NJ to communicate a symbolic message. The message is one of free access to God for both Jews and Gentiles in God's kingdom.[32]

There are three key passages, found outside the NJ vision, that help to elucidate this debate and establish the NJ as symbolic of God's people.[33] The first is Rev 3.12, where the reward of the overcomer is to be made a pillar in the temple of God and to have not only God's name written on him/her but also "the name of the city of my God, the new Jerusalem that comes down from my God out of heaven." Gundry argues that this is clear evidence that Christ identifies the believer with the NJ.[34] The second is 19.7-8, where John equates the bride with the saints. This passage, taken together with 21.2-3, 9b-10, reveals that John is equating the NJ with the saints. The reference to the bride being "ready" in both 19.7 (ἡτοίμασεν) and 21.2 (ἡτοιμασμένην) unites these two passages and provides a clue to the symbolic identity of the NJ. The third passage is 22.17a in which John writes, "The Spirit and the bride say, 'Come.'" Here, as John concludes his apocalypse, he is responding to the promise of Jesus that he is "coming soon" and that his reward is with him (22.12). The context (reinforced by 19.7-8) implies that John is using "bride" as a metaphor for the saints. This eager invitation comes from both the Spirit and the saints, the Lamb's bride, of which John considers himself a part. The fact that this text follows the NJ vision further proves that John considers both the bride and the NJ as equivalent symbols for God's people.

---

[32] Beale, *Revelation*, 1099–100.

[33] Gundry, "New Jerusalem," 256–57. Gundry cites the first two passages discussed here along with 20.9. This latter text, however, seems unhelpful in making the above argument. Cf. Vogelgesang, "Interpretation of Ezekiel," 85.

[34] Cf. Stevenson, *Power and Place*, 270, who argues that 22.3-4 is the eschatological fulfillment of 3.12 and 7.15.

The best interpretation of the vision of the NJ, therefore, is to understand it symbolically as the people of God and not as a place. This interpretation is both consistent with the overall methodological approach to interpreting the visions of the Apocalypse and is confirmed by the clearly symbolic, antithetical vision of the whore of Babylon.[35] The key to the debate lies fundamentally in a consideration of the source material that stands behind John's visionary description. Revelation 21.9—22.5 is full of allusions to the OT prophetic tradition as well as subsequent centuries of Jewish tradition.[36] Although there are significant differences, John's overall vision of the NJ is clearly modeled on Ezekiel's vision (Ezekiel 40–48) of a restored and rebuilt temple in an eschatological Jerusalem. In addition, John mingles in references from the Isaianic tradition in his description of both the NJ and the new heaven and earth (Isa 54.11-12; 60.1, 3, 5, 11, 19; 65.17, 22). In short, John wishes for his hearers to understand him as standing in a long line of prophetic tradition and so attempts to bring together the best of this tradition in this final vision of his apocalypse. Therefore, the fact that John's city is a new Jerusalem, that the nations stream into it, that it is bedecked with jewels, and that it is called the wife of the Lamb is all language that has as its goal not only to adopt the language of the OT prophets but also to bring Israel's hope of an eschatological renewal under the umbrella of contemporary ecclesiastical expectation.

The language of the prophets is naturally earthly language. They expected not only the restoration of Israel to its land but more specifically the restoration of Jerusalem. Ezekiel reveals this expectation through his vision of the rebuilt temple from which life-giving water flows. Isaiah's new heaven and earth is one in which Israel "shall build houses and inhabit them; they shall plant vineyards and eat their fruit" and "the wolf and the lamb shall feed together, the lion shall eat straw like the ox" (65.22, 25; see all of 65.1-17). Zechariah (14) also expects the establishment of Jerusalem as the throne place of God to which all the nations would come each year to celebrate the Feast of Tabernacles. Although these texts have an escha-

---

[35] The indisputable symbolic nature of the vision of chapter 17 is evidenced by the angel's interpretation of the vision in 17.7-18. As has already been observed, the vision of the NJ bears marked literary and structural similarities to the vision of the whore and is clearly intended to be interpreted in contrast/comparison to the vision of the whore. Thus both visions should be interpreted symbolically. Cf. Beale, *Revelation*, 1064–65, who makes a similar observation.

[36] See Lee, *New Jerusalem*, who traces the development of the NJ and new creation motifs from the OT prophets through Second Temple literature to John's apocalypse.

tological tone, they are very much grounded in the idea of an earthly restoration. This motif, however, undergoes a shift during the Second Temple period, perhaps because of the corruption of the second temple[37] and later to its 70 CE destruction (e.g., *4 Ezra* 7.26; 8.52; 10.27, 44, 54-55).[38] Lee observes that in Second Temple literature there is increasing interest in a restored temple/Jerusalem and its connection with, a heavenly temple/Jerusalem.[39] Second Temple writers have a greater tendency to describe the heavenly Jerusalem in more apocalyptic and eschatological terms than those of the OT and there is a liberty in the exegesis of OT passages in Second Temple literature which Lee believes lays the ground-work for John's interpretation.[40]

This latter point is best illustrated in John's adaptation of Ezekiel's vision of the new temple in Ezekiel 40–48. In both visions, the prophets are taken in a visionary state to a very high mountain (Ezek 40.2; 43.5; cf. Rev 21.10),[41] where they observe the angelic measuring of a new temple (in the case of Ezekiel) or a new Jerusalem (in the case of John). Both prophets see a life-giving river along the banks of which grow trees that bear fruit monthly and whose leaves provide healing. In both visions, the glory of God permeates the envisioned structure and communicates the permanent presence of God with his people.[42] While these similarities show that John has modeled his vision on Ezekiel's, it is the subtle and not so subtle differences between these two visions that reveal John's reinterpretation.[43] John's vision, of course, is considerably shorter than Ezekiel's and, unlike Ezekiel, John's focus is on the city rather than the temple compound. In fact, the most radical difference between John and Ezekiel is John's declaration that there is no temple within the NJ (21.22). Stevenson believes that this latter difference is best explained by observing that John has merged the city and the temple into one image.[44]

---

[37] This is evidenced through the Qumran community, which saw itself as the new temple and new Jerusalem (1QS 5.5; 8.1-10; 4.3-6; 4Q164). See the discussion; Lee, *New Jerusalem*, 127–28.

[38] See the discussion; ibid., 129–39.

[39] Ibid., 223–24.

[40] Ibid., 229.

[41] Beale, *Revelation*, 1065, believes that John has combined Ezek 40.1-2 and 43.5, in Rev 21.10, in order to make a connection with Ezekiel's new temple vision.

[42] Ibid., 1065.

[43] See Vogelgesang, "Interpretation of Ezekiel," 76–78, for a list of differences between these two visions. Cf. Deutsch, "Transformation," 114.

[44] Stevenson, *Power and Place*, 269–71.

Stevenson's observation seems a correct one. In John's vision the city is said to be permeated with the glory of God (21.11; 23) and is the location of the throne of God (22.3). Indeed, the cubic measurements of the city are an allusion to the holies of holies found in the original temple (1 Kgs 6.20). This merging of the city with the temple lends credence to the interpretation that the NJ symbolizes the people of God, since in the NT, the church is the temple of God in which his Spirit dwells (1 Cor 3.16; 2 Cor 6.16; Eph 2.21).[45] "In the new Jerusalem, the fullness of what the temple symbolized is realized."[46]

John envisions an eternal state in which God's presence infuses his people in such a way that the traditional barriers are removed. In this manner, he has universalized Ezekiel's message. The temple in Jerusalem had the advantage of symbolizing God's presence among his people, but also the disadvantage of reminding them of their separation from him. This separation is maintained even in Ezekiel's temple-centered vision where there is a clear delineation between God's presence and his people—only the Zadokites may enter his presence (Ezek 44.5). In John's vision, however, God's dwelling is among his people (21.3). Indeed, in Ezekiel's vision the nations are excluded from the sanctuary of God (Ezek 44.9), but not so in the Apocalypse where they have full access to his throne (Rev 21.24, 26; 22.2).[47] In addition, for Ezekiel, all the promises are for Israel and its inhabitants; but in the Apocalypse, John has universalized Ezekiel's language, incorporating all peoples into the promises of God (Rev 21.3, λαοὶ; cf. Ezek 37.27).[48] The NJ serves to merge the church and Israel into one people of God, thus including the nations in God's covenant community.[49] The similarities, and more importantly the differences, between John and Ezekiel show that while John's vision may model Ezekiel's vision, he has purposely adapted it to disclose his own message.[50] Both prophets see a future in which God's presence is universally among his people, but John's vision interprets Ezekiel's vision in light of the Christ event.[51]

---

[45] On this point see Mounce, *Revelation*, 382, who believes that 1 Cor 3.16-17 establishes a precedent for understanding the NJ as people rather than place.

[46] Stevenson, *Power and Place*, 269.

[47] Note as well that John has changed Ezekiel's description of the fruit bearing trees from "leaves for healing" (Ezek 47.12) to "leaves . . . for the healing of the nations" (Rev 22.2).

[48] Vogelgesang, "Interpretation of Ezekiel," 83–85.

[49] Stevenson, *Power and Place*, 272.

[50] Vogelgesang, "Interpretation of Ezekiel," 80.

[51] Robert A. Briggs, *Jewish Temple Imagery in the Book of Revelation*, SBLit 10 (New York: Lang, 1999) 104–10, calls this shift in prophetic viewpoint from the OT to John's

Since John wishes to invoke the ancient prophetic tradition, he adopts much of the language of the OT prophets. He is, however, particular in the language that he adopts and specific in his adaptation of it. Therefore, John uses language of an earthly nature to describe a heavenly vision. This heavenly vision, however, is not a vision of a place but of a people. It is not a vision of an eternal dwelling, but of a state of dwelling eternally with God. This is the eschatological inheritance of all who hold faithfully to the testimony of Jesus.

The Bride, the Wife of the Lamb

In 21.10, John sees the NJ descending "out of heaven from God" which serves to communicate a variety of messages concerning the nature of God's new creation. This descent is a fulfillment of the theophanic declaration of 21.3 since the dwelling place of God is now with humanity. The separation between heaven and earth has been removed, for heaven now descends to be united with earth. This union of heaven and earth serves to demonstrate the eventual dissolution of the previous dichotomy between the "earth-dwellers" and God's dwelling,[52] which only comes with the removal of evil (21.8, 27; 22.3).

The equating of the NJ with a heavenly Jerusalem is consistent with Jewish tradition (e.g., *1 En.* 14.8-17; 90.29-38; 4Q554; *4 Ezra* 7.26; 10.27, 42-44, 53-55; Gal 4.26) and reveals the belief that the eschatological restoration of Jerusalem will be a divine act. The fact that the heavenly Jerusalem is with God provides a sense of security for those who have put their hope in the eventual triumph of the people of God.[53] This theme of protection, which has already been developed throughout the Apocalypse (7.3-8; 9.4; 11.1-13), comes to completion here in the descent of the NJ. The people of God, who are symbolized in the NJ, have been kept spiritually secure through their perseverance and now inherit the new heaven and earth.

The descent of the NJ also speaks to the marriage union. According to 19.7-8, it is time for the marriage supper of the Lamb and the bride is

apocalypse "progressive revelation." The first coming of Christ has brought about a clearer understanding of God's eschatological plan previously realized by the OT prophets.

[52] Schüssler Fiorenza, *Vision*, 109.

[53] Lee, *New Jerusalem*, 138, observes that in the case of *4 Ezra* the dissonance caused by the destruction of Jerusalem in 70 CE is dealt with by turning to the apocalyptic concept of a heavenly Jerusalem/temple. A heavenly Jerusalem provides the concept of an indestructible city and temple that are secure with God and will be revealed in the end not through human action but divine action.

now ready. The announcement made in this passage comes to fruition in 21.9—22.5. The use of nuptial language here provides three important symbolic images. First, it provides a link to the OT covenantal language that the prophets often used of Israel as the wife of God.[54] In this manner, John maintains continuity with the OT prophetic tradition and provides a link between the eschatological people of God—who are heirs of the new covenant (and thus the bride of the *Lamb*)—and the people of the old covenant. Second, John has already indicated that the bride of the Lamb has been clothed in "fine linen, bright and pure," which represents "the righteous deeds of the saints" (19.8). Hence the chastity of the bride is contrasted to the promiscuity of the whore.[55] Third, the most important message being communicated through the use of bridal imagery is "the intimacy and fruitfulness of the relationship between God and the redeemed in the apocalyptic age."[56] Deutsch suggests that John uses both bride and wife language in 21.9 to express newness and intimacy. Her suggestion is credible if one considers the imagery within the framework of both the Old and new covenants. Wife language, which depicts God's intimate relationship with Israel, is borrowed from the OT prophets, while bride language indicates the renewal and hope of the new covenant. Bridal imagery, however, is even found among the OT prophets when they speak of the post-exilic restoration of Jerusalem and Israel (e.g., Isa 49.18; 61.10; 62.5).

Twelve Gates and Twelve Foundations

The NJ "has the glory of God and a radiance like a very rare jewel, like jasper, clear as crystal" (21.11). This description of the city recalls John's opening throne room vision of chapter 4 where the one seated on the throne "looks like jasper" (4.2) and before whose throne is a sea "like crystal" (4.6).[57] In 21.18, John describes the walls of the city as made of jasper and the city as made of transparent gold. This transparent beauty not only reflects the glory of God but emphasizes the purity of the city. The fact

---

[54] See Muirhead, "Bride," 175–87.

[55] This is a contrast equally applied in the OT to Israel, who is depicted both as a faithful wife and a promiscuous woman (e.g., Isa 54.6; Jer 3.1, 20; Hos 2.1-13).

[56] Deutsch, "Transformation," 113. Note the use of similar language in Eph 5.21-33 for Christ and the church.

[57] Ladd, *Revelation*, 281.

that the city reflects the glory of God also implies that it is permeated with his presence.[58]

Within the walls of the city are twelve gates named after the twelve tribes of Israel. This is only the second mention of the twelve tribes in the Apocalypse, with the first being in the vision of the 144,000 of chapter 7 (7.3-8). Their appearance in both of these visions serves a similar purpose in that John is able to unite imagery of God's covenant people Israel with the eschatological people of God—the church. This portion of the NJ vision is modeled on Ezekiel's vision of the temple; however, Ezekiel's twelve gates of the temple have become John's twelve gates of the city. John adapts Ezekiel's vision to focus on the city rather than the temple complex.

A most striking feature in John's NJ vision is his detailed description of the foundations that are inscribed with the names of the "twelve apostles of the Lamb" (21.14). This feature of the city departs from Ezekiel's vision, and is the first to indicate messianic symbolism. John spends a significant part of his vision detailing the foundations of the NJ because he wishes to emphasize this new aspect of his city (21.14, 19-20). John's Jewish heritage, as well as historical precedent, might lead one to expect the names of the twelve tribes to be inscribed on the foundations of the city, but the fact that the NJ is founded on the twelve apostles illuminates John's intention to identify the city as "eschatological Israel"—the church.[59] The designation of the twelve gates after the twelve tribes and the foundation stones after the twelve apostles is not intended to communicate a continued distinction between the two, but that the fulfillment of Israel's hope and covenant promises rests on Christ and the testimony of the apostles (cf. Eph 2.20).[60] John has taken Ezekiel's prophecy of a restored Israel and reinterpreted it in light of the redemptive work of the Lamb.

---

[58] Beale, *Revelation*, 1066. Beale believes that John alludes here to Isa 58.8; 60.1-2, 19, where God's glory, as another expression for his presence, is said to reside in latter-day Jerusalem.

[59] Prigent, *L'Apocalypse*, 471; cf. Beale, *Revelation*, 1070; contra Walvoord, *Revelation*, 322, who believes that the NJ represents a city inclusive of all the saints through the ages, but not the church as the new Israel; cf. Ladd, *Revelation*, 281, who says that the gates and the foundation stones show that "Israel of the Old Testament" and the "Church of the New Testament" have a part in the NJ—"the city encompasses both dispensations."

[60] Hirschberg, *Das eschatologische Israel*, 259–60, makes an interesting comparison at this point, drawing an analogy between the teacher of righteousness as the foundational character of the Qumran community and the twelve apostles as foundational for the eschatological Israel. Just as those who held to the teachings of the teacher of righteousness belonged to the Qumran community, so also those who hold to the teaching of the apostles share in Christ's eschatological kingdom.

The detailed description of the foundations and the gems from which they are made demonstrates the importance of this particular feature to John's vision. Each one of the foundations corresponds to one of the twelve stones that John is careful to list in his description of the celestial city. This detail implies that there is within John's description of the foundation stones a symbolic significance. What this significance is has, of course, been a matter of some debate.

There are primarily three interpretations[61] of the significance of the gem stones listed in 21.19-20. A number of scholars associate the gem list with the twelve signs of the zodiac.[62] Others have equally observed that eight of the twelve gem stones correspond to the stones in the breast piece of Israel's high priest (Exod 28.17-20; 39.10-13), with the rest being dubbed semantic equivalents.[63] Finally, because of the difficulties associated with the previous theories, some scholars argue that the stones simply imply the glory or reward of the people of God.[64] This latter interpretation is recommended when one considers the contrasted wealth of the whore of Babylon (17.4, 16).

The first and second interpretations are those held by most scholars, and it is between these two that the debate primarily divides. The third interpretation seems the least supported and can easily be dismissed as an insufficient interpretation to deal justly with the role of the gem stones in John's vision. This, of course, is not to deny that this latter interpretation has some validity, but simply to argue that it is insufficient to explain John's detailed description of each of the foundations of the wall. The rich ornamentation of the NJ certainly stands in contrast to the adornment of the whore in 17.4, 16; however, the detail and greater attention proportionately given to the adornment of the NJ implies that the list carries greater significance.

The views that the gems correspond either with the signs of the zodiac or the breast piece of the high priest are not mutually exclusive. The difference between these two views seems to be a matter of emphasis when speculating on John's primary symbolic message communicated through his listing and ordering of these gem stones. The association of the gem stones with the breast piece is complicated by the fact that it is difficult to

---

[61] These three interpretations are derived from the author's own research and the discussion in Osborne, *Revelation*, 756–58.

[62] Charles, *Revelation*, 2:165–68; Kiddle, *Revelation*, 433–34; Roloff, *Revelation*, 244; Vogelgesang, "Interpretation of Ezekiel," 98–99; Malina, *New Jerusalem*, 55.

[63] Mounce, *Revelation*, 393; Aune, *Revelation 17–22*, 1165; Beale, *Revelation*, 1080–81.

[64] Ladd, *Revelation*, 283, Gundry, "New Jerusalem," 261.

correlate the names of the gems, particularly since the names must cross from Hebrew into Greek; however, as observed above, there is some possible correspondence between at least eight of the names in the two lists. Another equally difficult problem is arranging a one-to-one correspondence between the order of John's list and those of Exod 28.17-20 and 39.10-13.

Charles and Vogelgesang both see a possible reference in John's list to the breast piece of the high priest but see a primary allusion to the zodiac.[65] Charles justifies his conclusion based largely on a supposed correspondence in antiquity between the signs of the zodiac and specific gem stones.[66] Although Charles does believe that the gem stones correspond to the breast piece of the high priest, he observes that the order of the stones in John's list is different from that in Exod 28.17-20 and 39.10-13. Charles solves this problem by taking the list of gems in Rev 21.19-20 and coordinating it with the compass directions in 21.13 and the list of tribes in 7.5-8. He then deduces that John has listed the gems in the reverse order of the zodiac. Charles finds two favorable results from his method. He believes that this method provides a link between key passages in the Apocalypse and that through the reversal of the zodiac, John denudes his cosmic city of any resemblance to either a Jewish or pagan concept of a "city of the gods."[67]

Vogelgesang, who believes that the NJ is a redeemed Babylon, would not agree with Charles' negative conclusion.[68] He proposes that John has integrated allusions to the city of the gods and other secular models into his NJ description.[69] However, he would agree with the association of the stones with the zodiac. He also acknowledges that the stones may reflect

---

[65] Charles, *Revelation*, 2:165–68; Vogelgesang, "Interpretation of Ezekiel," 98–99; cf. Roloff, *Revelation*, 244, who also finds a reference to the breast piece possible, but believes the association with the zodiac is purposeful. Malina, *New Jerusalem*, 55–56, takes a position similar to that of Vogelgesang.

[66] Charles' argument is based on the thesis of A. Kircher, *Oedipus Aegyptiacus* (Rome: Mascardi, 1653) 2. 2. 177–78 (as cited by Reader, "Twelve Jewels," 451, n. 45), who claimed to have discovered an Arabic document that outlined an ancient Egyptian correspondence between the zodiac and precious stones. There is, however, serious debate over the authenticity of Kircher's discovery since no such document has ever been produced. See the discussion in Reader, "Twelve Jewels," 451–52; Beale, *Revelation*, 1082, particularly n. 119.

[67] Charles, *Revelation*, 2:165–68; cf. 1:315–16, where Charles makes a similar connection between the crown of twelve stars of Revelation 12.

[68] Vogelgesang, "Interpretation of Ezekiel," 98–99.

[69] Ibid., 128.

the high priest's breast piece, but, given Josephus' (*Ant.* 3.162-187) and Philo's (*Moses* 2.124, 133; *Spec. Laws* 1.84-94; *QE* 2.112-15) association of the stones of the breast piece with the zodiac and what Vogelgesang sees as other allusions to Babylon and Babylonian mythology, he believes that John's primary reference is to the zodiac.

Charles' idea of a reversed zodiac seems to have been largely abandoned in recent scholarship,[70] although the association with the zodiac has not. Vogelgesang's approach is more plausible, but seems unlikely since it relies heavily on John's preoccupation with secular material and his desire to demonstrate a redeemed Babylon. He believes that the universal flavor of the NJ imagery indicates that John made use of multiple sources (e.g., the perfect Hellenistic city from Hippodamus of Miletus, the layout of Babylon from Herodotus, the cubical shape of the Tower of Babel, and Solomon's holy of holies) in his description.[71] Vogelgesang's interpretation, however, seems to be less a product of John's design and more Vogelgesang's desire to read into John his own universalism.[72] Schüssler Fiorenza similarly believes that John had a broad knowledge of Jewish apocalyptic literature, deuterocanonical literature, Greco-Roman motifs, and Babylon's architecture and made use of them in his description of the city.[73]

While one must acknowledge that John was a person of two cultures, one must ask which culture likely played the dominant role. The inherent assumption of the above viewpoint is that John would have knowledge of, or even a primary interest in, such secular allusions. This conclusion seems unlikely. Although the gem list, and even the shape of the city, may have some correlation to secular mythology, one must consider the author's primary socio-cultural background. John is a Jewish Christian. His attraction to allusions to the Jewish scriptures is undeniable, and his belief that Jesus is the Messiah is easily proven. It is this Jewish Christian perspective that dominates the Apocalypse. Although reference to John's Greco-Roman culture and its mythology may be in evidence at times, this is neither the primary circle of thought within which John operates nor should it stand on an equal plane with his Jewish culture. In considering John's use of secular material, one must not only consider geography and availability

---

[70] So Draper, "Twelve Apostles," 43–44.

[71] Vogelgesang, "Interpretation of Ezekiel," 93–94.

[72] Ibid., 107–8. Vogelgesang, for example, conceives of the entrance of nations (21.24-26) as a constant flow from the Lake of Fire into the NJ (103–8).

[73] Schüssler Fiorenza, *Vision*, 111–12.

but one should also assume that John is first immersed in his own culture and scriptures, and it is these that take precedent over secular sources.[74]

With this perspective in mind, one must conclude that John's list of gem stones finds its source in the Jewish scriptures. The stones not only allude to the breast piece of the high priest but also to the prophetic promises of a restored Jerusalem (Isa 54.11-12). Prigent suggests that 4Q164 provides precedent for the idea that John has connected the gems of the breast piece with those of restored Jerusalem.[75] The difference in order between John's gem list and that of Exodus is inconsequential since Josephus himself lists the stones in differing order (*Ant.* 168; cf. *J.W.* 234).[76] Indeed, Reader concludes that there was no standardized list in Hellenistic Judaism, but simply "a living flexible tradition of twelve gems" that resulted in a list not based on any original Hebrew one.[77]

Even more telling, however, is John's adaptation of this gem stone tradition in his description of the NJ. Each of the stones in the priestly breast piece had engraved on it one of the names of the twelve tribes of Israel. In John's vision, each of these precious stones bears one of the names of the twelve apostles. This replacement of the twelve tribes with the twelve apostles affirms that John sees the church as God's new spiritual Israel.[78] They are the foundation upon which the church is built (Eph 2.20); they are the founding heads of the renewed tribes of Israel. However, John does not divorce the church from its Jewish roots. The extensive allusions to Jewish cultic imagery, the Ezekiel-like naming of the twelve gates after the twelve tribes, and, of course, the fact that this vision of God's end-time people is a new Jerusalem all suggest that John sees the church as the realization of his Jewish heritage.

The connection of the priestly gem stones with the Apostles and in turn the church also serves John's intention to symbolize the priestly function of God's eschatological people (cf. 1 Pet 2.5).[79] Access to God's presence is no longer the sole right of a select few but the privilege of all of God's people; as John writes, "His servants will worship (λατρεύσουσιν)[80]

---

[74] Briggs, *Jewish Temple Imagery*, 42–43.

[75] Prigent, *L'Apocalypse*, 476–77.

[76] Beale, *Revelation*, 1080. Cf. Prigent, *L'Apocalypse*, 474–77, who believes that John's list evokes images of the priestly breast piece but offers a more complicated and, in the final analysis, inadequate explanation for the disorder.

[77] Reader, "Twelve Jewels," 439–40.

[78] Beale, *Revelation*, 1080–81.

[79] So Beale, *Revelation*, 1080–81; cf. Aune, *Revelation 17–22*, 1165.

[80] This term is used in the sense of cultic service to God (cf. 7.15). See "λατρεύω," 586,

him; they will see his face, and his name will be on their foreheads" (22.3-4). The foundation of Solomon's temple was laid with costly stones (1 Kgs 7.9-10), God promised to restore and rebuild Jerusalem with jewels (Isa 54.11-12), and John finds this promise of restoration fulfilled for all of God's people in the NJ.

The Wall and Its Measurements

John's detailed description of the foundations of the Holy City is preceded by an equally detailed description of its walls, in particularly their measurements. The measuring of the city recalls John's earlier vision of the temple in 11.1-2, where he is given a measuring rod and told to measure the temple, the altar, and the worshipers there. This latter vision, as well as the present one, alludes to Ezekiel's own vision of the measuring of the restored temple (40.3). As has already been noted in the previous discussion of 11.1-2, measuring can denote judgment, preservation, sanctification, or even restoration.[81] The themes of preservation and sanctification are likely in mind in 11.1-2. John is conveying to the saints assurance of preservation in the midst of opposition from the nations, and the command to measure performs the symbolic function of communicating this message. The measuring of the NJ, however, is intended to communicate a broader message than simply the ideas of preservation, sanctification, or even restoration. While these ideas may be possible sub-themes,[82] the detailed description of the city's measurements convey within themselves a message concerning the identity of the NJ.

In 21.16, John writes that "the city lies foursquare, its length the same as its width." The length of the sides of the city is 12,000 stadia, making the city approximately 1,500 miles square. In addition, John states at the end of 21.16 that the city's "length and width and height are equal," giving the city a cubical shape. The enormous size of the city and its shape have led to considerable speculation concerning the meaning of these measurements and the significance of the shape of the city.

BDAG on CD-ROM. Version 1.0d. 2000, 2001.

[81] See the discussion in chapter 4, 125–26.

[82] See Beale, *Revelation*, 1072, who believes that the measuring symbolizes the preservation and purity of God's end-time people (21.27; 22.14-15); cf. Mounce, *Revelation*, 393; Vogelgesang, "Interpretation of Ezekiel," 92, who believes the purpose of measuring is to "show" the city to John, as in the case of Ezekiel, and to indicate "perfection, plan and eternal preservation;" Osborne, *Revelation*, 752–53, who suggests the measuring symbolizes God's presence, protection, and restoration.

Of course, one's interpretation depends on one's view of the city as either literal or symbolic. Walvoord, who interprets the city literally, postulates that the enormous size of the city is necessary in order to hold the large number of saints who inhabit it eternally.[83] Osborne agrees, although he also accepts that the measurement of 12,000 stadia is symbolic of perfection, as in 7.4-8.[84] Gundry develops the symbolic interpretation exclusively by proposing that the 12,000 x 12,000 stadia of the NJ are reminiscent of the 144,000 of chapter 7 (cf. 14.1-5). If one combines these measurements of the city with its cubical shape, then the resulting cube would project twelve edges of 12,000 stadia each, which, when multiplied, equal 144,000.[85]

Gundry is following a more reasonable line of interpretation by emphasizing the symbolic nature of the numbers. John clearly has an affinity for the number twelve and its multiples and seems to use it symbolically for the people of God (e.g., 144,000 sealed, twelve tribes, twelve stars, twelve gates, twelve apostles). The 12,000 stadia, like the 144,000 sealed, are symbolic numbers and are multiplied times 1000 to indicate perfection, vastness and innumerability.[86] As in the case of the twofold vision of chapter 7, John uses the 12,000 from the twelve tribes to show the vastness of God's people, which he affirms later in the vision of the innumerable multitude. The enormous measurements of the NJ perform the same function. They are symbolic of the vastness of God's people portrayed in the image of the NJ. In addition, the use of multiples of twelve and the appearance of the twelve tribes of Israel in both visions suggest a common interpretation of the two. Both visions are symbolic of the church as eschatological Israel. The vision of the NJ makes this particularly clear, with the city founded on the twelve apostles of the Lamb.

Revelation 21.17 confirms this symbolic interpretation, as John here writes that the wall measures 144 (12 x 12) cubits. It is not clear whether John intends this measurement to indicate the thickness or the height of the wall.[87] Whichever the case may be, the wall is clearly disproportionate

---

[83] Walvoord, *Revelation*, 324.
[84] Osborne, *Revelation*, 752–53.
[85] Gundry, "New Jerusalem," 260; cf. Beale, *Revelation*, 1076–77. Also see the discussion in chapter 3, 101.
[86] See Bauckham, *Climax*, 36, in this regard concerning the 144,000. Cf. Mounce, *Revelation*, 392, on the NJ measurements.
[87] Osborne, *Revelation*, 753–54; Aune, *Revelation 17–22*, 1162, opt for the measurement being the width of the wall. Aune cites Neh 3.8; 12.38; Jer 51.58 and Herodotus 1.178, where the width of the wall is given priority over its height. Beale, *Revelation*, 1076–77,

in size compared to the enormous measurements of the city. The wall is not likely intended to be an outer defense of the city against the wicked[88] or a means to delineate between the clean and unclean.[89] These problems are not even issues in John's new heaven and earth (20.15). The disproportionate size of the wall rather indicates its symbolic importance.[90] Many cities of John's day had walls and this would be an expected part of an ideal city.[91] This aspect of the city is only an incidental part of the city's description; it is the measuring of the city that is the focus in this section of the vision, and thus far it has been the measurements that have held symbolic significance—no less is true of the 144 cubits.

The size of the wall may seem absurd to a literalist but within John's numeric schema it makes perfect sense. The number one hundred forty-four is another multiple of twelve and stands in perfect harmony with the square of 12,000 stadia and even the 144,000 sealed.[92] Indeed, the multiplication of the twelve apostles times the twelve tribes, both associated with the wall, suggests this numeric product. "Accordingly, it is right to see that the wall signifies that the new Jerusalem includes the perfect number of God's people."[93] In order to achieve his symbolic message, John maintains numeric and symbolic consistency to the detriment of the city's

opts for the height.

[88] Contra Charles, *Revelation*, 2:164.

[89] Contra Vogelgesang, "Interpretation of Ezekiel," 106–7. See the discussion in Lee, *New Jerusalem*, 277, against an interpretation of the wall as a delimiting symbol.

[90] Lee, *New Jerusalem*, 278, also says that in addition to its symbolic meaning the wall serves as a link to the Zion tradition upon which John draws, and signifies Zion's security which was paramount in the OT (Isa 26.1; 33.16; Ezek 36.12b-15; 38.8; Jer 30.10-11; Zech 9.8; 12.1-9; 14.10-11) and early Jewish literature (*2 Bar.* 4.1-7; 6.1-9; 1QH 14.18-38). This sense of security serves to assure the Asian believers of their eschatological security in the face of their present sufferings. This is a possibility since John's description of the NJ has affinity with OT (Isa 54.11-12) and early Jewish texts (Tob 13.16-17; 4Q164; 554; 5Q15) and is a motif consistent with the previous visions examined in the present study.

[91] So Mounce, *Revelation*, 379.

[92] So Prigent, *L'Apocalypse*, 473; cf. Beale, *Revelation*, 1076–77. Bauckham, *Climax*, 388–400, makes an additional observation with regard to the significance of 144. He postulates that John has set it in contrast to the number of the beast, 666, using Pythagorean arithmetic in which numbers are related to shapes. Six hundred sixty-six is a triangular number and 144 is a square number. The latter is indicated in John's vision by the square of twelve and John's own description of the NJ as square and then cubical (21.16). In addition, by means of Hebrew gematria, 666 is the sum of θηρίον when transliterated into Hebrew, and ἄγγελος, when transliterated into Hebrew, sums to 144. Bauckham argues that John invites such a comparison by using a similar expression in 21.17 as that of 13.18, "the measure of a human being, that is, of an angel" (21.17 translation his; cf. similar phrasing in 13.18).

[93] Lee, *New Jerusalem*, 279.

proportions, proving once more that the NJ is intended to be a symbol and not a literal place.

The measurements of the NJ also indicate a cubical shape to the city, and there has been some controversy as to how to interpret the meaning behind this shape. Scholars usually see in this image evidence of either John's Jewish or Hellenistic background or a combination of both. Schüssler Fiorenza believes that the cubic measurements of the city recall Herodotus' (1.178) "foursquare" description of ancient Babylon, suggesting that John wished to communicate to his readers that God's city stands in antithesis to historic Babylon.[94] This interpretation is particularly strengthened by the visionary antithesis John has established with metaphorical Babylon in Revelation 17–18.[95]

Vogelgesang pursues a similar line of interpretation, but instead understands John to be depicting the NJ as a redeemed Babylon rather than its antithesis.[96] He too cites the parallelism between 21.9—22.5 and 17–18, but believes that John wishes to show the redemption of the former enemies of God and their wealth. Vogelgesang finds marked similarities between the description of the NJ and that of Babylon in ancient literature. Its cubic shape recalls the Babylonian ziggurat and the repeated reference to the number twelve implies a reference to the zodiac. The city also not only lies foursquare like ancient Babylon but also has a river running through it (Rev 22.1-2; cf. *Herodotus* 1.180). Vogelgesang believes that John has modeled his city on the ideal Hellenistic city, showing that the NJ has achieved the idealistic universal world at which Greco-Roman cities had failed.[97]

Malina, who interprets the Apocalypse as an astronomical/astrological document, also finds many similarities between John's description of the NJ and his Hellenistic culture. He postulates that the cubic shape of the city is in keeping with the doctrine of astrology concerning the figures of the zodiac.[98] He notes that the square, which John specifically mentions in 21.16, is considered in ancient astral mathematics to be a symbol of

---

[94] Kraft, *Offenbarung*, 270–71, would agree on this point. He does not believe that there is enough evidence in the text to determine if John wishes to propose a cubic shape of the city. Equal sides and height are not enough. He does, however, believe that although no shape is intended here, John does wish to communicate an antithetical reference to the ziggurat of Babylon.
[95] Schüssler Fiorenza, *Vision*, 111–12; cf. Beale, *Revelation*, 1075.
[96] Vogelgesang, "Interpretation of Ezekiel," 127.
[97] Ibid., 126.
[98] Malina, *New Jerusalem*, 54–56.

perfection or completion. This astral interpretation is in keeping with the repeated reference to the number twelve, which he also views as symbolic of the zodiac.

Malina and Vogelgesang do not completely ignore John's Jewish background and acknowledge that the cubic shape may also be a reference to the holy of holies of Solomon's temple (1 Kgs 6.20). In fact, Vogelgesang believes that multiple images lie behind John's description of the NJ, indicating the international flavor of John's image.[99] However, he places greater emphasis on the NJ as a portrayal of a redeemed Babylon. Malina too likens the shape of the city to the holy of holies, intimating that the city, like Solomon's gilded holy of holies, stands in cubic perfection as a glorious bride for her husband.[100]

While comparisons between the NJ and Babylon are intriguing, they fall short of communicating the message that John is intending to convey. John does not wish to communicate that God has created the ideal city or that Babylon has in some way been redeemed. Antithetical comparisons are possible, especially in view of the fact that the vision of the NJ and the whore in Revelation 17–18 are clearly set in contrast to one another; but this is not the central message of the vision. This vision is of the *new Jerusalem*, not the new Babylon. The vision of the NJ, like those previously examined in the present work, is rich with Jewish imagery. John no doubt wishes to call upon Jewish prophetic and apocalyptic tradition to portray a new Jerusalem symbolic of the redeemed people of God. Although one does not wish to deny John's Hellenistic culture, the features of the vision and its affinity with OT scripture persuasively argue that his Jewish background takes precedent.[101] The cubic shape of the city implies that the entire city is a holy of holies, not a Babylonian temple.[102] The enthronement of God and the Lamb there, as well as the fact that his people have unhindered access to his presence, affirms this idea (22.3-4). The merging of the city with the temple in this fashion brings to completion the NT

---

[99] Vogelgesang, "Interpretation of Ezekiel," 93–94.

[100] Malina, *New Jerusalem*, 54–56.

[101] Briggs, *Jewish Temple Imagery*, 42–43, and Stevenson, *Power and Place*, 304, both argue methodologically that John's Jewish tradition takes precedent in the study of his apocalyptic imagery. Stevenson writes, "The primary literary and conceptual context for Revelation is Jewish thought and tradition (including apocalyptic) and the Old Testament." However, neither Stevenson nor Briggs suggests that John's Greco-Roman culture should be ignored.

[102] Gundry, "New Jerusalem," 261; Mounce, *Revelation*, 392; Prigent, *L'Apocalypse*, 473; Osborne, *Revelation*, 759–60.

idea of God's people as his temple and also communicates that the temple area, once off limits, has now become accessible to all.

The merging of the city with temple imagery also furthers the notion that the foundation stones are reminiscent of the priestly breast piece. Kline observes that the breast piece itself was designed as a miniature holy of holies, with its square shape corresponding to the cubical shape of the room and as the receptacle of the Urim and Thummim, it was "the locus of the divine judgment" (Exod 28.15).[103] In addition, both Prigent and Reader observe that the stones of the breast piece became connected in Targumic literature with the encampment of the Israelites in the wilderness.[104] This connection may be an image that John has in mind in his description of the NJ. John's detailing of three gates on each side of the city, each inscribed with one of the names of the twelve tribes of Israel, invokes this image of Israel's wilderness encampment, where the tribes camped three on each side facing the Tabernacle of God (Num 2.2, 17).[105] The declaration of Rev 21.3 that God's "tabernacle" (σκηνή) is among his people and that he will "tabernacle with them" (σκηνώσει μετ' αὐτῶν) reinforces this link. This combination of OT temple and tabernacle allusions provides John with the imagery he needs to communicate the eternal fellowship between God and his people.

Stevenson, who has done extensive research into the temple imagery of the Apocalypse, argues that the temple in Revelation is a place of "identity and power."[106] He observes that each time John uses temple imagery, it is usually heaven-centered (11.1-2 may be an exception); it serves as a place of identity for God's people (e.g., 3.12); and it is a place of access to his power.[107] The throne room scene of chapters 4 and 5 is couched in temple-like language (cf. Isa 6.1-8), and it is at the altar in heaven where both the prayers of the saints are received and from which God's judgment proceeds (8.3-5; 11.19; 14.17-18; 15.5-8; 16.1, 17). This association of

---

[103] Meredith G. Kline, *Images of the Spirit*, BBMS (Grand Rapids: Baker, 1980) 45.

[104] Prigent, *L'Apocalypse*, 474, cites 4QMMT 58-62, which equates the stones with Israel's camp. See particularly the extensive references and comparative analysis in Reader, "Twelve Jewels," 440–42. *Tg. Ps.-Jon.* Num 2.3, 10, 18, 25, is particularly illustrative. Reader notes that *Tg. Ps.-Jon.* Num 2.3, 10, 18, 25, lists the stones not as "four parallel rows, but rather in connection with the quadratic order of the camp, namely three per side (cf. Rev 21.13, 16, 19-20)." In light of the NJ measurements, it is also interesting to observe that *Tg. Ps.-J* Num 2.3, describes the camp of Israel as twelve miles in length and width.

[105] John's compass directions are, however, in a different order from Num 2.1-34.

[106] Stevenson, *Power and Place*, 305.

[107] Ibid., 305–6.

the temple with heaven provides a link between God and his people and contributes to the separation between the earth-dwellers (the followers of the beast) and the faithful of God (note the language of 13.6).[108]

Although the temple imagery throughout the Apocalypse provides a place of identity for both Jewish and Gentile Christians, the imagery itself is primarily Jewish.[109] Stevenson argues that temple language permeates the Apocalypse because John is making the claim that Christians are "Jews." John has taken the temple, which was a place of identity for the Jews, and has transferred it to Christians.[110] The NJ serves to merge the church and Israel into one people of God; God's covenant community is comprised of both Jews and Gentiles (Rev 21.24, 26; 22.2).[111] In the NJ, John's temple imagery has been merged into his description of the city, which descends from heaven to earth. The presence of God—located in the heavenly holy of holies—is now fully accessible to his people. As Stevenson writes, "In the New Jerusalem . . . the full meaning of what the temple is and what it does has been realized in the direct and immediate presence of God."[112]

No Temple There

This transformation of the city into a temple itself appears to contradict one of the most startling statements in John's description of the NJ, "I saw no temple in the city" (Rev 21.22). Although by the time of the writing of the Apocalypse the temple had been destroyed, any ancient Israelite, particularly of Ezekiel's day, would have found a restored Jerusalem without a temple to be inconceivable. What is it, then, that John is trying to say? Does such a statement actually nullify the concept of the NJ being modeled on the holy of holies or that God's servants serve him as priests eternally?

Throughout John's description of the NJ he has invoked allusions to the Jewish prophetic tradition and has primarily modeled his description on Ezekiel's vision of the rebuilt temple. John, however, has demonstrated interpretive freedom in his own description, departing from Ezekiel and other Jewish traditions to communicate his christocentric message. As has been noted, one of the major differences between John's and Ezekiel's vi-

---

[108] Ibid., 305.

[109] See ibid., 267–68. Note particularly the presence of the Ark of the Covenant (11.19) and the reference to the "tent (or tabernacle) of testimony" in 15.5.

[110] Ibid., 238–39.

[111] Ibid., 272; cf. 224; cf. Lee, *New Jerusalem*, 280.

[112] Stevenson, *Power and Place*, 306.

sions is that Ezekiel is preoccupied primarily with a detailed description of a restored temple while John describes a new Jerusalem. In the mind of any Jew and perhaps some Gentiles, the link between Jerusalem and the temple was inseparable. To speak of one was to imply the other.[113] John, however, while evoking cultic imagery in his description of the city, does not wish to imply that the temple is present in his new Jerusalem. The reason for his clarity is that while the temple evokes memories of God's presence among his people, it also communicates a sense of separation and limited access to that same presence. John wishes his message to be clear that the eternal state of God and his people is unhindered fellowship. As Deutsch writes, "The temple, as a symbol of access to the divine presence, is replaced by the Presence itself."[114] Thus John completes the statement of 21.22 by writing, "for its temple is the Lord God the Almighty and the Lamb."

The double entendre cannot be overlooked here. The city, a symbol for God's people, is itself in the shape of the holy of holies, which suggests that it is a huge temple where God's presence dwells. As Stevenson points out, in the Apocalypse the "temple and the throne room are interrelated"; "Revelation conceives of the throne as being in the temple"[115] (cf. 22.3). Indeed, the city itself is infused with and reflects the glory and presence of God (21.11). Such a message is consistent with the idea of God's people being his spiritual temple and also communicates the intimacy achieved in the eternal state; however, the city has no temple because God's presence is fully among his people. As in Ezekiel's vision John's city could be fittingly called, "The LORD is There" (Ezek 48.35).[116]

The introduction of the central place of God and the Lamb leads naturally into a discussion of the effects of their presence in the city. There is no need for sun or moon, for the glory of God and the Lamb will be its light and the nations shall walk by this light. In 21.23-26, John appeals to the prophetic tradition of Isa 60.1-3, 5, and 11 concerning the restoration of Israel, where Isaiah prophesies that God's glory shall rise upon his people and the nations of the earth will stream into restored Jerusalem. Indeed Isa 60.11 states that Jerusalem's gates will always be open and the wealth of nations shall be brought into it. John adopts much of Isaiah's imagery but

---

[113] Ibid., 5, remarks that in the OT the mention of the temple normally implies Jerusalem or vice versa since one would be unimaginable without the other.

[114] Deutsch, "Transformation," 115; cf. Hirschberg, *Das eschatologische Israel*, 241.

[115] Stevenson, *Power and Place*, 233. Stevenson cites a number of passages that illustrate this point, the most striking of which is the throne room scene of chapters 4 and 5.

[116] Osborne, *Revelation*, 759–60.

noticeably adapts the language for his own purpose.[117] The most striking difference between John and Isaiah is John's universalistic language.

According to Isa 60.11-12, the nations will bring their wealth into Jerusalem with "their kings led in procession," and those who do not serve Israel will "perish" and will be "utterly laid waste." For John, however, the people of God are now the people of the nations. They will bring in, not their wealth, but their glory, thus honoring God. They are also not led as captives, but enter freely, walking by the light of the glory of God.[118] This is a radical change from John's previous treatment of the nations elsewhere in the Apocalypse (2.26; 6.15-17; 10.11; 11.2, 9, 18; 12.5; 13.7; 14.6-8; 15.9; 17.15; 18.3, 23; 19.12; 20.3, 8),[119] but it is not inconsistent with his belief that the redeemed are comprised of those from every nation (5.9; 7.9). John is perhaps aware of this change of image for the nations and adds the qualifying statement, "But nothing unclean will enter it, nor anyone who practices abomination or falsehood, but only those who are written in the Lamb's book of life" (21.27).

Paradise Regained (22.1-5)

Although John introduced the idea of a new heaven and a new earth in 21.1, thus far he has been preoccupied with a description of the NJ. He now turns in his description to characteristic elements of the new creation. What is significant, however, is that his description of the new creation is an extension of his discussion of the NJ, for the NJ encompasses the new creation.[120] In 22.1-5, John reacquires his Ezekelian model as he blends imagery of the NJ with the new heaven and earth. The conflation of the NJ with the new creation is a natural outgrowth of John's vision, since its descent from heaven to earth serves to unite these two spheres.

John models this portion of his vision on Ezek 47.1-12; however, his adaptation of Ezekiel's language is again revealing. In Ezekiel's vision, the angel brings him back to the entrance of the temple, where he sees a

---

[117] Ibid., 761–63.

[118] For the latter comment see Aune, *Revelation 17–22,* 1170.

[119] Vogelgesang, "Interpretation of Ezekiel," 103.

[120] There is some debate as to whether the NJ is intended to be the center of the new creation or encompass it. The latter seems more likely, especially if the city symbolizes the people of God. The astronomical dimensions may also suggest such a conclusion. For support of this idea, see Vogelgesang, "Interpretation of Ezekiel," 95, 126; Schüssler Fiorenza, *Vision,* 110; Beale, *Revelation,* 1109–11; Malina, *New Jerusalem,* 56. Contra Lee, *New Jerusalem,* 272, who sees the NJ as the center of the new creation, where the features of the "latter are more intensively given to the former."

life-giving river flowing from underneath the threshold of the temple's east gate. Along the banks of this river are trees that bear their fruit monthly and whose leaves are "for healing" (47.12). John, too, sees a life-giving river in his vision, which he calls "the river of the water of life" (22.1). This river, however, flows not from the temple, but from the throne of God and the Lamb, the temple of the NJ.[121] Unlike Ezekiel, the tree, which John sees growing along the river of life, is not just any tree; but it is the "tree of life," and its leaves are not just "for healing" but for the "healing *of the nations*" (22.2; emphasis mine). Here, John has adapted Ezekiel's language to conform to his own christocentric perspective—that the ultimate goal of God's salvific plan is the redemption of a people from every nation (5.9; 7.9).[122]

The tree of life and the river of life call to mind images of a restored Eden (Gen 2.9-10).[123] Lee argues that there is a close connection between the new temple, NJ, and new creation throughout Jewish literature.[124] He concludes that "the new Jerusalem/temple, Garden of Eden, and the New Creation are the triple pillars of the message of restoration in the OT."[125]

---

[121] Beale, *Revelation*, 1103–4, suggests that John may have combined allusions to both Ezekiel's vision and Zech 14.8 (cf. Joel 3.18), where Zechariah sees a river of life flowing from Jerusalem.

[122] So Bauckham, *Climax*, 316; Beale, *Revelation*, 1107–8. Bauckham specifically notes John's addition to Ezekiel's description of the trees as bearing "twelve kinds of fruit" (22.2) and that their leaves are for the "healing *of the nations*" (emphasis mine), as suggesting that John has combined the number of God's people (twelve) with a reference to the nations to show the inclusion of the nations in the covenant people. Beale offers that John's use of twelve here and throughout the vision symbolizes the completeness of the redemptive plan.

[123] So Vogelgesang, "Interpretation of Ezekiel," 108–10; Deutsch, "Transformation," 116–17; Mounce, *Revelation*, 398; Aune, *Revelation 17–22*, 1187–88; Beale, *Revelation*, 1103–4; Osborne, *Revelation*, 768.

[124] Lee, *New Jerusalem*, 223–25; 271–72; cf. Deutsch, "Transformation," 116–17. The idea of a heavenly new temple/Jerusalem and particularly a heavenly paradise is more a development of Second Temple literature than of the OT, although the idea of the new temple/Jerusalem, new creation, and paradise coexisting can be found in the OT (Ezek 47.1-12; Isa 11.6-9; 51.3; 54.11-12; 65.17-25). As observed earlier, the hope of an earthly restoration of the temple/Jerusalem became increasingly focused heavenward during the Second Temple period with the perceived corruption of the temple hierarchy and its subsequent destruction.

Second Temple texts that connect the NJ with Eden: *2 Bar.* 4.1-7; 32.1-6; *1 En.* 24–26; 28–36; *T. Dan* 5.12-13; *4 Ezra* 8.52; cf. 1QH 14.15-17, where the community as temple is described in terms of Eden. Texts that speak of a new creation: *2 Bar.* 72–74; *Apoc. Ab.* 9.8-10; see also Lee, *New Jerusalem*, 224, for other references.

[125] Lee, *New Jerusalem*, 52.

John has indeed combined these elements in his description of the NJ. The restoration of Eden is the restoration of a lost relationship between God and humanity. It is the goal of God's salvific plan to restore this relationship lost through Adam's sin. Whereas angels once blocked entry into the Garden of Eden, angels now hold open the gates of the NJ, giving free access to the tree of life and healing for the nations.[126]

As Beale comments, the Garden of Eden is the place where Adam and Eve had fellowship with God and where they functioned in a priestly role.[127] They were to guard and serve in Eden and extend its boundaries throughout the earth (i.e., "subdue the earth").[128] They failed to keep sin out and lost their priestly role. The restoration of this relationship and their priestly role has been accomplished in the Second Adam, Jesus Christ (Rom 5.12-21; 1 Cor 15.22). This already-not-yet relationship has begun in the believer (2 Cor 5.17), who is the temple of God's Spirit (1 Cor 6.19-20; 2 Cor 6.16; cf. John 2.19), from which life-giving water flows (John 4.14; 7.37-39),[129] and will find its culmination in the eternal state symbolized in the NJ.

John summarizes the culmination of this relationship in 22.3-5, where he describes again in cultic language the intimate communion of God with his saints. With the removal of the curse a certainty, the saints in high priestly fashion serve God, look upon his face, and bear his name eternally in his presence (cf. Exod 28.36-38). In addition, the saints will reign eternally with God in his new creation since the fellowship and dominion envisioned in the Garden of Eden has been restored in the eternal state. This is the reward of the faithful and is the guarantee of all those who overcome (3.12; 7.2-3; 7.15).

Conclusion

The vision of the NJ follows on the heels of final judgment to assure believers of their promised reward. It is set in contrast to the judgment of the whore in chapters 17 and 18 and thus maintains the apocalyptic dichotomy between the earth-dwellers and God's faithful. It is also the pinnacle vision in John's overall call to persevere. It is the faithful who will "inherit these things" (21.7) and enjoy eternal fellowship with God (22.3-4).

---

[126] Beale, *Revelation*, 1099–100.
[127] Ibid., 1109–11.
[128] Cf. Lee, *New Jerusalem*, 292.
[129] So Aune, *Revelation 17–22*, 1125; Beale, *Revelation*, 1052; Osborne, *Revelation*, 737.

Revelation 21.1-8, which forms a transitional passage between the preceding judgment of 19.11—22.15 and the NJ vision that follows in 21.9—22.5, introduces three important themes that are united in John's description of the NJ. They are a new creation, the NJ, and the tabernacle of God among humanity (21.3). The idea of a new creation is prevalent throughout, as heaven and earth are united with the descent of the NJ. The throne voice declares in 21.3-8 that all things have been made new and that evil has been eradicated from this new world—something John consistently reiterates throughout the vision (21.26; 22.3; cf. 22.11). It is the absence of evil that allows the union of heaven with earth and the presence of God among his people in this restored Garden of Eden (22.1-5).

The details of the NJ vision are particularly rich for the present study in that they offer a glimpse into John's view of the role and composition of the new covenant people of God. John's vision of a restored heavenly Jerusalem stands solidly within Jewish expectation found both in the Hebrew Scriptures and Second Temple literature. The vision itself is modeled primarily on Ezekiel 40–48, with imagery and language borrowed from other Hebrew prophets. John clearly sees himself as one who stands in a long line of Jewish prophetic tradition. What are particularly telling, however, are the idiosyncratic additions and adaptations that John makes to the images and Jewish texts to which he alludes. Most of these modifications are the result of John's own understanding of the nature of the people of God in light of the redemptive work of the Lamb.

John's description of the NJ as reflecting the glory of God and as housing the throne of God and the Lamb makes clear that the NJ *is* the tabernacle of God. Indeed, its cubical shape indicates that it is modeled on the holy of holies of God's earthly tabernacle/temple, and the fact that God's servants serve him there in cultic fashion completes this image (22.3-4). Although John uses this cultic imagery throughout, he makes clear that within the NJ there is no temple. God and the Lamb are its temple. This is a startling declaration for a Jew describing a restored Jerusalem, but John's purpose is to make a point. The first temple symbolized God's presence among his people, but it also was a constant reminder that access to his presence was limited because of sin. In his vision of the NJ, John wishes to demonstrate that access to God's presence is unhindered. Therefore, this Jerusalem has no temple, yet it *is* a temple. It is a temple because it is where God's presence is located and it is where God's servants serve him as priests. Indeed, John takes his imagery one step further by identifying the NJ *as* the people of God. The NJ is the "bride, the wife of the Lamb" (21.9). This bride, who is equated with the saints elsewhere in the

Apocalypse (19.7-8; 22.17a), has prepared herself for the consummation of marriage. This consummation is illustrated in the imagery of the NJ.

As in Ezekiel's vision, John's NJ is bounded on all sides with twelve gates named for the twelve tribes of Israel; yet, the city is founded on twelve gemstone foundations named for the twelve apostles of the Lamb. These gemstones from which the twelve foundations are made likely correspond to the stones in the breast piece of the Jewish high priest and evoke not only the NT idea of a priesthood of believers but also imply that the twelve apostles are the new patriarchs of God's eschatological people. In addition, the vast measurements of the city, in multiples of twelve, and the streaming of the redeemed of the nations into its gates affirm the identity of the city as an innumerable multitude from every nation (7.9), who have been redeemed by the blood of the Lamb (5.9). This people of God are none other than the saints who comprise the church.

The blending of Jewish and Christian imagery in the vision of the NJ is consistent with a pattern already observed in the previous visions considered. This pattern reveals that John sees a consistent redemptive line of activity beginning with Israel and now fulfilled in the church. God's people are no longer determined by ethnicity, but by faithfulness to his redemptive plan, consummated in the redemptive work of the Lamb. God's new covenant people are from every race and people and are subsumed in, and a full extension of, God's covenant people Israel. No vision in the Apocalypse makes this point clearer than the vision of the NJ. The Holy City of Zion has now become a heavenly symbol for the eschatological people of God, both Jew and Gentile. The transformation of this symbol from a wholly Jewish one to one that encompasses all of the redeemed of the Lamb argues persuasively that John sees this new covenant people of God, the church, as God's new spiritual Israel.

6
Conclusion

THE foregoing discussion has outlined in some detail, through careful analysis of key vision passages within the Apocalypse, a consistent line of interpretation with regard to John's view of the church as God's new spiritual Israel. The purpose of the discussion was to establish John's perception of the relationship between the church and Israel in light of the redemptive work of the Lamb and then make some attempt to place this perception against the backdrop of the developing schism between Jews and Christians during the period from 70 to 150 CE.

In chapter 1, an overview of the factors that contributed to the developing schism was considered in order to provide some historical background against which to place John's apocalypse. Much of the evidence from this period is derived from Christian sources and paints a picture of an emerging Christian movement that is distancing itself from its mother religion Judaism. This separation is by no means uniform and will not be complete for centuries. However, the period between 70 and 150 CE is a particularly volatile and definitive time in this separation. Although many factors contributed to the hostility between Christians and Jews, a major break is perceptible after the Bar Kokhba revolt.

The extant Christian literature of the period reveals that the church's effort to distance itself from Judaism was accomplished primarily through a two-pronged approach. The church Christianized the Jewish scriptures and usurped the Jewish claim to be the covenant people of God. The Christians worshiped the same God and used the same scriptures as Judaism, but Judaism's failure, from the church's perspective, was not to recognize Jesus as the Messiah. This failure to recognize their Messiah offered the emerging church an excuse to wrench from Judaism its claim to be the covenant people of God. Thus the church adopted the Jewish scriptures by arguing that it alone interpreted them correctly and by arguing that the Jewish rejection of Jesus meant God's rejection of Israel.

The church eventually found evidence of this rejection in part with the destruction of the temple in 70 CE and the expulsion of the Jews from Jerusalem in 135 CE.

Chapters 2 through 5 offered an in-depth analysis of key passages within the Apocalypse that arguably reveal John's perspective on the relationship between Jews and Christians in God's redemptive plan. The synagogue of Satan accusations in Rev 2.9 and 3.9 suggest two conclusions in developing a composite sketch of John's view of the relationship between the church and Judaism. These passages reveal historically that these two churches were in conflict with elements of the Jewish communities in Smyrna and Philadelphia, and they also imply that John has theologically redefined who a Jew is. Those Jews who have aligned themselves with Satan in opposition to the followers of the Lamb are not true Jews; that is, they are not part of the covenant people of God. John no longer defines a Jew according to ethnicity, but whether a person is a "Jew" (i.e., a member of the covenant people of God) is measured through spiritual faithfulness to God, a standard that John applies equally to both Jews and Gentiles. Therefore, faithfulness is the litmus test of those who belong to God, of those who will enjoy the preservation and reward that he promises.

It is this paradigm of faithfulness through which John establishes an apocalyptic dichotomy that first emerges in the seven messages and extends through the entire Apocalypse. It is those who belong to God and those who belong to Satan who are separated into mutually exclusive groups and whose fate is tracked throughout John's apocalyptic visions. The former are those who persevere and whose dwelling is in heaven, and the latter are the earth-dwellers who follow the beast to their destruction. The followers of Jesus are encouraged to persevere; and those who have already compromised are admonished. Those who remain faithful will enjoy God's spiritual preservation through the coming ordeal but will not be preserved from suffering. However, they will in the end in God's presence be vindicated. These faithful saints embody John's concept of the church, and it is this group that he encourages throughout his apocalyptic visions.

Although much of the Apocalypse is preoccupied with the judgment of God upon the followers of Satan or his emissary the beast, several visions throughout offer a message of hope to the saints who currently suffer. These visions are those that have been examined in some detail in the present study: the visions of the 144,000 and the innumerable multitude (7.1-17; 14.1-5), the measuring of the temple and the two witnesses (11.1-13), the heavenly woman (12.1-17), and the new Jerusalem (21.1—22.5).

Each of these visions offers the saints hope of preservation, vindication, and eventual reward in the presence of God.

Each of these visions also discloses a consistent view of John's perception of the church as God's new spiritual Israel. This interpretation is recommended because of John's use of Jewish imagery and scriptures uniquely adapted for this purpose. For example, the 144,000 sealed out of the twelve tribes of Israel are guaranteed protection from the judgments that are about to be unleashed through the sounding of the seven trumpets. These "Israelites," however, are not ethnic Jews but are all believers who remain faithful to God. John implies this interpretation by offering several clues within the vision narrative. For example, the anomalies of his tribal list reveal his own hand through the messianic promotion of Judah and through the exclusion of tribes that have possible association with unfaithfulness (i.e., idolatry). In addition, the subsequent vision of the innumerable multitude further confirms the identity of the 144,000 as a symbolic number for the redeemed "from every nation" (7.9), indicating once again that John has broadened his definition of the people of God beyond ethnic boundaries. His reintroduction of the 144,000 in 14.1-5 as followers of the Lamb "redeemed from humankind" (14.4) standing on Mount Zion also serves to equate this group with the innumerable multitude who are equally shepherded by the Lamb (7.17). In both visions of the 144,000, John appropriates symbols that lie at the very core of Jewish national and cultic identity (the twelve tribes and Mount Zion) and freely applies them to God's new eschatological people, comprised of both Jews and Gentiles, the church.

This pattern is not unique but can be seen as well in other vision passages within the Apocalypse. The measuring of the temple, the two witnesses, and the heavenly woman of chapters 11 and 12 are all symbols of God's people and all contain the same message of preservation and vindication. Each of these images has been borrowed and developed primarily from Jewish tradition and indicates not only John's cultural and religious heritage but also his own view that God's eschatological people, the followers of the Lamb, are an extension of God's covenant people Israel and full heirs of the covenant promises. It is the church, God's temple and God's lampstands, that must, in the same tradition as the Hebrew prophets, witness to the nations but will equally follow the Lord in suffering, death, and resurrection.

The appropriation of Jewish symbols for the church is not the only indication that John views the church as God's new spiritual Israel. His adaptation of the Jewish scriptures is also revealing. The present study has discussed at length the OT sources behind John's visions. This is particularly evident, for example, in John's visions of the measuring of the temple (11.1-2), the two witnesses (11.1-13), and the vision of the new Jerusalem (21.1—22.5). All three visions have obvious parallels to a number of OT texts. The vision of the new Jerusalem is particularly telling, for John has not only once again borrowed a decidedly Jewish national and cultic symbol, but he has clearly adapted it for his Christian audience. The hope of a restored and rebuilt Jerusalem and temple is drawn from both the Hebrew scriptures and Jewish apocalyptic tradition and has been altered to conform to John's Christian perspective. This new Jerusalem is built on the foundation of the twelve apostles of the Lamb and surprisingly has no temple. In addition, the old covenant language used in this vision has been altered to reflect John's international perception of God's new covenant Israel. The singular "people" of Ezek 37.27 has now become "peoples" in Rev 21.3, and the nations, which eschatological Israel conquers and leads in procession in Isa 60.11-12, enter John's new Jerusalem freely as heirs of the redemption purchased by the Lamb (21.7, 26).

This entire study has implied that John sees continuity between Israel and the church in that the church is subsumed in, and a clear extension of, God's covenant people Israel. In this sense, the church is God's new spiritual Israel. It is not Israel's replacement but its fulfillment. The church is both Israel and the nations as one people of God; however, it is not Israel ethnically but spiritually. Thus John freely appropriates Jewish national and cultic symbols for the church. He also appropriates as Jewish covenant promises and eschatological hopes and believes them fulfilled in and on behalf of the followers of the Lamb—the church. John has altered his understanding of a "true Jew" by not only broadening its scope beyond ethnic boundaries but also by redefining it theologically. Spiritual faithfulness is now the mark of a "true Jew," which implies keeping the commandments of God and holding the testimony of Jesus (12.17).

In this respect, John is similar to other NT writers, particularly Paul, who view the church as God's temple (1 Cor 3.16-17; 6.19; 2 Cor 6.16; Eph 2.21; cf. 1 Pet 2.4-5, 9-10) and define a Jew theologically rather than ethnically (Rom 2.28-29; Phil 3.3). Indeed, John is in harmony with the Hebrew prophets, who themselves understood the faithful of Israel to be the true people of God and anticipated the gathering of the nations to Jerusalem. John's perspective, however, unlike the Hebrew prophets is developed in light of the advent of Christ.

What is of particular interest is how much John's view of the church as God's new Israel is in harmony with some of his Christian contemporaries who are quite direct in their subordination of Israel and their exaltation of the church as the true people of God. Revelation 2.9 and 3.9, which have been studied extensively along this vein, illustrate that John is able to criticize and even condemn his fellow Jews. This being said, however, as was pointed out in chapter 2 of the present study, John never uses the term "Jew" in a pejorative sense. It is still a term of honor that he apparently reserves for those who are faithful to God and the Lamb.

Another passage that may be revealing is Rev 11.8. Here, John identifies earthly Jerusalem not only as Sodom and Egypt but also as the place where the Lord was crucified. This description is important because John betrays a negative appraisal of an important Jewish symbol and by implication cultic Judaism. How much this remark reflects a post-70 Christian attitude toward the destruction of the temple is difficult to say. Does John imply here that the destruction of the temple is God's eschatological judgment on unfaithful Israel? This question is impossible to respond to definitively, but what can be said is that John has placed earthly Jerusalem and "the great city" Babylon together in one metaphorical description as partners in opposition to God and his people. However, just as with the designation "Jew," John does not completely abandon Jerusalem but reserves its heavenly counterpart as a symbol for God's redeemed people (cf. Gal 4.25-26; Heb 12.22-24; cf. 11.10). Once again, one can observe that John's perception of the people of God has moved beyond ethnic boundaries or geographic markers and has been redefined through spiritual faithfulness.

John is, therefore, free to criticize and even condemn as a "synagogue of Satan" Jews who persecute the church or crucified the Lord because they have failed in their faithfulness to the covenant plan of God and thus have aligned themselves with Satan. Such condemnation, however, is not reserved for just ethnic Jews but is similarly heaped on errant Asian Christians who are admonished as followers of Balaam and Jezebel (2.14, 20). Thus John's condemnation of certain elements in the Jewish communities of Smyrna and Philadelphia does not imply that John is drawing a distinction between Jews and Gentiles or even Jews and Christians. He is making a distinction between the faithful and the unfaithful. John never makes a distinction in the Apocalypse between Jews and Gentiles, but sees them both comprising God's eschatological people, the church. This perception is clear from the visions analyzed in the present work in which John adopts and adapts Jewish imagery for this new people from every nation, tribe, language and people.

The implication of the preceding discussion is that John sees the church in continuity with Israel. For him, the church is the extension of God's covenant people Israel. This "new Israel" is not a replacement of ethnic Israel but an extension of the covenant promises of Israel to the nations through the Lamb. Being a Jew is, therefore, not an automatic guarantee of membership in the covenant community. God's "Israel" is defined through spiritual faithfulness not ethnicity and, thus membership is open to all. Hence, John interprets Jewish symbols and prophetic tradition in light of the Christ-event and freely applies these symbols and tradition to the universal people of God, the church.

It is this appropriation and reapplication of Jewish symbols and scripture for the church that may imply that John reflects to some degree the emerging trend within Christianity to appropriate the Jewish scriptures and covenant place as the people of God. It is unwise, however, to draw such a conclusion. Certainly one might say that John does to some degree "Christianize" the Jewish scriptures and his redefinition of the people of God, indeed who a "true Jew" is, might even suggest a supersessionist theology. However, it would be better to say that John does not see such a clear line of distinction between the church and Judaism. For John, the church is the fulfillment of Judaism. It represents the Jewish hope of the ingathering of the nations as one people of God. His perception, however, is not like the ethnically oriented prophecies of the Hebrew Scriptures, but he sees one new people from all nations comprised of brothers and sisters, Jews and Gentiles, who follow the Lamb.

The title "new spiritual Israel" has been applied in this work to John's eschatological people, but it is not done in the sense suggested by Justin Martyr. John does not see Israel replaced by the church nor does he ever imply the Jewish people are abandoned by God. John's perception of the church also does not imply, as in some other Christian writers, any attempt to be anti-Jewish, and is certainly not anti-Semitic. This latter statement, of course, places him out of step with the trend that was developing within some segments of the Christian church between 70 and 150 CE. His perception of the church as God's new Israel, however, may have been misunderstood and later used as fodder in Christianity's vicious struggle to overcome its Jewish rival. John never makes evident his position on the fate of ethnic Israel, but his hope, no doubt, is that all Jews (as well as Gentiles) will come to recognize the redemption purchased by the Lamb and will find through faithfulness to God's new covenant a place in his new Jerusalem, the church, God's new spiritual Israel.

Selected Bibliography

Primary Sources

Bell, H. Idris, editor. *Jews and Christians in Egypt*. London: Oxford University Press, 1924.
Blackman, Philip, translator. *Mishnayoth*. 7 vols. London: Mishna, 1951–56.
Cassius Dio. *Dio's Roman History*. Translated by Earnest Cary on the basis of the version of Herber Baldwin Foster. 9 vols. LCL. Cambridge: Harvard University Press, 1914–27.
Chadwick, Henry. *Origen: Contra Celsum*. Cambridge: Cambridge University Press, 1953.
Charlesworth, James H., editor. *The Old Testament Pseudepigrapha*. 2 vols. Garden City, N.Y.: Doubleday, 1983, 1985.
Clarke, Ernest G., translator. *Targum Pseudo-Jonathan: Numbers*. The Aramaic Bible: The Targums 4. Collegeville, Minn.: Liturgical, 1995.
Danby, Herbert, editor and translator. *The Mishnah: Translated from the Hebrew with Brief Introduction and Explanatory Notes*. 1933. Reprinted, London: Oxford University Press, 1950.
Danker, Frederick W., Walter Bauer, W. F. Arndt, and F. W. Gingrich. *Greek–English Lexicon of the New Testament and Other Early Christian Literature on CD-ROM*. Libronix Digital Library System Version 1.0d. 2000, 2001. Print ed.: *Greek-English Lexicon of the New Testament and Other Early Christian Literature*. 3d ed. Chicago: University of Chicago Press, 1999.
Epstein, Isidore, editor. *The Babylonian Talmud*. 35 vols. London: Soncino, 1935–52.
Eusebius. *The Ecclesiastical History*. Translated by Kirsopp Lake and J. E. L. Oulton. 2 vols. LCL. Cambridge: Harvard University Press, 1926–32.
Freedman, H. and Maurice Simon, editors. *Midrash Rabbah*. 10 vols. London: Soncino, 1939.
Hayward, Robert, translator. *The Targum of Jeremiah*. The Aramaic Bible: The Targums 12. Wilmington, Del.: Glazier, 1987.
Herodotus. Translated by A. D. Godley. 4 vols. Rev. ed. LCL. Cambridge: Harvard University Press, 1926–28; 1938.
Holmes, Michael W., editor. *The Apostolic Fathers: Greek Texts and English Translations*. Rev. ed. Grand Rapids: Baker, 1999. Updated edition of *The Apostolic Fathers: Greek Texts and English Translations of Their Writings*. 2d. ed. Edited and translated by J. B. Lightfoot and J. R. Harmer. Edited and revised by Michael W. Holmes. Grand Rapids: Baker, 1992.

James, M. R., translator. *The Biblical Antiquities of Philo*. 1917. Reprinted, The Library of Biblical Studies. Edited by Harry M. Orlinsky. New York: Ktav, 1971.

Josephus. Translated by H. St. J. Thackeray et. al. 10 vols. LCL. Cambridge: Harvard University Press, 1926–65.

Kircher, A. *Oedipus Aegyptiacus*. Rome: Mascardi, 1653 [not seen].

Kittel, Gerhard, and Gerhard Friedrich, editors. *Theological Dictionary of the New Testament on CD-ROM*. Libronix Digital Library System Version 1.0d. 2000, 2001. Print ed.: *Theological Dictionary of the New Testament*. Translated by G.W. Bromiley. 10 vols. Grand Rapids: Eerdmans, 1964–76.

Klijn, A. F. J., and G. J. Reinink. *Patristic Evidence for Jewish-Christian Sects*. NovTSup 34. Leiden: Brill, 1973.

Louw, J. P. and E. A. Nida, editors. *Greek–English Lexicon of the New Testament: Based on Semantic Domains on CD-ROM*. Libronix Digital Library System Version 1.0d. 2000, 2001. Print ed.: *Greek–English Lexicon of the New Testament: Based on Semantic Domains*. 2d ed. New York: United Bible Societies, 1989.

Metzger, Bruce M. *A Textual Commentary on the Greek New Testament*. 2d ed. Stuttgart: United Bible Societies, 1994.

Munier, Charles. *Saint Justin Apologie Pour Les Chrétiens Édition et Traduction*. Paradosis: Études de littérature et de théologie anciennes 39. Friboug: Éditions Universitaires, 1995.

Musurillo, Herbert, translator. *The Acts of the Christian Martyrs*. OECT. Edited by Henry Chadwick. Oxford: Clarendon, 1972.

Neusner, Jacob, translator. *Genesis Rabbah: The Judaic Commentary of Genesis a New American Translation*. 3 vols. BJS 104–106. Atlanta: Scholars, 1985.

———. *Pesiqta deRab Kahana: An Analytical Translation*. 2 vols. BJS 122–123. Atlanta: Scholars, 1987.

———. *Sifre to Deuteronomy: An Analytical Translation*. 3 vols. BJS 98, 101. Atlanta: Scholars, 1987.

———. *The Talmud of the Land of Israel: A Preliminary Translation and Explanation*. 35 vols. CSHJ. Chicago: University of Chicago Press, 1982–94.

———. *The Tosefta*. 6 vols. New York: Ktav, 1977–81.

Philo. Translated by F. H. Colson, G. H. Whitaker, and Ralph Marcus. 10 vols. 2 supp. LCL. Cambridge: Harvard University Press, 1929–43.

Roberts, Alexander and James Donaldson, editors. *Ante-Nicene Christian Library: Translations of the Writings of the Fathers down to A. D. 325*. 1885–1887. 10 vols. 1909. Reprinted, Peabody: Hendrickson, 1994.

Smith, John Clark, translator. *Origen: Homilies on Jeremiah; Homily on 1 Kings 28*. FC 97. Washington D. C.: The Catholic University of America Press, 1998.

Sparks, H. F. D., editor. *The Apocryphal Old Testament*. Oxford: Clarendon, 1984.

Suetonius. Translated by J. C. Rolfe. 2 vols. LCL. Cambridge: Harvard University Press, 1913–14.

Tcherikover, Victor A., and Alexander Fuks, editors. *Corpus Papyrorum Judaicarum*. 2 vols. Jerusalem: Magnes, 1957, 1960.

Vermes, Geza. *The Complete Dead Sea Scrolls in English*. New York: Penguin, 1997.

Williams, A. Lukyn. *Justin Martyr, the Dialogue with Trypho*. London: SPCK, 1930.

Commentaries

Aune, David E. *Revelation 1–5*. WBC 52A. Dallas: Word, 1997.
———. *Revelation 6–16*. WBC 52B. Nashville: Nelson, 1998.
———. *Revelation 17–22*. WBC 52C. Nashville: Nelson, 1998.
Barrett, C. K. *The Gospel According to St. John: An Introduction with Commentary and Notes on the Greek Text*. 2d ed. Philadelphia: Westminster, 1978.
Beale, G. K. *The Book of Revelation: A Commentary on the Greek Text*. NIGTC. Grand Rapids: Eerdmans, 1999.
Beasley-Murray, G. R. *The Book of Revelation*. NCB. Rev. ed. Grand Rapids: Eerdmans, 1981.
Beckwith, Isbon T. *The Apocalypse of John: Studies in Introduction with a Critical and Exegetical Commentary*. 1919. Reprinted, Grand Rapids: Baker, 1979.
Brown, Raymond. *The Gospel According to John (I–XII): Introduction, Translation, and Notes*. AB 29. Garden City, N.Y.: Doubleday, 1966.
Caird, G. B. *A Commentary on the Revelation of St. John the Divine*. 1966. Reprinted, *The Revelation of Saint John*. BNTC. Peabody, Mass.: Hendrickson, n.d.
Charles, R. H. *The Revelation of St. John*. 2 vols. ICC. New York: Scribner, 1920.
Court, John M. *Revelation*. NTG. Sheffield: JSOT Press, 1994.
Feuillet, André. *The Apocalypse*. Translated by Thomas E. Crane. Staten Island: Alba, 1964.
Fitzmyer, Joseph A. *The Acts of the Apostles: A New Translation with Introduction and Commentary*. AB 31. New York: Doubleday, 1998.
Ford, J. M. *Revelation*. AB 38. New York: Doubleday, 1975.
Hort, F. J. A. *The Apocalypse of St. John I–III*. London: Macmillan, 1908.
Kiddle, Martin. *The Revelation of St. John the Divine*. MNTC. New York: Harper, 1940.
Koester, Craig R. *Revelation and the End of All Things*. Grand Rapids: Eerdmans, 2001.
Kraft, Heinrich. *Die Offenbarung des Johannes*. HNT 16a. Tübingen: Mohr/Siebeck, 1974.
Ladd, George Eldon. *A Commentary on the Revelation of John*. Grand Rapids: Eerdmans, 1972.
Lohmeyer, Ernst. *Die Offenbarung des Johannes*. HNT 16. 2d ed. Tübingen: Mohr/Siebeck, 1953.
Malina, Bruce J., and John J. Pilch. *Social-Science Commentary on the Book of Revelation*. Minneapolis: Fortress, 2000.
Michaels, J. Ramsey. *Revelation*. IVPNTC. Downers Grove, Ill.: InterVarsity, 1997.
Mounce, Robert H. *The Book of Revelation*. NICNT. Rev. ed. Grand Rapids: Eerdmans, 1998.
Murphy, Frederick J. *Fallen Is Babylon: The Revelation of John*. NTC. Harrisburg: Trinity Press, 1998.
Osborne, Grant R. *Revelation*. BECNT. Grand Rapids: Baker, 2002.
Prigent, Pierre. *L'Apocalypse de Saint John*. CNT 14. Rev. ed. Geneva: Labor et Fides, 2000.
———. *Commentary on the Apocalypse of Saint John*. Translated by Wendy Pradels. Tübingen: Mohr/Siebeck, 2001.
Roloff, Jürgen. *The Revelation of John*. CC. Translated by John E. Alsup. Minneapolis: Fortress, 1993.
Rowland, Christopher. "The Book of Revelation: Introduction, Commentary and Reflections." In *Hebrews, James, 1 & 2 Peter, 1, 2 & 3 John, Jude, Revelation*, 503–744.

The New Interpreter's Bible: A Commentary in Twelve Volumes. Edited by Leander E. Keck et. al. Vol. 12. Nashville: Abingdon, 1998.

———. *Revelation.* Epworth Commentary. London: Epworth, 1993.

Schüssler Fiorenza, Elisabeth. *Revelation: Vision of a Just World.* PC. Minneapolis: Fortress, 1991.

Sweet J. P. M. *Revelation.* PNTC. London: SCM, 1979.

Thompson, Leonard L. *Revelation.* ANTC. Nashville: Abingdon, 1998.

Walvoord, John F. *The Revelation of Jesus Christ.* Chicago: Moody, 1966.

Monographs

Barnard L. W. *Studies in the Apostolic Fathers and Their Background.* Oxford: Blackwell, 1966.

Bauckham, Richard. *The Climax of Prophecy: Studies in the Book of Revelation.* Edinburgh: T. & T. Clark, 1993.

Beagley, Alan James. *The 'Sitz im Leben' of the Apocalypse with Particular Reference to the Role of the Church's Enemies.* BZNW 50. Berlin: de Gruyter, 1987.

Beale, G. K. *John's Use of the Old Testament in Revelation.* JSNTSup 166. Sheffield: Sheffield Academic, 1998.

Borgen, Peder. *Early Christianity and Hellenistic Judaism.* Edinburgh: T. & T. Clark, 1996.

Briggs, Robert A. *Jewish Temple Imagery in the Book of Revelation.* SBLit 10. New York: Lang, 1999.

Cadoux, Cecil John. *Ancient Smyrna: A History of the City from the Earliest Times to 324 A.D.* Oxford: Blackwell, 1938.

Cohen, Shaye J. D. *The Beginnings of Jewishness: Boundaries, Varieties, Uncertainties.* Berkeley: University of California Press, 1999.

———. *From the Maccabees to the Mishnah.* LEC. Philadelphia: Westminster, 1987.

Collins, Adela Yarbro. *The Combat Myth in the Book of Revelation.* HDR 9. Missoula, Mont.: Scholars, 1976.

———. *Crisis and Catharsis: The Power of the Apocalypse.* Philadelphia: Westminster, 1984.

Corwin, Virginia. *St. Ignatius and Christianity in Antioch.* New Haven: Yale University Press, 1960.

Davies, W. D. *The Setting of the Sermon on the Mount.* Cambridge: Cambridge University Press, 1964.

Dunn, James D. G. *The Partings of the Ways: Between Christianity and Judaism and Their Significance for the Character of Christianity.* London: SCM, 1991.

Flusser, David. *Judaism and the Origins of Christianity.* Jerusalem: Magnes, 1988.

France, R. T. *Matthew: Evangelist and Teacher.* Grand Rapids: Zondervan, 1989.

Gager, John G. *The Origins of Anti-Semitism: Attitudes toward Judaism in Pagan and Christian Antiquity.* New York: Oxford University Press, 1983.

Harvey, Graham. *The True Israel: Uses of the Names Jew, Hebrew and Israel in Ancient Jewish and Early Christian Literature.* AGAJU 35. Leiden: Brill, 1996.

Hemer, Colin J. *The Letters to the Seven Churches of Asia in Their Local Setting.* 1986. Reprinted, Grand Rapids: Eerdmans; Livonia, Mich.: Dove, 2001.

Herford, R. Travers. *Christianity in Talmud and Midrash.* Clifton, N.J.: Reference Book, 1965.

Hirschberg, Peter. *Das eschatologische Israel: Untersuchungen zum Gottesvolkverständnis der Johannesoffenbarung.* WMANT 84. Neukirchen-Vluyn: Neukirchener, 1999.

Kline, Meredith G. *Images of the Spirit.* BBMS. Grand Rapids: Baker, 1980.

Lee, Pilchan. *The New Jerusalem in the Book of Revelation.* WUNT 2/129. Tübingen: Mohr/Siebeck, 2001.

Le Frois, Bernard J. *The Woman Clothed with the Sun: Individual or Collective.* Rome: Orbis Catholicus, 1954.

Lieu, Judith. *Image and Reality: The Jews in the World of the Christians in the Second Century.* Edinburgh: T. & T. Clark, 1996.

Malina, Bruce J. *The New Jerusalem in the Revelation of John: The City as Symbol of Life with God.* Collegeville, Minn.: Liturgical, 2000.

Marshall, John W. *Parables of War: Reading John's Jewish Apocalypse.* Studies in Christianity and Judaism/Études sur le christianisme et le judaïsme 10. Waterloo, Ontario: Wilfrid Laurier University Press, 2001.

Martyn, J. Louis. *History and Theology in the Fourth Gospel.* 3d ed. NTL. Louisville: Westminster John Knox, 2003.

Mathewson, David. *A New Heaven and a New Earth: The Meaning and Function of the Old Testament in Revelation 21.1—22.5.* JSNTSup 238. London: Sheffield Academic, 2003.

Overman, J. Andrew. *Matthew's Gospel and Formative Judaism: The Social World of the Matthean Community.* Minneapolis: Fortress, 1990.

Prigent, Pierre. *Apocalypse 12: Histoire de l'exégèse.* BGBE 2. Tübingen: Mohr/Siebeck, 1959.

Ramsay, W. M. *The Letters to the Seven Churches.* Updated ed. Edited by Mark W. Wilson. Peabody: Hendrickson, 1994. Orig. ed. *The Letters to the Seven Churches of Asia and Their Place in the Plan of the Apocalypse.* London: Hodder and Stoughton, 1904.

Richardson, Peter. *Israel in the Apostolic Church.* SNTSMS 10. Cambridge: Cambridge University Press, 1969.

Robinson, J. A. T. *Redating the New Testament.* Philadelphia: Westminster, 1976.

Rowland, Christopher. *Christian Origins: From Messianic Movement to Christian Religion.* Minneapolis: Augsburg, 1985.

———. *The Open Heaven: A Study of Apocalyptic in Judaism and Early Christianity.* New York: Crossroad, 1982.

Sanders, Jack T. *Schismatics, Sectarians, Dissidents, Deviants: The First One Hundred Years of Jewish-Christian Relations.* Valley Forge, Pa.: Trinity, 1993.

Schüssler Fiorenza, Elisabeth. *The Book of Revelation Justice and Judgment.* 2d ed. Minneapolis: Fortress, 1998.

———. *Priester für Gott: Studium zum Herrschafts- und Priestermotiv in der Apokalypse.* NTAbh 7. Münster: Aschendorff, 1972.

Simon, Marcel. *Verus Israel: A Study of the Relations between Christians and Jews in the Roman Empire (135–425).* Translated by H. McKeating. 1986. Reprinted, Littman Library of Jewish Civilization. New York: Vallentine Mitchell, 1996. Orig. ed.: *Verus Israel: Étude sur les relations entre Chrétiens et Juifs dans l'Empire Romain (135–425).* Paris: de Boccard, 1964.

Smallwood, E. Mary. *The Jews Under Roman Rule from Pompey to Diocletian: A Study in Political Relations.* 2d ed. SJLA 20. Leiden: Brill, 1981.

Stevenson, Gregory. *Power and Place: Temple and Identity in the Book of Revelation.* BZNW 107. Berlin: de Gruyter, 2001.

Thompson, Leonard L. *The Book of Revelation: Apocalypse and Empire.* New York: Oxford University Press, 1990.
Trebilco, Paul R. *Jewish Communities in Asia Minor.* Cambridge: Cambridge University Press, 1991.
Vogelgesang, Jeffrey Marshall. "The Interpretation of Ezekiel in the Book of Revelation." Ph.D. diss., Harvard University, 1985.
Wilson, Stephen G. *Related Strangers: Jews and Christians, 70–170 C.E.* Minneapolis: Fortress, 1995.

Articles

Applebaum, Shimon. "The Legal Status of the Jewish Communities in the Diaspora." In *The Jewish People in the First Century.* CRINT 1, edited by S. Safrai et al., 420–63. Philadelphia: Fortress, 1974.

———. "The Organization of the Jewish Communities in the Diaspora." In *The Jewish People in the First Century.* CRINT 1, edited by S. Safrai et al., 464–503. Philadelphia: Fortress, 1974.

Alexander, Philip S. "'The Parting of the Ways' from the Perspective of Rabbinic Judaism." In *Jews and Christians: The Parting of the Ways A.D. 70 to 135,* edited by James D. G. Dunn, 1–25. 1992. Reprinted, Grand Rapids: Eerdmans, 1999.

Bauckham, Richard. "The List of the Tribes in Revelation 7 Again." *JSNT* 42 (1991) 99–115.

———. "Revelation as a Christian War Scroll." *Neot* 22 (1988) 17–40.

Barrett, C. K. "Jews and Judaizers in the Epistles of Ignatius." In *Jews, Greeks and Christians: Essays in Honor of William David Davies,* edited by Robert Hamerton-Kelly and Robin Scroggs, 220–44. SJLA 21. Leiden: Brill, 1976.

Borgen, Peder. "Polemic in the Book of Revelation." In *Anti-Semitism and Early Christianity: Issues of Polemic and Faith,* edited by Craig A. Evans and Donald A. Hagner, 199–211. Minneapolis: Fortress, 1993.

Bredin, Mark R. J. "The Synagogue of Satan Accusation in Revelation 2:9." *BTB* 28 (1999) 160–64.

Bruns, J. Edgar. "The Contrasted Women of Apocalypse 12 and 17." *CBQ* 26 (1964) 459–63.

Carey, Greg. "The 'Synagogue of Satan' (Rev 2:9; 3:9)—What's at Stake for Us?" Paper presented at the Annual Meeting of the Society of Biblical Literature. Toronto, Canada, November 23, 2002.

Collins, Adela Yarbro. "Insiders and Outsiders in the Book of Revelation and Its Social Context." In *"To See Ourselves as Others See Us": Christians, Jews, and "Others" in Late Antiquity,* edited by Jacob Neusner and Ernest Frerichs, 187–218. Scholars Press Studies in the Humanities. Chico, Calif.: Scholars, 1985.

———. "Vilification and Self-Definition in the Book of Revelation." In *Christians among Jews and Gentiles: Essays in Honor of Krister Stendahl on His Sixty-Fifth Birthday,* edited by George W. E. Nickelsburg with George W. MacRae, 308–20. Philadelphia: Fortress, 1986.

Considine, Joseph S. "The Two Witnesses: Apoc. 11.3-13." *CBQ* 8 (1946) 377–92.

Deutsch, Celia. "Transformation of Symbols: The New Jerusalem in Rv 21:1—22:5." *ZNW* 78 (1987) 106–26.

de Villiers, P. G. R. "The Lord Was Crucified in Sodom and Egypt: Symbols in the Apocalypse of John." *Neot* 22 (1988) 125–38.

Draper, Jonathan A. "The Twelve Apostles as Foundation Stones of the Heavenly Jerusalem and the Foundation of the Qumran Community." *Neot* 22 (1988) 41–63.

Evans, Craig A. "Root Causes of the Jewish-Christian Rift from Jesus to Justin." In *Christian-Jewish Relations through the Centuries,* 20–35. JSNTSup 192. Sheffield: Sheffield Academic, 2000.

Feuillet, André. "Les 144,000 Israélites Marqués d'un Sceau." *NovT* 9 (1967) 191–224.

Fox, Kenneth A. "The Nicolaitans, Nicolaus and the Early Church." *StRel/ScRel* 23 (1994) 485–96.

Frankfurter, David. "Jews or Not? Reconstructing the 'Other' in Rev 2:9 and 3:9." *HTR* 94 (2001) 403–25.

Gaston, Lloyd. "Judaism of the Uncircumcised in Ignatius and Related Writers." In *Anti-Judaism in Early Christianity: Separation and Polemic* 2, edited by Stephen G. Wilson, 33–44. Studies in Christianity and Judaism 2. Waterloo: Wilfrid Laurier University Press, 1986.

Geyser, Albert. "The Twelve Tribes in Revelation: Judean and Judeo Christian Apocalypticism." *NTS* 28 (1982) 388–99.

Gundry, Robert H. "The New Jerusalem People as Place, Not Place for People." *NovT* 29 (1987) 254–64.

Hill, C. E. "Antichrist from the Tribe of Dan." *JTS* 46 (1995) 99–117.

Horbury, William. "The Benediction of the *Minim* and Jewish-Christian Controversy." *JTS* 33 (1982) 19–61.

Horn, Friedrich Wilhelm. "Zwischen der Synagoge des Satans und dem neuen Jerusalem: Die christlich-jüdische Standortbestimmung in der Apokalypse des Johannes." *ZRGG* 46 (1994) 143–62.

Joubert, Stefan J. "A Bone of Contention in Recent Scholarship: The 'Birkat ha-Minim' and the Separation of Church and Synagogue in the First Century A.D." *Neot* 27 (1993) 351–63.

Judge, E. A. "Judaism and the Rise of Christianity: A Roman Perspective." *TynBul* 45 (1994) 355–68.

Katz, Steven T. "Issues in the Separation of Judaism and Christianity after 70 CE: A Reconsideration." *JBL* 103 (1984) 43–76.

Kimelman, Reuven. "*Birkat Ha-Minim* and the Lack of Evidence for an Anti-Christian Jewish Prayer in Late Antiquity." In *Jewish and Christian Self-definition: Aspects of Judaism in the Graeco-Roman Period* 2, edited by E. P. Sanders et al., 226–44. Philadelphia: Fortress, 1981.

Kraemer, Ross S. "On the Meaning of the Term "Jew" in Greco-Roman Inscriptions." *HTR* 82 (1989) 35–53. Reprinted, in *Diaspora Jews and Judaism: Essays in Honor of and in Dialogue with A. Thomas Kraabel,* edited by J. Andrew Overman and Robert S. MacLennan, 311–29. South Florida Studies in the History of Judaism 41. Atlanta: Scholars, 1992.

Lampe, G. W. H. "A.D. 70 in Christian Reflection." In *Jesus and the Politics of His Day,* edited by Ernst Bammel and C. F. D. Moule, 153–71. Cambridge: Cambridge University Press, 1984.

Lambrecht, Jan. "Jewish Slander: A Note on Revelation 2,9-10." *ETL* 75 (1999) 421–29.

———. "Synagogues of Satan" (Rev 2.9 and 3.9) Anti-Judaism in the Book of Revelation." In *Anti-Judaism and the Fourth Gospel,* edited by R. Bieringer et al., 279–92. Louisville: Westminster John Knox, 2001.

Lieu, Judith M. "Accusations of Jewish Persecution in Early Christian Sources, with Particular Reference to Justin Martyr and the *Martyrdom of Polycarp*." In *Tolerance and Intolerance in Early Judaism and Christianity*, edited by Graham N. Stanton and Guy G. Stroumsa, 279–95. Cambridge: Cambridge University Press, 1998.

McDonald, Lee Martin. "Anti-Judaism in the Early Church Fathers." In *Anti-Semitism and Early Christianity: Issues of Polemic and Faith*, edited by Craig A. Evans and Donald A. Hagner, 215–52. Minneapolis: Fortress, 1993.

Muirhead, I. A. "The Bride of Christ." *SJT* 5 (1952) 175–87.

Paul, Ian. "The Use of the Old Testament in Revelation 12." In *The Old Testament in the New Testament: Essays in Honor of J. L. North*, edited by Steve Moyise, 256–76. JSNTSup 189. Sheffield: Sheffield Academic Press, 2000.

Reader, William W. "The Twelve Jewels of Revelation 21.19-20: Tradition History and Modern Interpretations." *JBL* 100 (1981) 433–57.

Rowland, Christopher. "Moses and Patmos: Reflections on the Jewish Background of Early Christianity." In *Words Remembered, Texts Renewed: Essays in Honour of John F. A. Sawyer*, edited by Jon Davies et al., 280–99. JSOTSup 195. Sheffield: Sheffield Academic, 1995.

Sanderson, G. V. "In Defence of Dan." *Scripture* 3/4 (1948) 114–15.

Schiffman, Lawrence H. "At the Crossroads: Tannaitic Perspectives on the Jewish-Christian Schism." In *Jewish and Christian Self-Definition: Aspects of Judaism in the Graeco-Roman Period* 2, edited by E. P. Sanders with A. I. Baumgarten, and Alan Mendelson, 115–56. Philadelphia: Fortress, 1981.

Smith, Christopher R. "The Portrayal of the Church as the New Israel in the Names and Order of the Tribes in Revelation 7.5-8." *JSNT* 39 (1990) 111–18.

———. "The Tribes of Revelation 7 and the Literary Competence of John the Seer." *JETS* 38 (1995) 213–18.

Stern, M. "The Jewish Diaspora." In *The Jewish People in the First Century*, edited by S. Safrai et al., 117–83. CRINT 1. Philadelphia: Fortress, 1974.

Strand, Kenneth. "The Two Witnesses of Rev 11:3-12." *AUSS* 19 (1981) 127–35.

Sumney, Jerry L. "Those Who 'Ignorantly Deny Him': The Opponents of Ignatius of Antioch." *JECS* 1 (1993) 345–65.

Townsend, John T. "The Gospel of John and the Jews: The Story of a Religious Divorce." In *Antisemitism and the Foundations of Christianity*, edited by Alan T. Davies, 72–97. New York: Paulist, 1979.

Wilson, J. Christian, "The Problem of the Domitianic Date of Revelation." *NTS* 39 (1993) 587–605.

Winkle, Ross E. "Another Look at the List of Tribes in Revelation 7." *AUSS* 27 (1989) 53–67.

www.ingramcontent.com/pod-product-compliance
Lightning Source LLC
Chambersburg PA
CBHW070316230426
43663CB00011B/2157